RISE AND SHINE

45 years in the Land of the Rising Sun

RISE AND SHINE

45 years in the Land of the Rising Sun

ISBN 978-1-387-81461-9

Mary Klassen Derksen

Alvin Ens - Editor, Cover design
Mary Klassen Derksen - Photos
Dave Loewen - Layout, Publisher

Cataloguing Information
Peter and Mary Derksen
Japan missions
Missionary family
Commission on Overseas Mission of the
General Conference Mennonite Church
Mennonite Missions

RISE AND SHINE

45 years in the Land of the Rising Sun

Mary Klassen Derksen

Mary, Rickie, Vangy, Peter
Ready for Japan

Dedication

Dedicated to our strongest mission supporters,
our children:

Evangeline Helen
Richard John
Rosaline Hilda
William Paul
Wanda Marie
Lillian Ruth

PREFACE

I had no intention of publishing a book when I started to write our story. After we retired in 1999 from 45 years in Japan, we decided to collect all the prayer letters we had written every year and make a letter-sized book. Fortunately, we found the letters among our boxes that had crossed the Pacific. Oh, oh. Some years were missing. We checked with Helene, Peter's sister who always kept everything. Yes! She had a pile! We were still three years short. I had started writing **Our Story** for our family. Each part was a five-year term and a furlough. The result was ringed folders of approximately fifty pages each. "When are we getting the next one?" someone asked.

Peter's health deteriorated and I spent more time taking care of his needs, doctor appointments and hospital stays. My writing took a big break. Ten days after Peter's funeral in November, 2014, I was in the hospital for five blood transfusions. Next my doctor told me he suspected cancer in one of my kidneys. The following spring I had a major operation to remove the bad kidney. Imagine the joy when we got the results. The specialist told us, "Out of one hundred patients who have this same operation, only one, or possibly two, are benign." I was one of a hundred!

I received a letter from the Oita Mennonite Church asking me to write my testimony. I was quite put out. I did not feel like writing anything, let alone a testimony. They persisted, and finally I began to write. To my surprise, I found it quite therapeutic to share our experiences. I wrote a long testimony in Japanese.

Now it is time to write again. This book is my expression of thanks to God for restoring my health, and for His marvelous presence throughout our life, my life. It is also a thank you to our family, our many friends and churches in Canada and the US who supported us for forty-five years in Japan.

We were missionaries blundering our way in a strange culture and language among highly educated people. Missionaries are ordinary people. ***RISE and SHINE! 45 Years in the Land of the Rising Sun*** is the story of one ordinary Christian missionary family's life with an extraordinary God in a beautiful land that has become home, Japan.

Mary Klassen Derksen

Table of Contents

Dedication ---------- *v*

Preface ---------- *vi*

Preamble ---------- *ix*

Chapter 1: Our Roots ---------- *1*

Chapter 2: Japan, Here We Come; 1954 ~ 1956 ---------- *27*

Chapter 3: Aburatsu-Nichinan; 1956 ~ 1959 ---------- *45*

Chapter 4: Hyuga; 1960 ~ 1965 ---------- *81*

Chapter 5: Hyuga; 1966 ~ 1967 ---------- *127*

Chapter 6: Oita; 1967 ~ 1971 ---------- *149*

Chapter 7: Oita; 1972 ~ 1978 ---------- *205*

Chapter 8: Beppu; 1978 ~ 1988 ---------- *245*

Chapter 9: Minami-Oita; 1988 ~ 1989 ---------- *292*

Chapter 10: Hakata-Fukuoka Ken; 1990 ~ 1999 ---------- *306*

Acknowledgements ---------- *337*

PREAMBLE

GONE – 45 YEARS!

"What have we done?" my husband Peter asked, as we settled in the jumbo jet. Teary-eyed, I looked out on the tarmac of Fukuoka International Airport, but people and vehicles became a blur. The jumbo roared to life! I wiped my eyes so I could get a last look at Japan, our home for the past 45 years. As the plane lifted into the air, I felt my insides bursting, and my body began to shake with heaving sobs! What had we done?

For years we had known that someday we would have to leave. Today – July 5th, 1999 - was that day, and we were being swept into the sky away from our beloved Japan. There had been little time to absorb it all, but now the reality hit us. Were we really leaving our adopted land of Japan to return to Canada?

"Love"

Chapter 1

OUR ROOTS OUR CALL

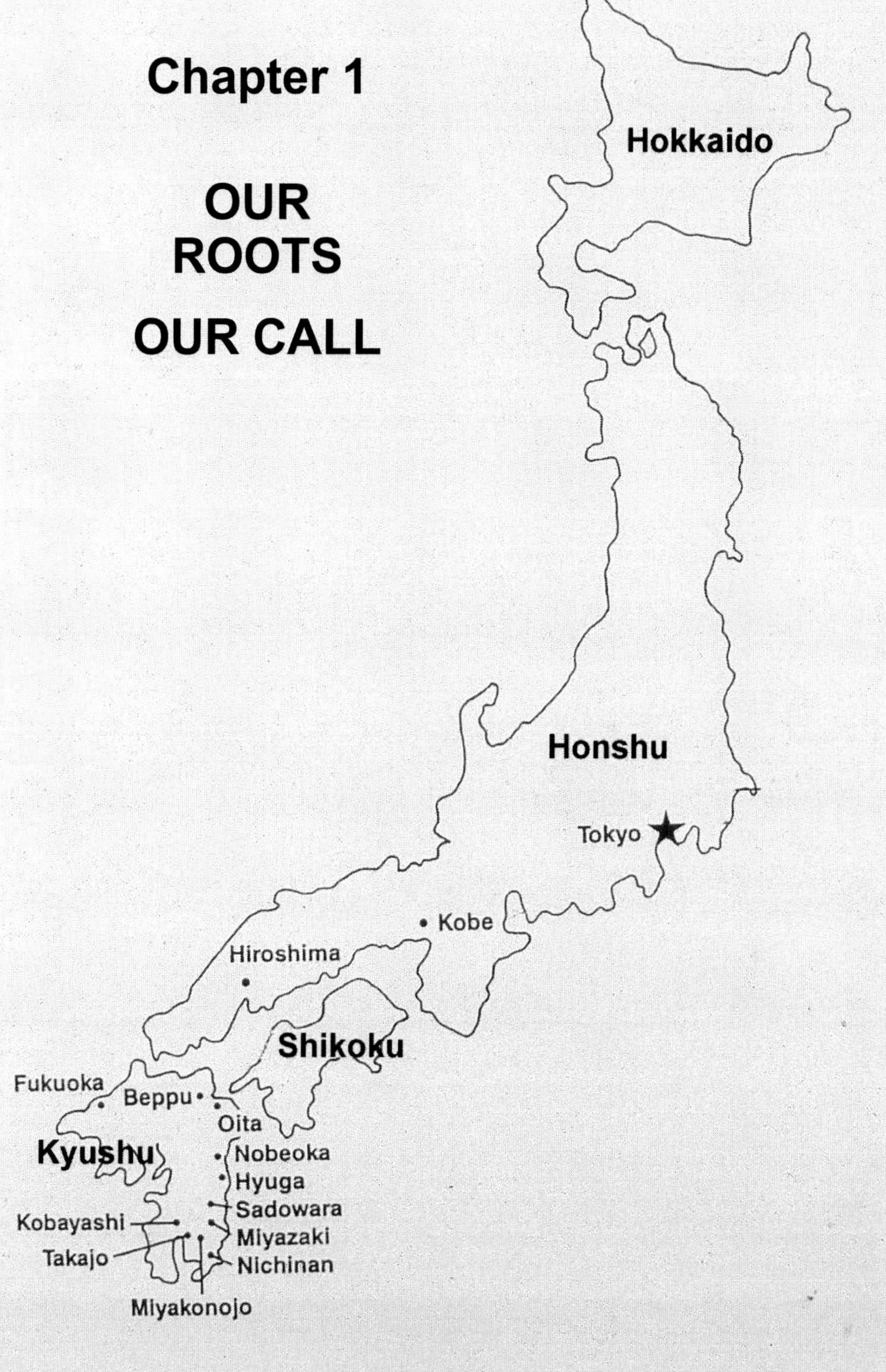

GROWING UP

What miracle could possibly have brought our paths together? Peter Derksen from Abbotsford, British Columbia, and Mary Klassen from Virgil, Ontario? Both were born in 1928, Peter in Reinland, Manitoba, and Mary in Kronstal, Ukraine. Peter's family immigrated to Canada in 1925, and Mary's family fled on the last train from Moscow that went through the Red Gate before the Iron Curtain came down in Russia in 1929.

We grew up in Christian homes, with daily devotions, prayer, and much love. We attended Sunday School and church from earliest childhood. We lived thousands of miles apart. Peter's parents, Peter and Maria Derksen, were chicken and berry farmers in Abbotsford, BC. Mary's parents, Dietrich and Agatha Klassen, were fruit farmers in Virgil, Ontario. Mary's father was also a lay minister in the Virgil Mennonite Brethren Church. Peter was in the middle of five siblings, Erna, Melita, Helene and Henry. Mary was the oldest of six, Walter, Helmut, Martha, Hilda and Frieda.

Peter's parents were pioneers who moved to Abbotsford in 1936. They bought ten acres on Marshall Road, and proceeded to build their own house. They ate mostly what their garden produced, which was a big help financially.

While growing up, Peter's strongest influence was his Christian home. Every evening the family gathered around the small pump organ to sing, enjoy Bible stories, and kneel to pray. His family was one of the founding members of the West Abbotsford Mennonite Church. They had no vehicle, so they walked to church more than a mile away every Sunday.

The children also attended meetings in a small mission close to their home. when Peter was twelve, he followed the invitation to accept Jesus into his heart. Years later he wrote, "I can still remember how the whole world seemed different next morning as I was walking to school. Jesus Christ had become real to me. I now wanted to live for Him. Most of my classmates were not Christians, and I realized that I could not do many of the things they were doing. I was in God's world, and I wanted to live as a child of God's world. I read biographies of famous evangelists, and in my heart I had a deep desire to become an evangelist." In Bible college he came to the decision to follow Christ at any cost.

Peter also had a mischievous bent. He told me how once he had grabbed an arm full of one of his sister's clothes, run down and outside to the potato cellar, with the sister running after him screaming!

PRIVATE HIGH SCHOOLS

Although they were poor, Peter's parents felt a Christian education, even though much more expensive, was important for their children, and sent Peter and his sisters to the new Christian high school, Mennonite Educational Institute, MEI.

Peter attended M.E.I. from the first year of its existence in 1944. He seldom got into trouble, but one day during choir practice, he whistled. F.C. Thiessen, the music teacher asked, "Who did that?" He was shocked when Peter raised his hand. "Peter, das haette ich nicht gedacht von dir!" (I would not have thought that of you) he said. German was still prominent.

Meanwhile, many young people in our churches in Ontario attended Bible schools. We didn't know of any Christian high schools in Ontario. When we heard about OBS, Ontario Bible School, a Christian high school in Fort Erie, enthusiasm spread like wildfire. I begged my parents to let me go. My father said, "Only if you take something you can finish in two years."

Sending me to a boarding school was a big concession, as my parents struggled to keep our family farm going. I registered for the two-year business course, and lived in the dormitory. Those of us from the Niagara community took turns taking the family car for the week, returning home weekends. We made the one-hour trip either Sunday evening or early Monday. Every weekend we passed the famous Niagara Falls, one of the Seven Wonders of the World. What a marvelous creation of God! How could those tons of water keep pouring over the falls day by day, year by year, century by century? I never tired of watching this extraordinary creation of God. Beyond Niagara Falls we drove along the scenic Niagara River to our school on its banks.

The building used to be a high-class three-story estate. What was once a dance hall became a chapel overlooking the Niagara River. Offices and classrooms were on the main floor and part of the second. The girls' dormitory was on second and third floors. The large attic was transformed into a boys' dormitory. Our dining room was in the basement. One hundred students from four Mennonite denominations made one big happy family in one big building. Most students were from southern Ontario, Niagara, St. Catharines, Welland, Vineland, and Leamington areas, and a few from Manitoba and Alberta.

The business course proved useful immediately. After my first year, at sixteen, I was offered a summer job in the office of the Niagara Fruit Co-op, where I took shorthand letters from my boss, typed, and helped with bookkeeping. I held that summer job for two years.

Several of us in the two-year business course graduated together with the grade twelve students. I begged my father to let me continue high school, so reluctantly he allowed me to return for grade eleven. Then my best friend Rose and I decided to attend St. Catharines Collegiate near home for grade twelve. This was much cheaper. However, I had missed out on the math and science subjects while taking business, so I never graduated from high school.

LINKS

Our call to Japan had come like a chain - one link at a time.

Link one: I had my first experience with First Nations people at OBS. Ruth and two cousins, aboriginals, had braved the white world of OBS, and found acceptance and friendship. Ruth became a close friend. Every fall and spring the school held a spiritual emphasis week. Bishop E.J. Swalm, one of the evangelists, called me aside and praised me for befriending Ruth. I didn't understand. She was a friend, so why should I be praised?

A second dubious link came with my father who was lay pastor of the large Virgil M.B. church. Missionaries on furlough from India or Africa often stayed with us. I don't remember what they shared in church, but I vividly remember the wild animal stories they told us at home! As a result, I had a horrible dread of lions, elephants, tigers, snakes and all wild creatures!

Bishop Swalm had altar calls every night for those who wanted to dedicate their lives to serve the Lord. Oh, yes, I wanted to, but oh no, what if God called me to India or Africa where they had all those fierce wild animals? No, please, God! But yes, if God called me to such a country, he would protect me, wouldn't he? After a long struggle I could release my fears and say "Yes, Lord!"

A third link, my first contact with Japanese was when I worked in the office of Boese Foods canning factory during the next four summers. A very friendly Japanese Canadian, George Hotta, worked on the Boese fruit farm, and brought the daily fruit in for weighing. He was the first Japanese I ever saw.

Peter's first link to Japan was with Japanese Canadians in junior high school. He often wondered what happened when they suddenly disappeared from school during WWII. Many years later he discovered that they had been sent to the internment camps for Japanese "enemies." Why had no one told the students?

OUR CALL

After high school graduation in 1947, Peter followed God's call to prepare for ministry at the Mennonite Brethren Bible College in Winnipeg, where we first met. He felt God calling him to be an evangelist/teacher in North America, and I felt God calling me to overseas missionary service. Peter was from the General Conference Mennonite Church and I was from the Mennonite Brethren Church. He had chosen this college because of the strong faculty and Bible emphasis. (omit and faculty.) I told friends Peter went to the wrong school.

I went to MBBC in January, 1949. Friends soon began linking our names. No dating was allowed during the school year. However, friends found ways to connect us. Sometimes it was in the pantry peeling potatoes for supper. Once it was taking the same street car to the Mennonite Symphony concert downtown. Always with a friend, mind you. Ben Horch, our music director, believed in getting involved. There I was, not only attending, but tinkling the triangle, and crashing the cymbals at the right places in the symphony. Scary!

Discovering a male and female student together would never do. But that didn't stop the furtive looks, catching a quick smile in passing, or studying in the library – at different tables, of course. Once, Peter and I were playing ping-pong with friends, Jake and Millie, when the dean walked in. "This is not allowed," he told us, "Playing together in a room raises the blood pressure!"

A Christian from Japan and I became good friends. Thielmans, Mennonite Central Committee workers in Osaka, Japan, after WWII, had arranged for her to attend MBBC in Winnipeg. When the Japanese student's mother sent a parcel of delicacies from Japan, she invited several of us to her room for a treat. The rice balls wrapped in seaweed tasted yucky. How could anyone enjoy such a "treat?" When she told us that her parents worshipped idols, my mind did a flip. Mind-boggling! I was hearing firsthand what we had been told – people worship idols made of stone!

Peter was studying the three-year theology course, and I was enrolled in the music course. One of his highlights in college was a study of the book of Acts, and how the Holy Spirit in the early church became alive was a great influence on his later ministry. One of my highlights was singing in the trio for the weekly GOSPEL LIGHT HOUR radio program. We both sang in the acapella choir under the direction of Ben Horch. For the Christmas concert we sang Handel's Messiah. It was the first time for many students to hear this great masterpiece.

Graduation brought the culmination of many a secret romance. With restraints gone, young grads hurried after lone women students walking back to their apartment or dormitory in the dusk. There were numerous surprises, but I don't think we surprised anyone.

Peter took me to a restaurant in a borrowed car. Everyone in school knew he was a vegetarian, but on this date he had a meat sandwich. I concluded I could make headway with that problem! However, at the end of our date, he shook hands with me and said our future was not to be together. I was heartbroken. He didn't even ask if I would marry him. He took for granted that my strict MB pastor father would never allow him to marry his daughter unless he became an MB, too. For Peter, that was out of the question, because he felt God was calling him to work in his own denomination.

OUR ENGAGEMENT

When Peter returned home to BC, his mother immediately sensed something was wrong and questioned him. Just as she had suspected, he was in love, but had decided it wouldn't work. Ma Derksen was bold, and encouraged him to go for it! He wrote this strict MB pastor to ask for his daughter. It was not quite so simple. Father told me about the letter, and asked, "Do you love Peter?"

When I responded in the positive, he said, "Then there is only one way!" He had thoroughly investigated this young upstart through his good friends who were MBBC college professors. Soon Dad received excellent reports about this would-be evangelist, by now a teacher at Bethel Bible Institute in Abbotsford, BC, and gave him permission to contact me. Peter and his brother Henry made the long trip by car from BC to Ontario that summer, and we were engaged.

That was not as simple as it sounds. No way would my minister father allow me to be seen with this young man from BC in church on a Sunday morning without an engagement announcement! So instead of waiting for the romantic afternoon Peter had planned, Father arranged for us to meet in his study on Sunday morning. Peter was waiting for me and asked me right there to be his bride. Our engagement was announced in church an hour later!

After the worship service friends congratulated us. A friend grabbed my left hand to see my engagement ring. My hand was empty! Peter had told me that all he owned was an extra pair of pants and a small Austin car. Would I still marry him without any guarantee of making a living? Oh yes, I certainly would. After our tragic first date, I had told my roommate Helen, "If I can't marry Peter, I will never marry!"

In spite of these obstacles we still had a lovely afternoon at Glen Park on the Niagara River, but the surprise and romance of the moment were lost. My friend's search for a ring on my finger had not gone unnoticed. A few weeks after Peter returned to BC, I received a small parcel in the mail. I eagerly opened the box, and inside found the most beautiful diamond engagement ring! He had borrowed money from his parents to purchase it.

After graduating from MBBC, Peter was hired to teach at Bethel Bible Institute in Abbotsford, BC. At twenty-two, he was the youngest teacher, and felt the challenge of teaching the Bible and related subjects to young people who were eager to learn and grow and prepare for lives of service.

Peter was also the school's choir director. They practiced *The Hallelujah Chorus* from **Handel's Messiah** and sang it for the afternoon spring closing program in Peter's home church. In the evening the program would be presented once more. Peter's mother warned him, "Do not sing the Hallelujah song in the evening. People have told me they will walk out. Too much repetition!"

However, this young choir leader did not give in. A few years later, *The Hallelujah Chorus* became a tradition in his church every Christmas morning for over 50 years! One furlough Peter was asked to conduct *The Hallelujah Chorus* Christmas morning. Our oldest daughter, Vangy, then a teenager, and I also sang in the choir that Daddy conducted! A highlight!

During the two years after Peter's graduation, he took part in a weekly radio program. The Wiebe quartet sang, Betty Suderman was pianist, and Peter preached for The Messengers of Peace broadcast live from Bellingham, WA, every Sunday afternoon. The radio staff at KPUG compared the quartet to the Haven of Rest Quartet in California, and Peter to Billy Graham.

The East Chilliwack Mennonite Church (now Eden Mennonite), asked Peter to be choir leader. Twice a week we drove to Chilliwack for choir practice, and again for Sunday services. Many choir members had attended the Bible school where Peter taught. He loved this added connection. It seemed to be mutual. Many years later when I met former students, they would say, "Mr. Derksen was my favorite teacher!"

OUR WEDDING

In the fall of 1950 Peter heard a report by William Voth, missionary from China. The Voths, along with all foreign missionaries, had to leave China when the Communists came to power. The General Conference Mennonite Mission Board asked Voth to make an exploratory trip to Japan to investigate the possibility of opening mission work there. At the end of the meeting, Peter was asked to make the closing remarks. God had challenged him, and he said, "If God should call me to serve in Japan, I am willing to go."

I still had one year of Bible College before our wedding, which was planned for August, 1951. Peter sent me a sleeper train ticket to come B.C. to spend Christmas with his family. I was so excited about being together again. I had never seen mountains. At night I kept looking out of the window and could hardly imagine that those looming dark shadows against the sky were actually mountains!

This was my first meeting with Peter's family. I don't remember much except for one happening. They served frozen strawberries for a night snack and set the sugar dish on the table. I sprinkled sugar on my strawberries, ate one small spoonful, and waited. When one of them started eating strawberries with sugar, what a commotion! Someone had mistakenly put salt into the sugar bowl!

A college friend, Elsie Lenzmann and I were both planning weddings in the summer of 1951. We found the most beautiful lacy material for our wedding dresses on sale at Eaton's for $8.00. A friend's mother made my dress with small delicate covered buttons from the waist to the neck, a peter-pan collar, long sleeves, and a train.

If the dress could talk, it would have interesting tales to tell. We took it with us when we went to Japan three years later, and when our first pastor planned to get married, I offered my dress to his bride. She accepted gratefully. However, I had cut the train off to make a dress for our baby Rosie! After we retired one of our granddaughters asked if she could use it for Halloween! I hesitated, then reluctantly consented. Now the dress is packed away in a suitcase, yellowing with age. I tried wriggling into it without success after we had been married 50 years.

August 18th, 1951, our wedding day, was perfect! We had scheduled it for six days after Peter's 23rd birthday, so that we would be the same age. Perhaps most brides and bridegrooms have doubts during engagement time, and so did I. After all, next to receiving Christ as Savior, this was the biggest decision of my life. We would promise "till death do us part." That was a long time into the future. Would we make it? We didn't really know each other. But there is the anticipation, and then there is the gift of love. On this day all my doubts vanished. My heart warmed with a deep love for Peter. Strange that each felt a different calling – Peter for evangelism in North America, and I, for overseas missions. Yet we knew that the Lord had brought us together, and He would lead.

The wedding was in my home church in Virgil, Ontario. Simplicity ruled. No attendants, not even a flower girl. My father married us. I do not remember his message, but I do remember a very quiet peace and joy in my heart.

The church ladies helped prepare food for the reception in the church basement. About 400 people were invited. Naturally, this included the whole congregation. Peter's Mother and younger sister Helene had come from B.C. His older sister Melita was an MCC volunteer in Washington, DC at the time, so she was also able to attend.

We spent the first week after our wedding in my home in Virgil. During that time we packed, and then left for our new home in BC. The farewells with my family were difficult. After all, I was moving clear across Canada, but for our family it might as well have been to another continent. When would we see each other again?

The trip west to B.C. was our honeymoon, but Mother Derksen and Helene drove with us, sleeping in the car while Peter and I slept in motels. Not very conducive for building close family relationships! This new bride struggled. However, I learned to love my Mother-in-law as much as my own Mother. We just needed some time and space.

OUR FIRST HOME

Our first home was a three room apartment in the Bethel Bible Institute dormitory next to our church. Now the facility is King Haven, a drug rehabilitation centre in Abbotsford. Our luxuries consisted of cold running water, a wood stove, a piano which was a wedding gift from my parents, and an outdoor privy. We often went to Peter's home for meals, but also had guests in our small apartment.

Rev. H.H. Janzen, one of our professors from MBBC, was a night visitor in our humble apartment one wintry night. Rev. Janzen was one reason we were together, since he had told my Father what a wonderful young man Peter was! After breakfast, I needed to use the outhouse. As soon as I stepped outside I noticed the icy path. Too late! Both feet slid and I landed smack on my seat. I forced myself up, and when I went in, I didn't let on how much it hurt. No way would I show any discomfort, let alone pain. I still have a lumpy tailbone!

At MBBC I had loved singing in the a'capella choir, piano, and voice lessons. In Abbotsford I felt quite lost. Then I found a good voice teacher in Vancouver and drove to lessons once a week. That was before the freeway was built, so it was a time-consuming drive. At BBI I taught a few voice lessons. One of my students still likes to make me feel special that I taught him. I sang an occasional solo, although performing was always a nervous experience.

Morning and evening Peter and I had devotions. One evening the Bible passage from Romans 10:13-15 gripped us with an urgency that we had never experienced. *Everyone who calls on the name of the Lord will be saved. How, then, can they call on the one they have not believed in? And how can they believe in the one of whom they have not heard? And how can they hear without someone preaching to them? And how can they preach unless they are sent?*

We both had a deep desire to share the good news of our Lord and Savior with others. That evening God was tugging us together towards overseas mission. In Canada people who wanted to hear the Gospel could find a church, or hear it via radio. In many countries, neither was an option. Millions were without Christ.

Bethel Bible Institute had a six-month school year. We moved to Vancouver in spring so Peter could find a job. A funeral home looking for a driver hired Peter. He had three days of training, and saw some of the inner workings of the funeral business, including embalming a body. The boss was very pleased, until Peter told him he could work only for a few months. He fired Peter immediately. They could not afford to train a new worker for a few months. What a disappointment!

God provided another job, unloading grain cars by the harbor. At the end of the first week Peter told them he would not work on Sunday. The foreman told him, "Don't bother coming back on Monday!" But Peter bravely returned Monday morning, and nothing was said! He did back-breaking grain shoveling all summer.

In our search for God's plan for our life, we consulted our mission board in Newton, Kansas. They encouraged Peter to get his BA degree and some seminary training. Thus, after teaching at BBI for two years, we packed our car and moved to Newton, Kansas, to study at Bethel College for a year. Then we moved to New York City, where Peter attended New York Biblical Seminary for one year.

OUR FAMILY GROWS

On Sunday, July 30, 1952, Evangeline Helen was born. When Peter arrived at the meeting place in Abbotsford to drive to Bellingham for the radio program, the Wiebe quartet was waiting on the sidewalk and sang,

"Evangeline Helen's just come 'long ...to ring dem charmin' bells!"

Vangy was the first grandchild for both our parents. The small cottage hospital was overcrowded, and after a long painful night of labor I ended up in the hallway opposite the noisy kitchen. When Peter's mother came to the hospital and found me in the hallway, she was not pleased. She immediately told the hospital that I was going home with her!

Mother was thrilled with her first grandchild and insisted that we leave Vangy with her for the first few nights so that she would learn to sleep through the night. Probably Mother slept little those nights, but the training worked! We spent most of that month in Peter's home and returned to our apartment for nights while Oma kept Vangy.

When Vangy was a month old, we packed everything we owned, except our piano and a bookcase made for Peter by a favorite Sunday School teacher, Peter Unger, into our car, and put Vangy in her basket. We said good-bye to family and friends. Oma Derksen finally had her wish for a grandchild fulfilled only to have her taken away.

BETHEL COLLEGE, KANSAS

In North Newton we lived behind the post office in an upstairs apartment of the Barnettes. It used to be a barn and looked like a barn! Peter just had to walk across the street to classes at Bethel College. We made many new friends, and Peter was busy with studies. He was also asked to be assistant pastor of the Walton Mennonite Church, so we worshipped in that little country church not far from Newton.

Both Peter and I grew up in very conservative churches. What a shock to see women in a Mennonite church wearing lipstick! And a woman teaching Sunday School, chewing gum in front of the class as if her life depended on it! What a difference between Canadian and U.S. Mennonite cultures! However, they welcomed us warmly and we gained lifelong friends and mission supporters.

Peter graduated from Bethel College with his BA in the spring of 1953. Erwin Goering resigned as pastor of the Walton Church, and the church asked Peter to be interim pastor for the summer. The dry heat of Kansas was almost unbearable as I was due to give birth in September. Mrs. Linscheid, the post office manager, invited us to move into her basement which was much cooler than our apartment.

In July, Vangy and I boarded a train for Chicago, where my parents from Ontario picked us up to attend my brother Walter's wedding in Steinbach, Manitoba. His bride was Grace Warkentin. In my condition it was not an easy trip. However, it was one of only two siblings' weddings I attended. Peter missed all of his. On our trip home to Ontario with my folks, we stayed in motels. One night I awoke to Vangy's cries, and all of us scratching! When we turned on the light, we found the place jumping with fleas! I don't think we ever packed so quickly. We left at 4 AM and carried a few fleas with us until all were finally eradicated.

What a happy summer on the farm in Virgil with my parents. Peter joined us at the end of August. On Sept. 9, 1953, Richard John was born in the Hotel Dieu hospital in St. Catharines. When we brought him home from the hospital, Peter was holding Vangy, and I was holding her new baby brother. Her welcome was a quick slap on his face.

SEMINARY IN NEW YORK

Dr. Erland Waltner, who had become a good friend during our year at Bethel, recommended that Peter attend New York Biblical Seminary in New York City. Peter applied and was accepted. Classes would begin in mid-September. We left Virgil, Ontario, in September in our old Buick. Vangy was one, and Rickie nine days old. Ma (as the Derksen family called her), had come from BC to help for a month.

The seminary had indicated that they would have an apartment for us. When we arrived on 33rd street in the teeming asphalt jungle of Manhatten, Peter went to the office to announce our arrival. Dean Ahern said, "I hope you didn't bring your family!"

When Peter said, "They are outside in the car," he was quite concerned.

"I thought of sending you a telegram to come alone," he said. Too late! They had nothing for us, and sent us to a hotel. I had not recuperated from Rickie's birth yet and cried and cried. Fifteen dollars a night! Our meager savings of $400 would be eaten up in no time.

The next day Peter returned to the seminary and found out that God was already solving our problem. Rev. George Hardy, a part-time student at the seminary, pastor of a Baptist church in the Bronx, had heard of our plight. He and his wife offered to take this homeless family in until we found something. It was a long drive through the skyscraper jungle of Manhattan to the Bronx. They had a hot meal waiting for us. This young couple hosted our large family of five for ten days before we found an unexpected solution.

On the first Sunday the seminary sent us to a Presbyterian church in Long Island. The church wanted a seminary student as interim pastor for the year. They had a lovely parsonage next to the church. However, during the morning worship service they had infant baptism. Peter knew he might be required to perform that ceremony. After the service he met with the board of elders in a room with thick swirls of blue smoke circling above their heads. Definitely not a church for us! The dean was quite disappointed that Peter turned down this wonderful offer.

Another blow hit us that night. When Peter reached into his pocket for his wallet, it was gone. He immediately cancelled the $400 check. We knew our savings would not last long in New York, but we had launched out in faith that the Lord would provide. We got the money back some time later.

During our stay at the Hardy's, I was quite sick for a few days. What a life-saver that Ma was there to help with the children! Peter was already in classes, but nothing was opening up for living quarters. One day Rev. Hardy bravely made an offer. Their church was looking for a janitor, with free accommodations in a small apartment on the fourth floor of the church tower. The pay was $25 a month. Would we care to look at it? We were ready to try anything, and I slowly climbed the three flights of stairs. When Mr. Hardy opened the door, the sun streaming in welcomed us warmly! It was small, but there were windows all around, and I told Peter we could manage. We accepted the offer, and moved in.

APARTMENT

The apartment consisted of one large room, a tiny bathroom, and a cramped bedroom. The bedroom held a double bed and a baby's crib which had to be moved to get at the closet. Rickie would sleep in his baby basket on the floor. The living room had furniture on every side. Ma would sleep on the couch. A small fridge, table and chairs, and a washing machine filled the wall space. No dryer. We hung diapers and other laundry in the church balcony one floor below.

We looked down on the lively Italian neighborhood. Small grocery stores sent aromas of Italian garlic sausages and cheeses through their open doors. Our favorites were the bakeries, with a new treat for us, cannoli, a rich scone stuffed with a delicious cream cheese filling.

It was 1953, and we still didn't know what our future held. When the seminary planned a day of prayer and fasting for November 18, we decided to spend the day separately, praying for God's direction. That day we both felt with certainty that God was calling us to serve Him in Japan. We wrote the mission board about our decision. Within two weeks we received a letter from John Thiessen, secretary of the mission board. The missionaries in Japan had asked for two couples. Bob and Alice Ruth Ramseyer from Bluffton, Ohio, and we had responded. The mission board wanted us to leave for Japan the following summer. At last! An assignment, and not to a country with fierce animals! What a relief!

Peter was busy with classes, school assignments, family, and janitor work. I helped where I could, dusting church benches and typing Peter's term papers. The church people were mostly Italians with a Catholic background. Here we gained a whole new set of friends. We also spent many happy hours with the Hardy's.

At Christmas, quite unexpectedly, Pastor Hardy resigned and took a pastorate in a different area of the city. What a shock! The church asked Peter to be interim pastor until the end of the school year. They moved us into the parsonage next door. What luxury to have a whole house when most people in our neighborhood lived in tenements where laundry was hung from windows. We even had tiny front and back yards. The famous Bronx Zoo was within walking distance, and on Sunday afternoons we took the children in the buggy. Peter continued the janitor job, and preached on Sundays. His salary rose to $125 a month, so we had more money when we left New York than when we came!

The folks at St. John the Baptist church were very friendly, but the culture was so different. Some would leave the service shaking Peter's hand, holding a lit cigarette with the other, saying, "That was a wonderful sermon, Pastor." There were also dedicated Christians who shared in our excitement of going to Japan as missionaries.

When we first drove through the teeming streets of New York, I thought, never could I drive there. But before we left I had mastered the art of driving in the largest, at that time, city in the world! Quite an accomplishment! Peter had his own firsts, one of which was conducting a funeral. His short experience with a Vancouver funeral company came in handy.

PREPARING FOR JAPAN

Preparations for moving overseas were endless. Dental work, medical check-ups, shots for typhoid, smallpox, cholera, and tetanus. Passport applications. Shopping for clothes, household and food items. Missionaries in Japan sent orders. Correspondence to the mission board and to our families. We ordered prayer cards with a family picture for our prayer partners. April the 22 Peter's picture and write-up appeared in the New York Post. Sixty-three years later I still have a copy of that article. How could such an unknown student pastor's picture appear in a New York newspaper?

April 28 we received notice from our mission board that we were booked to leave from Seattle, Washington on the freighter S.S. OCEAN MAIL August 30. In the midst of all the preparations, Vangy suddenly had the measles.

The last months flew by and, before we knew it, we were packing our earthly possessions into the old Buick once more. Tears ran freely as we said good-bye to our friends at St. John the Baptist church in the Bronx on May 21 and left for the cross-country trip. that would take us to BC. Our first stop was Virgil, Ontario, to spend a few weeks with Mary's family, and then home to BC.

Missionaries are put to work immediately, and during our short time in Ontario we visited many churches, sharing our call to Japan and showing slides of Japan from the mission board. We spoke in eleven meetings.

The mission board had arranged orientation meetings at the Mission Center in Chicago for new missionaries going out under our conference to Japan, India, Columbia, Congo, and Taiwan. We heard speakers from various missions and enjoyed wonderful fellowship. Missionaries whom we met there became lifelong friends, including Bob and Alice Ruth Ramseyer, our new coworkers.

It was hot and humid, and the children were restless. Rickie was feeling sick. We thought he was teething. However, a few days later he developed a red rash over his whole body. Measles! The following day he cut his first tooth.

Finally, on June 29, we left for Abbotsford, BC in our bulky '41 Buick, every nook and cranny full. There was just enough room for Vangy and Rickie on top of the baggage. The first day we were caught in a cloud burst resulting in wet spark plugs. In spite of the delays, we drove 630 miles that day. The next day we visited a former Bible college roommate in ND and drove 603 miles. The third day we ran out of gas in the mountains and had a flat tire. This trip was a good learning experience in accepting hassles along with our own bungling. When we reached Everett, WA, the car began to sputter. We managed to putter to Abbotsford. Two miles from our parents' home, the car coughed once more and then gave up, refusing to drive up that last long hill! We phoned our folks to get us and arrived home July 2, 1954.

LAST WEEKS IN CANADA

During our short time in BC we were scheduled for sixteen meetings in churches and schools. We shared at a church camp for children. The last night 31 children received Jesus as their Savior. What joy in the camp and in heaven! And what a preparation for mission work!

On July 11, Peter had the children's feature in church, and also preached. In my diary I wrote, "Peter's new sermon inspiring." In all our years of missionary service and furloughs, I never tired of Peter's preaching even though I heard some of his sermons over and over again.

Weekdays we helped on the farm. I drove tractor for the men loading hay. We ordered a fridge, washing machine, crib, and locker from Sears-Roebuck across the border. There was no end of shopping, as we were warned that we might not find shoes and clothes to fit us in Japan. We discovered, since we were both short, that was not a problem. We spent hours searching for metal drums for packing, and made detailed lists of contents. Thinking we would not need fancy things, we left many of our beautiful wedding gifts stored with our folks. Wrong thinking! During our two years of language school we often entertained Japanese friends and travelers. After our first furlough, we took our gifts to Japan.

On Sunday, August 22' the West Abbotsford Church and Chilliwack churches celebrated a Missionsfest and commissioned us for ministry in Japan. Bishop J.J. Thiessen from Saskatoon, the guest speaker, laid hands on us for the commissioning. Blessing upon blessing. We felt so unworthy but so rich with all our Christian brothers and sisters and many friends from other churches. Bishop Thiessen surprised us when he bent to plant a kiss on my forehead! In those days such things were not done. But he made me feel like family!

In our files I found a paragraph about our last week in Canada, written August 22, 1954. "*This is the day the Lord hath made; let us be glad and rejoice in it.* We had looked forward to this important day with much joy and anticipation. Our commissioning as missionaries was to take place at 2 p.m. The West Abbotsford Mennonite Church had set the day aside for a Missionsfest. It was raining, and as God poured His blessings on the fields, He also showered us with bountiful blessings in the church. The preaching, the choir singing and quartet, and the many verses of Scripture touched our hearts. We felt grateful as never before for the many prayer partners God was giving us. O, Lord, may the knowledge of our dear friends praying for us keep us humble, and make us worthy to be called Your servants. And may this day serve to draw many Christians into closer fellowship with Christ, so that young people choose to follow You all the way."

DEPARTING

Suddenly Vangy got the flu. Ma Derksen became sick. Our family doctor couldn't find any cause, but presumed it was the stress of her oldest son and family leaving perhaps for a seven year term, as we thought at the time. To her it seemed like forever. She had often taken care of children of sick moms in church. Now she finally had her own grandchildren, and they were going to the other side of the world. It might as well have been to the moon! Much as Ma wanted us to serve the Lord, she found it very difficult. She remained in bed until two days before our departure. A constant stream of friends and relatives dropped in to say good-bye. Some stayed for meals. With a sick toddler, a baby, a sick mother, and people coming all day, how did we ever manage to pack?

Saturday August 28, 1954, departure day. Peter's brother, Henry, took us to Seattle by truck to Pier 88 with our baggage. That evening I felt sick and tired. Sunday we attended a Baptist church. In the afternoon we said good-bye to Henry who returned to BC.

Monday, August 30, family and friends came from BC to see us off.

What a special time of singing, praying and saying farewells on the deck of the Ocean Mail. A young oriental lady stood nearby, watching us with keen interest. Realizing that we were new missionaries leaving for Japan, she introduced herself as Seiko Kuroda, a Christian kindergarten teacher who was returning to Japan after two years of study in Chicago. She asked to say a few words and gave a warm testimony in English, thanking our family and friends for sending missionaries to her country to share the Good News of Jesus Christ. What an encouragement!

All too soon the announcement came, "All visitors must leave the ship!" We felt both the pain of separation from loved ones, and the anticipation of our life that stretched before us like the wide ocean. We were eager to be on our way.

We threw paper streamers to the folks on the pier. At 9 PM the ship gave three deafening blasts, and the gangplank was raised. Slowly the ship began to move. We waved to family and friends and tugged at the streamers, wanting to hold on to the final connections as long as possible. As the last streamers dropped into the water, our last physical ties with North America were gone. Soon those on the pier faded into small dots in the distance, leaving the blinking lights of NA bidding us farewell. Farewell loved ones! Farewell North America.

Peter and Maria Derksen Family

Dietrich and Agatha Klassen Family

Peter and Maria Derksen—
Abbotsford pioneers

Peter and Mary's Wedding, 1951

Cousins; Peter wearing hat

Peter's (front center) high school graduation from MEI

Ontario Bible School Choir

Ontario Bible School with Niagara River in foreground

Messengers of Peace Radio Program; Peter at mic

Bethel College graduation

Chapter 2

Japan, Here We Come 1954~1956

OFF TO JAPAN

Off to Japan, Land of the Rising Sun! We had chosen our motto: "Your Servants for Jesus' sake." Little did we know how that motto would challenge us.

The Ocean Mail was a freighter with cabins for twelve passengers. On ship we spent time getting acquainted with Bob and Alice Ruth Ramseyer and son Mark, six months old. We had met at missionary orientation in Chicago, and now were going out under the same General Conference Mennonite Board of Missions. Later the name of our mission board was changed to The Commission on Overseas Mission (COM) of the General Conference Mennonite Church of North America As we became acquainted with missionaries from other missions, we began to realize that our mission board must be the best! We were often overwhelmed with the care and support we received.

After the victory over Japan at the end of WWII, General McArthur sent out an urgent message to the churches in North America. "Send 1,000 missionaries to Japan!" Ramseyers and we were a small fraction of the response to that challenge. Hundreds of missionaries had already responded.

Seiko, the Japanese lady, soon became a good friend to these young green horns going to her country to evangelize! Why, we didn't know a single Japanese word, not even "Ohio gozaimasu," (Good Morning). She patiently taught us some introductory words – greetings, thank you, please, yes and no, and other important phrases. We kept up contact with Seiko and her husband throughout the years, although we met only a few times. The last time was in their home in Tokyo when Mr. Kuroda was in his nineties.

The first day at sea the ocean was calm but foggy. Our captain called it a millpond. The twelve passengers, including three Ramseyers, Seiko, and four Derksens, had meals with the captain. The food was delicious, and so far, no one was seasick. Rickie was quite restless day and night. Vangy loved the deck, and we walked around and around. The fifth day we ran into a storm, and Vangy was seasick.

Poor Peter lost his land legs, and felt quite sick much of the time. He was very happy when air travel became less expensive. However, I always enjoyed the relaxed two-week ocean trips, where I had time to adjust to the other culture again whether we were coming or going. One added bonus of ship travel was the stop in Hawaii for a day, when we could go ashore and see a bit of this exotic country that we had only heard about.

Sunday Peter spoke at a worship service for the passengers. Besides our two missionary families and Seiko, there were two young Christian men on board. Every day we pushed our clocks ahead. Monday, September 6, we crossed the date line, and lost a day! By Tuesday we had gained five hours. September 9 we celebrated Rickie's first birthday with a cake that I baked in the galley.

LAND OF THE RISING SUN

We rose with excitement when the freighter neared Japan, and we spotted the land of the rising sun in the early morning hours after thirteen days at sea. This was the beginning of a new journey that would last a lifetime!

Japan! Land of the Rising sun! The land to which God had called us. Time to **"*Rise and Shine*!"** Our hearts were filled with awe and anticipation, and a deep desire to share the marvelous light of our Savior, Jesus Christ. We saw the first lights of Japan at 6 PM and soon arrived in Yokohama harbor, where the freighter stayed overnight.

This was not the end of our trip. Our destination was Kobe, but the Ocean Mail would be in Yokohama for a few days. Don McCammons, who had been Mennonite missionaries in China but had relocated to Japan when Communism deported all missionaries, took us to their home in Tokyo for the night.

Evenings we had wonderful fellowship at the McCammons, where Pete Willms, a former Ontario Bible School classmate, joined us. Pete and his wife Mary had come to Japan as missionaries under the Brethren in Christ mission, and served in the town of Hagi on the western tip of Honshu Island.

I wrote first impressions for ***Missionary News and Notes*** on October 20, 1954:

"Monday morning of September 13th the Ocean Mail anchored in Yokohama harbor for a short stay before going on to Kobe, our destination. The harbor was buzzing with activity. As soon as the customs launch left our ship, numerous barges flanked us on all sides, and in a few minutes the decks were swarming with little men in baggy pants and padded sock-shoes scurrying around like busy ants unloading cargo. How hard those longshoremen shoveled grain twelve hours in a stretch for very little pay!

"Soon the small passenger launch arrived at our ship and took us to the docks. McCammons took us to their home in Tokyo by car. We didn't have enough eyes to see all the new and strange sights. From the harbor, Yokohama had looked like any other port city, but as we drove through the suburbs the sights bombarded us. No room for lawns in Japan! However, trees and shrubs thrived wherever they found a tiny spot. Houses, buildings, and fences were not painted. Except for a few plastered houses, it looked drab. Homes, schools, and parks were surrounded by high wooden or stone fences. This afforded privacy but didn't satisfy our curiosity!"

Once more we boarded our freighter for the last lap of our journey. Normally, this would have been a one-day trip, but a typhoon was nearing Japan, and in order to avoid the worst of the storm, our freighter headed far out to sea again. As we plunged up and down, Peter could not stomach the upheaval; his legs let him down.

After three days of rough seas, bright sunshine welcomed us as we neared Kobe, Japan, on Monday, September 20. Kobe is a narrow harbor city in the shape of a crescent. The high mountains almost squeeze the city into the bay. We caught our breath at the beauty. Tears filled my eyes. This was our new country, our new home where we wanted to serve the Lord with all our hearts. Little did we realize how important our motto, ***Servants for Jesus' sake,*** would be. Little by little we discovered that it was not easy to be servants for Jesus' sake!

In the distance we spied a small group of people on the pier. As the specks grew, we recognized our missionaries, Bernard and Ruby Thiessen, Ferd and Vi Ediger, Anna Dyck and Martha Giesbrecht, from pictures we had seen. They had been in language school for one year already, and helped us through immigration and customs. No duty. Thank you Lord! Finally, we were finished with the red tape. Those of us who couldn't fit into the mission van piled into a taxi and the driver took off with horn blaring! The streets got narrower and narrower. The driver kept his hand on the horn. Chickens, dogs, and people scattered in all directions. I closed my eyes and prayed, "Please, Lord, don't let us kill someone before we even begin our work here!"

Traffic was frightening! Vehicles drove on the left side of the road. It looked dangerous! The business center of the city was like any N.A. city, except that we couldn't read billboards or store signs. As we drove into the residential areas, sidewalks disappeared, streets narrowed, and open sewers were visible on either side of the street. Pedestrians walked on the roads. Children played in the path of cars, bicycles and motorcycles. How could the taxi possibly get through? The horn and brakes kept our driver going. Small Japanese taxi cabs were here, there and everywhere, a real menace to pedestrians. The drivers seemed to think that if they blew their horns every few seconds their duty was done. And they kept up their speed. Surprisingly, accidents happened seldom.

OUR FIRST HOME IN JAPAN

What a relief when the taxi finally stopped in front of 122 Yamamoto Dori in Kobe. The Japan GC mission had bought this western-style house in 1951 for $5,000. U.S. A high cement wall surrounded the large square yellow two-story wooden house. A typical Japanese gate with double wooden doors, shielded by a small tile roof, led into the courtyard.

Thirteen of us spilled out of the vehicles that brought us from the harbor. Our first-floor furnished apartment had two rooms, one on either side of the main entrance and hallway. The entrance separated our two rooms. This was the thoroughfare for all who entered the building. Since we usually left the door into our living room open, our children thrived on the extra attention.

Everyone took off their shoes and lined them neatly along the hall. We learned to appreciate this custom so much that our family always took off shoes in every house where we lived. Some customs were not as easy to follow. Our mission chairman, John Thiessen, had told us, "Look and listen for the first two years without criticizing." Excellent advice!

We were exhausted. After the excitement of meeting our fellow missionaries and arriving in our new home in this new land, the children and I lay down for a nap, Rickie in his crib, and Vangy and I on our bed. I awoke feeling dizzy and dripping wet. I thought I had perspired during my nap, but soon discovered that I had forgotten to put a diaper on Vangy! Later in the evening Martha Giesbrecht came to help make the bed. I found a tiny red bug on the pillow and asked, "What is that?"

"A bedbug!" said Martha. No wonder I was all bitten up! The mattress was full of them. We hauled the mattress outside and slept on air mattresses until we could find a better bed.

Each floor shared the "ofuro," bathroom facilities. The missionaries had hired a carpenter, Abe San, who had transformed the house into four apartments, two downstairs, and two upstairs. The missionaries couldn't wait for the end of language study to evangelize, so they started worship meetings in the garage. Abe San became a dedicated Christian and later led his wife to the Lord.

This house was home to all our missionaries for two years while attending Japanese language school. This was great for rubbing off our sharp edges!

Although the mission board had beds on suggested items to take to Japan we decided the Japanese must sleep, so we would, too. However, we discovered that Japanese sleep on cotton mats spread on thick straw mat floors, but our apartments had cold hardwood floors. We bought beds with straw mattresses at an old army and navy store. There was no central heating, so in winter we carried the portable kerosene heater into the bedroom to warm it before putting the children to bed.

One dark winter night I crossed the hall to switch on the bedroom light. Darkness prevailed. Electricity off? Gradually the dim naked bulb came into view, and I shouted for Peter. The room was black with smoke from the little heater! Needless to say, the doors and windows stayed wide open for some time before we finally went to bed. Brrr, was it cold! We washed black linens and scrubbed black walls for hours the next day. After that we never left heaters unattended.

SIGHTS AND SOUNDS

A loud clop, clop, clop, greeted our ears early the first morning. What could that be? Ah, this was the music of the wooden clogs on the streets of Japan! These geta, as they are called, looked uncomfortable and awkward to us, but they were worn by old and young, rich and poor, and the children could even run and jump with them. Perhaps soon we would try them out!

In the mornings Vangy often crawled into bed with us and lay quietly until Rickie opened his eyes. "Hi!" was his jolly greeting, and the two would play. One morning he leaned over the railing after his usual greeting, and toppled head over heels onto the floor. We thanked the Lord for protecting him from major injury. Was somebody praying?

The mission board had sent us a list of things we should take along to Japan, such as a refrigerator, oven, washing machine and beds. We had left our beautiful wedding gifts such as dishes and lamps in storage with our parents. Imagine our surprise when our missionaries had a welcome dinner for us and the table was set with beautiful dishes on a lovely linen tablecloth. We had brought only our melmac dishes. Fortunately, Japan had beautiful dinner sets much cheaper than they would be in N.A. We bought a set for twelve that served us well for forty-five years. During our stay in Japan hundreds of guests graced our table throughout the years. Now our daughter Vangy uses the set in Canada.

There were fascinating little shops on every street. Most of them had open fronts that closed with wooden sliding doors for the night. Fruits, vegetables, meat, bread, candies and cookies, china, hardware, stationery, drugs, and geta, were artistically arranged, each in different shops. The fish markets and open sewers provided the aroma.

A few days after arriving, Typhoon 16 hit Japan. Five ferryboats sank, with a death toll of over 1500. In Kobe we felt only the lesser effects of the typhoon, wind and rain. The terrible loss of life touched us deeply. We were too late for these people. How many of them were ready to meet their Maker?

LANGUAGE SCHOOL

Then came the unthinkable! We had to hire a full-time helper to care for the children, cook, shop, and clean while we attended language classes. Our only consolation was that we would be giving a family the means to live.

Takumi San had worked for missionaries already, and the children loved her. She and her son conveniently lived in a small apartment at the back of the house. Every morning Takumi San and the other helpers lined up all the missionary children outside the gate to wave good-bye to parents as they drove off to the Naganuma Japanese Language School, operated by the Japan Presbyterian Church.

We attended classes all morning and did homework for the rest of the day. The school was a melting pot for missionaries from many denominations and many countries. A sampling of the western world met here: Canada, America, Holland, Germany, France, Sweden, England, Switzerland, and Austria.

The school took an excursion to Nara, a city teeming with shrines and temples. Nara boasts Japan's largest indoor Buddha statue, weighing 5000 pounds. We found it difficult to understand how the educated people of Japan could worship idols made with their own hands.

Learning the Japanese language became a life-long challenge. Someone remarked that the devil invented this difficult language to keep people from learning about the Lord Jesus Christ! Gradually the strange sounds began to take on meaning. In chapel we learned to sing from the Japanese hymnbooks, even though we didn't know what we were singing! We learned to read the simple forms of writing, hiragana and katakana. However, that did not help when confronted with Japanese language newspapers, where these simple forms of writing were just prefixes or suffixes to myriads of Kanji picture words. In order to read the daily newspapers, one needed to know 1,900 basic Kanji. Students had to master these by the time they finished middle school (grade 9). God gave grace to persevere in this difficult language. It didn't take long to discover the talented linguists in our midst. I was not one of them.

BLUNDERS

A veteran Lutheran missionary in Japan shared his experiences with our mission group. "The first thirty years the language is difficult," he said. "After that you are over the hump." What a shock for young missionaries eager to get going!

Peals of laughter rang out at missionary gatherings when we shared language blunders! One missionary had gone out to distribute tracts, and instead of saying, "Oyom**i** ni natte kudasai," which means, "Please read this," he said, "Oyome ni natte kudasai," meaning, "Please become my bride!" Once I sent Takumi San to market to buy a dozen eggs. In language school that morning I had asked a teacher the word for eggs. Takumi San brought me a tiny box of raisins. We had a good laugh. I had used the word "hoshibudo," meaning raisins, instead of "tamago," meaning eggs. Instead of a dozen in Japan they use ten.

Another day Peter asked Takumi San the name for an axe. I had just been reading the Bible, and remembered the word for Acts of the Apostles, so I blurted out "Shitogyoden!" I was quite proud of myself. Imagine my surprise as we entered a hardware store later that day, and Peter asked the clerk for a "Shitogyoden!" It so happened that the clerks were Christians, and we all burst out laughing. Poor Peter had no idea why, until he learned the difference between an axe, "ono," and Acts of the Apostles, "Shitogyoden."

After the first fifty lessons, each student had to give a short talk during morning devotions in language school in both Japanese and English. Two years seemed like a long time to spend learning a language when we were eager to share the Good News.

ROSALINE HILDA ARRIVES

Moms were busy with the little ones. Some of us gave birth to babies during language school. Our third child, Rosaline Hilda, was born May 2, 1956, in the Presbyterian mission hospital in Osaka, just an hour from our home in Kobe. This was at the end of our second year in language school. What a beautiful, sweet baby, always content. In no time she was sleeping through the night. Ramseyers also had a baby, Joy, the same month, and our children became best friends. During this time in Japan our family grew to five.

FAILURES AND OPPORTUNITIES

A Mennonite Brethren missionary, Roland Wiens, phoned from Osaka one day and asked if I would meet a young lady who was interested in Christianity. Exciting! I tried to lead Maki to a decision the first time we met. Alas, she never returned. Too late I realized that my misplaced enthusiasm had turned her off. I also learned that God continues to follow people even though I often bungled my opportunities. I prayed that someone with a little more tact may have led her to the Lord at some time in her life.

The mission house boasted a small garage, which doubled as shelter for the mission van during the week and a church meeting place on Sundays. A small group of Christians and seekers gathered in the garage for services every Sunday. Most of them were young people, and often stayed afternoons for fellowship, praise and prayer. Missionaries took turns preaching.

One Sunday afternoon we heard ***O happy day, that fixed my choice on Thee my Savior and my God.*** Our hearts skipped a beat! A university student had just given his heart to Christ. At our missionary meetings we had been praying for him and were thrilled that God had answered our prayers. Some of students went to Bible college in Tokyo and became the first pastors for our new churches in Kyushu. The mission never planned to begin a church in Kobe. Kobe was just a stopover for language study. Young people gave their hearts to the Lord and were bonded in Christian fellowship. And so the Kobe Garage Group church just "happened!" How can you block God's Spirit? With our combined missionary numbers, we realized that hundreds of our friends in Canada and the U.S. were praying.

After worship one Sunday we hiked up the mountains behind Kobe. Each missionary received an "obento" lunch box full of surprises; Japanese rice balls, fish, veggies and other goodies. Hmmm. We tasted and tried. Then they offered something that looked like fudge. We tried. Suddenly a sticky sweet blob filled my mouth that wouldn't go down. Peter swallowed his, but alas, the pasty stuff stuck in my throat. I managed to swallow part of it, but it came back! A quick drink of water drained it down to my gurgling stomach. That was our first taste of bean paste. The sushi with raw fish was better and became one of my favorites. But not for Peter. He remained a vegetarian.

Shortly after our arrival, Peter preached his first sermon through an interpreter. Later he would write his sermons out and have them corrected. After several years of that, he decided to launch out with just an outline. No doubt that helped him to absorb the language quickly. At his first language test in November, his grades were "superior!"

POST-WAR JAPAN

Japan was still recovering from WWII. We saw vast bombed out areas. Houses looked drab. Homeless people roamed the streets. They used cardboard, tin, boards and whatever they could find to make lean-to's, using the block walls of railway tracks for one side of their makeshift homes. They searched garbage bins for rags and paper to sell for recycling. Sometimes they came to the gate begging for food or clothes. One day when Peter answered the doorbell, a man stood at the gate. All he wanted was a pair of pants and a belt. Peter immediately took the belt from his pants and handed it to him. He got a pair of pants as well!

At Christmas Martha and I went to the slums to bring clothes and New Testaments to families in the huts. They couldn't invite us in, because there was no room to stand. We invited them to our mission house for a Sunday evening meal. Rice was still rationed in those days, but since our diet, unlike the Japanese diet, did not consist mainly of rice, this was no hardship for us. At the appointed time, eighteen men, women and children arrived. They ate as if starved, and we were happy that there was plenty of food. After the meal we sang gospel songs, and Yamada Sensei, lay leader of the Kobe Garage Church, used slides to tell the story of the feeding of the 5000. The next Sunday several came to the worship service. We prayed that they might find the "riches" we have in Christ Jesus.

One of the effects of the defeat in the war was a deep sense of emptiness and hearts hungry for spiritual food. When we handed out tracts on the streets, eager hands reached out.

In November of that first year, we were finally able to see where we would settle after language school. It was time for our annual missionary conference in southern Kyushu. Senior missionaries who were already church planters in several cities in Miyazaki Prefecture hosted us. Guests from the U.S. mission board joined us, and we had five wonderful days of fellowship and encouragement.

CHRISTMAS

Christmas came early overseas! If you wanted your family to receive presents on time, you had to mail parcels in October. We also looked forward to parcels from home. In those days cereal was unheard of in Japan, so we asked for corn flakes! Of course, our families included many other treats; chocolates, fruitcake, halvah, toys and clothes.

Peter and I had decided we would not introduce the Christmas tree tradition to Japan. Imagine our surprise when the church put up a Christmas tree! We invited neighbors and homeless people for meals and special treats. Japan did not celebrate Christmas, so it was not a holiday and people went to work as usual. But since school winter vacation began on December 24th, students were free. The church had acquired a small pump organ. Christians shared the Christmas story and we sang carols. Celebrating Christ's birth took on special meaning, knowing that most of these folks were hearing it for the first time.

COMMUNITY

There was no end to community events. When one festival was over, another started. The city's annual chrysanthemum show took place in a beautiful park within walking distance. Never had we seen so many varieties of mums. Tiny ponpons, giant single ones held in place with stiff wire frames, delicately trimmed mannequin ladies in kimono in a rainbow of color, animal flowers, and myriads of other designs showed Japanese talent for raising beautiful flowers.

Several of us braved the local ofuro, or bathhouse, one night. The men's and women's had recently been separated, although in some areas of Japan they were still together. A mammoth sunken square tile "ofuro" tub was in the centre, surrounded by a tile floor with drains. Small wooden basins sat in a row by the taps on the wall. People sit on a small wooden stool and dip into the ofuro with a basin, then scrub with soap from top to bottom. Next, rinse off the soap, dipping into the bath with the basin for water over and over. Washing is always done outside of the ofuro. When you are sure you are clean, you gingerly stick your big toe in – ouch! That's hot! Too hot!

Gradually you sink into the water until you sit in what feels like scalding water up to your neck. At first we could be in for only a few minutes. When I stepped out, my skin was beet red, and I felt quite faint! Not recommended for people with heart problems. We learned to appreciate the ofuro. It kept us warm through cold winter nights. Without an ofuro, you shivered for an hour or two before you finally warmed up. Japanese have an ofuro, hot bath, every night, summer and winter. Those who can't afford an ofuno in their home go to the public bath house. Toilets are always in a separate room in all Japanese homes and hotels.

Our children were a constant joy and challenge. At the clinic Vangy was diagnosed with worms. Worms in the diapers? Yuck! Rickie was teething, learning to walk and talk. He called Vangy "Wowie!" We tried to speak German at home as well as English, so the children could learn both. However, when the children started school, we gave up German. Occasionally we tried again, but soon realized that three languages were too much!

One day we visited Dave and Mary Balzer, MB missionaries in the neighboring city of Osaka. Peter, Dave and Mary had graduated from MBBC together. We also met my good college friend who was at home in Kyoto, an hour from Kobe. Later I had the joy of spending a night with her. Here I saw what had drawn me to Japan; except for my friend, this family worshiped idols. We prayed that one day they would join their daughter in worshipping the true God, our Lord and Savior Jesus Christ.

Two long years in language school finally came to an end. We packed our belongings onto a large truck that would deliver our worldly goods to our new home in southern Kyushu. Then we boarded a train with our family of five. The mission conference decided that our family should continue the work that Peter and Lois Voran had begun in Nichinan City in Miyazaki Prefecture. The Vorans were going on furlough after completing their first five-year term.

Ramseyers and Derksens off to Japan, 1954

Missionaries welcoming us to Japan

Our first Japanese friend, Seiko, whom we met on the ship

Takumi San, baby-sitter

COM Missionary Family in the 1950s

Kobe Garage Church

Rosie is born; Vangy & Rickie in front

Chrysanthemum Show

Yamada interprets for Peter

Chapter 3

Aburatsu-Nichinan 1956~1959

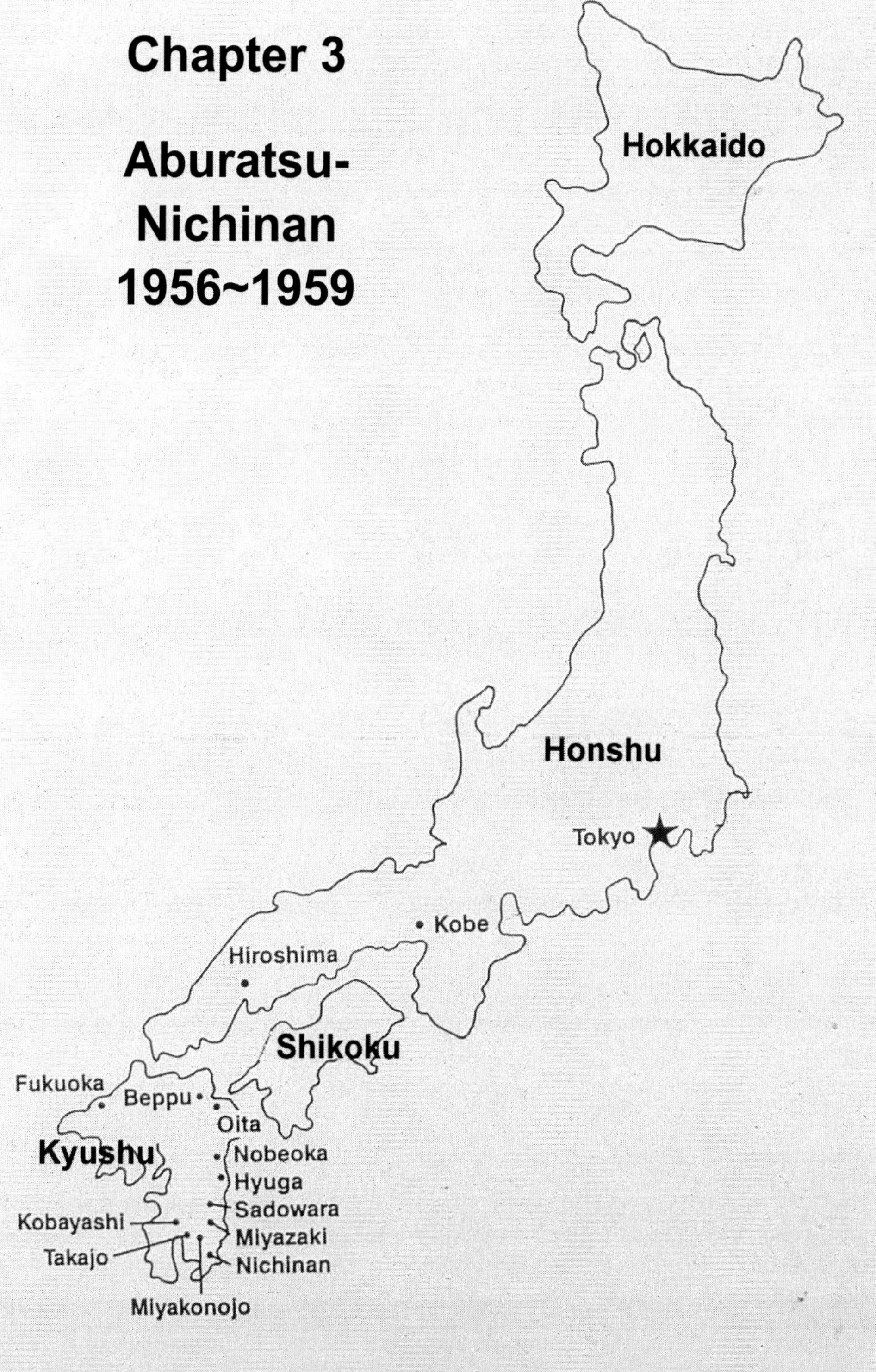

OUR NEW HOME 1956

Life in Nichinan began with a rush! The Aburatsu Kirisuto Kyokai, our area church in Nichinan had planned ten days of evangelistic meetings. A huge tent was set up on an empty lot nearby. Church young people loaded drums and loudspeakers onto a two-wheeled cart which they pulled by hand and marched through the town, advertising the meetings. They sang gospel songs to the beat of the drums. Some carried large posters around their necks. The posters were like a vest, called ad sandwiches!

Every night about 300 people crowded into the tent to hear the Japanese evangelist, perhaps also to see the foreigners and their kids! Summer holidays had begun, and children filled the tent for the afternoon meetings for children. Kindergarten teachers told Bible stories with flannelgraph and taught choruses.

When the evangelist asked for decisions for Christ in the evening meetings, the response was overwhelming! More than one hundred people signed cards. Later we learned that the Japanese people are so polite, that when someone serves you, you try to please that person. In this case, they signed cards. We were disappointed that only six people followed through. However, the seed of God's Word was planted in many hearts. There was great rejoicing when the six became Christians.

The church grew rapidly in those early years. Most of the thirty-seven baptized Christians were young people. They taught Sunday School, distributed tracts, and enthusiastically shared their faith in Christ. The kindergarten served as a church meeting place. We made many mistakes, both in language and culture, but the Japanese were very forgiving of these young inexperienced foreigners.

Most missionaries in those days began their ministry with tent evangelism. If all those who had made decisions at meetings in our various churches would have remained faithful, the churches would be packed. It was discouraging when new Christians lost interest and dropped out. Some returned years later. However, there were always those for whom the decision was real.

THE KINDERGARTEN

Peter and Lois Voran had planted the Aburatsu Mennonite Christian Church and opened Keiai (Faith Love) Kindergarten, during their three years in Nichinan.

The mission did not want to depend on institutions, but rather on outreach by the Christians. However, society put great weight on kindergarten education, so the Vorans had felt God calling them to open a Christian kindergarten in Nichinan. The seed of God's Word was planted in hundreds of children. At home these young ones would insist on praying before meals. The seeds kept growing.

Some mothers began attending church services. We started cooking classes and Bible studies in missionary homes. Christian kindergartens in Japan, including the Catholic ones, had a positive impact on society. The children from such kindergartens not only behaved better but were also better students as they moved on to elementary school. Families were eager to enroll their children in Christian kindergartens.

People often told us that they had attended a Christian kindergarten, even though they never became Christians. Many years later we met a young Christian in the Oita church who had attended the mission kindergarten in Nichinan. He had kept on attending Sunday School. Later he made a decision for the Lord and was baptized in the Oita Mennonite Christian Church.

Peter became the new principal of Keiai (Grace-Love) Yochien, the mission kindergarten, with 108 lively children and five dedicated Christian teachers, even though he had had no training for this type of work. Just before the fall semester was to begin, the staff realized they needed one more teacher to comply with the “mombushou” (the Education Ministry of Japan) rules for kindergartens. But there was no one to call on, and the only quick solution was that I also sign up as a teacher. Woe to me! First, Rosie was just four months old; secondly, I did not want to be a teacher and thirdly, in spite of studying Japanese language for two years, my communication skills were very limited. I could not understand the local dialect, so when older people talked to me, I just listened quietly, trying to look intelligent by nodding my head. Children's language was even more difficult. However, since there was no other solution, I reluctantly agreed.

In kindergarten I helped with the youngest class, the three-year-olds. My main talents were holding crying little ones on my lap and wiping runny noses! We hired Sahashi San, a gentle lady in the neighborhood, to care for our children during the morning hours. Her teenage daughters, Yoshie and Naoko, loved to play with our kids. We never lacked babysitters.

Before we arrived, the church had called Takashi Yamada, the first convert from the Kobe Garage group, to serve the Aburatsu church as their pastor. Takashi was single and had no Bible or seminary training. However, he was a gifted young man on fire for the Lord. He lived in a tiny hut on the yard of some friendly neighbors. We often invited him for meals, a welcome guest.

PROBLEMS

The home the Vorans had built was western style, except for one large tatami (solid straw mat) room upstairs for guests or children's meetings. We sat at a low Japanese table for meals. Sitting on your legs on a hardwood floor could become excruciatingly painful, even with cushions under our legs! Eventually we discovered a good carpenter in town and ordered a table. It was heavy, but well-built, and could be extended with two boards to accommodate twelve people comfortably. This table served us well throughout our life in Japan.

There were two large bedrooms downstairs, and we acquired second-hand beds. Rosie, the baby, slept in a crib in our room. One day I walked into the bedroom to check on her. Because of mosquitoes, we all slept under nets hanging from the ceiling. I froze when I spied a huge monster slowly creeping towards my sleeping baby! I hated killing creatures of any kind, and if it would have been a spider, I would have carried it out with a towel. But this creature had long sturdy legs and claws. Ugh! No way would this monster get to my baby! I grabbed a slipper, slowly moved towards the crib, and wacked the thing off the crib onto the floor. I wacked it once more and realized too late that it was a harmless crab. We lived close to the Pacific Ocean and later discovered more crabs finding their way into our home. That was the first and last time I ever killed a crab!

Nights were a big problem. The mosquito population would have made short work of us had it not been for the mosquito nets. Even so, if a mosquito got under the net, we switched on the light and chased it until we finally cornered it! Every night one or two found their way under the nets.

Another night problem was that I had to go to the kitchen for the baby bottles. I dreaded turning on the light! That resulted in a sudden skittering sound as dozens of enormous cockroaches that looked like Italian plums on legs scurried for shelter. I learned to keep bug spray handy, but what a solution for a squeamish mother. They were big and glossy and could fly! That was the closest I got to wild animals in Japan. Oh, how I hated those critters!

There was no central heating, so we used small portable kerosene heaters and moved them from room to room where we needed them. Except for fall, the climate was usually very damp. In summer we almost suffocated from the damp heat (no air-conditioning), and in winter we almost froze from the damp cold. Yet the temperature seldom went below freezing. When my father visited, he said he never froze as much in the Ontario cold winters outside pruning fruit trees as he did in Japan.

How we loved the ofuro, the Japanese bath. The bathroom had a built-in huge iron tub that was heated with wood from underneath in the laundry room. A fitted wooden lid kept the water hot. Fortunately we had cold water taps, so we added cold water as needed. The tub was built into a raised tile wall about two feet high. The whole family used the same hot water, but of course, each one washed off outside the tub before getting in. In Japanese families, the father was first; in ours, he was last!

In winter we heated the room with a small heater. However, after an ofuro, you were warm even in a cold bed, and stayed warm throughout the night. Oh, the delights of the ofuro! One cold winter night the water was too hot, and Peter fainted when he got out, nearly falling against the heater. After that we put up with the cold room rather than with the danger of a heater.

A NEW NEIGHBORHOOD

Living in a new neighborhood was challenging for our children as well as for us. One day when Rickie was three or four, I happened to look out of the bedroom window that faced the kindergarten playground.

Our son was throwing stones at the neighbor boys. I was appalled, and did what parents did in those days. He received a good spanking, with a stern warning. But he did it again. And again. Strange that each time I happened to be looking out of the window and caught him in the act. After the third time, the spanking finally seemed to sink in, and the boys became playmates.

I remembered hearing missionaries from Africa and India telling how they carried on mission work because they had nannies to care for their children. I decided that in our mission work my priority would be to my husband and children. At the same time, I felt I wasn't really a missionary yet, because I was not directly involved in evangelism and church work.

Evenings Peter often went to nearby villages with young Christians for meetings, so I was left alone with the children. I used flannelgraph Bible stories. Then we sang and prayed, and I tucked them into bed.

The church had many young eager Christians. Often, they came to our door, and I would invite them in. I thought that was the right thing to do, so I put the children to bed without our family devotion time. A no-win situation! I felt guilty, but I also felt guilty if I didn't invite them in. Peter and I discussed the problem and made a compromise. I would invite the callers in but ask them to sit off to the side of the room while I had devotions with the children. Not the best solution, but it was better than rejecting their visits. Gradually the children got used to having the occasional guests nearby during family devotions

Soon we began hearing remarks by the young people who came to visit evenings. "I want to marry a Christian so we can have family devotions," or "I'm going to tell my children about God when I get married," or "I want a Christian home, too." Gradually I realized that I was a missionary! I was involved. My heart was filled with gratitude to God. He showed me that our Christian home was serving as an example. A number of years later, a Japanese pastor said, "Your family may be your greatest contribution to Japan." We were humbly grateful.

CRISIS WITH ROSIE

The four Mennonite denominations in Japan arranged for an All-Mennonite missionary fellowship once in three years. Geographically we were thousands of kilometers apart. The Old Mennonites were on the northernmost island of Hokkaido, the Mennonite Brethren in the Kansai in Osaka, the Brethren in Christ in the western tip of the main island of Honshu in Yamaguchi Ken (prefecture,) and the General Conference Mennonites on the southernmost island of Kyushu. Each of the four groups took turns hosting this fellowship that lasted three or four days.

It was with great anticipation and excitement that we prepared for our first trip to Hokkaido, a long train trip of several days. Vangy was five, Rickie four, and Rosie was just beginning to walk.

First we travelled by bus to the city of Miyazaki, where we spent a few hours with Bernard and Ruby Thiessen before boarding the night train for Kobe. Thiessens had a small tricycle, and I set Rosie on it. I stood beside her reading a letter. Suddenly she tipped and fell over and screamed! When we took her to a doctor, he said she just had a cold. Well, I was sure that was not a cold, and that she must have hurt herself. We decided to board the night train anyway and take Rosie to the Presbyterian hospital in Osaka, the same hospital where she was born. We slept very little in our sleepers that night. I kept giving Rosie her milk bottle to pacify her. Every time I lifted her legs to change her diaper she screamed!

When we arrived in Kobe, we took her to a chiropractor first. Thankfully, this chiropractor immediately realized that our baby needed a doctor. He thought the leg was broken. So we took a local train to neighboring Osaka to the Presbyterian hospital. Dr. Marian Powell met us in the hallway and took Rosie in her arms.

"Looks like a broken bone," she said. Sure enough, the X-ray showed the leg was broken high above the knee. She put her in traction immediately. They allowed me to stay in the hospital the first night. Rosie would have to stay six weeks for the healing to be complete. What should we do? Our family certainly couldn't stay in the hospital.

Dr. Powell suggested we go to our conference in Hokkaido, because Rosie would adjust to her new circumstances much better if we weren't around. So, feeling very guilty, we followed the doctor's advice and continued our trip to Hokkaido, where we stayed for two weeks. When we returned, Rosie had almost forgotten us. She loved the nurses but cried every time Dr. Powell came into her room. After all, it was the doctor who had put her through so much pain putting her leg in traction. Her legs were both tied tightly and suspended from a bar above the bed so the broken one would be the same length as the good one. The pain was gone, and she was like a little monkey, pulling herself up and swinging around on the ropes that held her legs. Quite an amazing feat for a one-year old!

The doctor suggested we all return home and come back for her in one month. How could I leave my baby alone and carry on as if nothing had happened? There seemed to be no other choice.

A month later I boarded the train once more for Osaka. Rosie had forgotten me, and acted strange. However, after holding her for a while, she adjusted quickly. My problem was that I was holding her just as I had before the accident. Once she almost fell out of my arms backward. What a scare! I learned to support her back when holding her. What a relief to have our baby home again. Soon she was crawling around, and in a few months began to walk. That was the big test. No limping! We were thrilled. In Japan we had seen many children, young people, and older people limping due to a break when they were younger. How thankful we were for the Presbyterian mission hospital and dedicated Christian doctors and nurses.

DOUBLES

In the fall of 1957, God chose to bless us again. Ever since I was a child I had wished for multiple babies. When I was a first grader in elementary school in Beamsville, Ontario, the Dionne Quintuplets were born. Our teacher filled the walls with their pictures. I was mesmerized! Not that I wished for five at a time now, but I did pray for twins. At seven months I was so big that I looked ready to deliver. We decided to check at the local hospital. The doctor ordered an X-ray. And guess what? Finally, an answer to my prayers! Twins!

When we discovered that the local hospital didn't have incubators, we decided I would take the train to Kobe a week before my due date, which was to be in the beginning of June 1958. I will never forget that train ride! I had a sleeper, but fake contractions set in at night, and I was terrified! What if the twins would be born on the train? I felt so alone. I was reminded of the Apostle Peter walking on the water. That night I *walked on the water* and *sank in the waves* alternately. Oh me of little faith!

What a relief when morning came and I was still just me! Phyllis and Ray Reimer, our new missionaries, had graciously offered to host me during my wait. I slept in their bedroom and they slept in their only other room, the kitchen-living room! The other missionaries living in the Kobe house during language study took turns hosting me for meals. All were loving and concerned.

The next day I took the train to the Presbyterian mission hospital in Osaka for a check-up. Alas, my time was not yet. One day while walking along the street to the train station, two high school boys walking behind me were laughing and saying, “Okii, na!” (She’s huge!) And I was! They didn’t know I understood them. I felt as big as a house walking along the road. And I was lonely for Peter, but he had to stay at home to care for the other three. Rosie was two at the time. The Reimers did their best to make me feel welcome, but I was so uncomfortable.

The doctor also tried to comfort me, saying, “Don’t worry. They will come when they are ready!” A week passed, and they were still not ready!

Finally on Wednesday, June 11, the twins made their way into this world. A boy and a girl! It’s not often children get their wishes. Vangy wanted a girl, and Rickie wanted a boy. William Paul was born at 10:21 PM, and Wanda Marie followed fifteen minutes later. She came so fast, it was almost as though she had grabbed her brother’s ankle to help her out! Bill weighed seven pounds, and Wanda six and a half. No wonder I had been so uncomfortable with thirteen and a half plus pounds of babies in me!

I stayed in the hospital another ten days to regain my energy which I would certainly need. Dave and Mary Balzer, our friends in Osaka, had twin girls a year earlier. When Mary came to visit me in the hospital, she said, “I don’t know whether to laugh with you or cry for you!”

Laughingly I told her, “Just laugh with me. I’m so thrilled. I’ve always wanted twins!”

FAMILY OF SEVEN

Hospital nurses accompanied us to the airport ten days later. Peter, Vangy, Rickie and Rosie were waiting for us at the Miyazaki airport with the mission van. Since there were no seat belts in those days, we all fit in quite nicely for the two-hour drive home to Nichinan (I can’t imagine having to strap five children into car seats!). The children were so excited about our new twin babies! Rosie kept saying, "Me see! Me see!"

In Japan the young wife is allowed to return to her home a month before the birth of a baby and is allowed to stay for a month after the birth. How I wished I could have my Mother with me during this time! But the next best thing happened. Alice Ruth came to help for several days, and brought her youngest, Joy, who was born the same month as Rosie. Taking care of two babies was a full-time job. Feeding took twice as long, and so did changing diapers. I don't know what I would have done without Alice Ruth those first crucial days.

We had only one baby crib, but that was no problem. Billy and Wanda lay side by side across the crib, flailing hands and feet as babies do. How exciting the day their hands touched and they became aware of each other! I needed Sahashi San full-time now. She was such a pleasant helper in the home and we all loved her.

Vangy and Rickie attended our mission kindergarten next door, and Rosie stayed home with me. Sometimes we envied the ease with which the children adapted to this society and used the Japanese language. We were still using three languages, English, Japanese and German. One day Rickie asked quite seriously, "How do we laugh in Deutsch?"

Billy and Wanda brought much joy and laughter into our home. We had acquired a jolly jumper and a rocker, and these provided hours of fun as we switched them from one to the other. When they began to crawl the real fun started. Billy was faster and stronger than Wanda. He would crawl to the end of the hall, hide around the corner, and wait. When Wanda got to the corner, he called "boo" and they would laugh and laugh. They still needed Mom for changing diapers and feeding. There was no baby food in the stores, so we made our own. All this was time consuming. But I also felt jealous sometimes. They were so happy playing together that they hardly needed me!

Sunday worship services were in the kindergarten next door. If the twins were sleeping, I would leave them in the house and check on them occasionally. If they were awake, we took all five to church. I never lacked eager helpers wanting to hold the babies.

MOTORCYCLE

The mission van was available for anyone. However, Peter decided it would be easier for him to get around on a motorcycle, so he bought one. When the student evangelism team came to our city, Pete Voran and several young men took the van to a neighboring village, and Peter went by motorcycle. In those days, even the main roads were not all paved. After the evening service, Peter left on the motorcycle, and the van followed.

Suddenly the van lost sight of the motorcycle taillight. They stopped and began to search for Peter. Finally, they found him six feet down in a rice field! His wheel got into the gravel around the curve, and he knew that if he turned, he would fall. So he just went straight over the cliff. The place where he fell was the only spot that didn't have rocks at the bottom. God certainly had his hand over Peter.

The team helped get his motorcycle back on the road. He limped home walking with the motorcycle. What an agonizing night. Next day I insisted he go to the hospital. The leg was black and blue from top to bottom. X-rays showed no broken bones. The doctor laughed at him, and Peter vowed he was finished with doctors. He never went to a doctor again until he had his first heart problem twenty years later.

FIRST CHRISTIAN WEDDING

During the Vorans' first term the new young church they had established in Nichinan had called Takashi Yamada from the Kobe Garage Group to serve as their pastor. He fell in love with a lovely Christian kindergarten teacher. Helping with wedding plans was exciting. The young couple had very little in the way of earthly goods, and certainly not the means to have a traditional Japanese wedding, which would have been very expensive. I offered my wedding dress to the bride, which she gratefully accepted. It was a perfect fit! What a thrill to see this lovely Christian in my dress. Everybody wanted to help with preparations. The ceremony took place in the kindergarten, which was also the church meeting place. Verney Unruh, mission chairman at the time, officiated at the wedding. One hundred and fifty guests enjoyed a simple reception with tea and cake.

The bride's father was so impressed with the wedding and messages on "The Christian Home," that his former attitude of antagonism towards Christianity turned to interest.

We had invited family members and close friends to our home for a simple meal of rice and meat topping, along with salads and homemade cake. When I think of the simplicity of it now, I wish we could do it over and have a more elaborate meal. We had not attended a wedding in Japan yet, so we were quite unaware of wedding customs and food. However, it was a joyous occasion, and the church rejoiced in this new Christian home, a rarity in Japan. Single Christian women always outnumbered single Christian men.

CHURCH GROWTH

The young people of the Aburatsu Mennonite Christian Church were a constant challenge. Imagine our joy when eight asked for baptism! Pastor Yamada and Peter taught the new Christians about the different forms of baptism and gave them the freedom to choose. The choice was even. Four wanted pouring, and four wanted immersion. Thus, four were baptized by pouring during the morning worship service. After a lunch together, we walked to the river, and the other four were baptized by immersion. The form of baptism never became a problem in our churches in Japan.

Summers were ideal for evangelism. In most of the earlier meetings, we invited Japanese evangelists. The church people took care of the advertising. One year fifteen young people pedaled around the streets in tandem with handmade posters tied to their bicycles. That year we rented the city hall, and attendance was good. The seed of God's Word was sown widely during early years, and we praised the Lord for the many decisions for Christ.

Imagine the joy of a Christian serving in a lonely lighthouse away from home, learning that his entire family had become Christians at one of these evangelistic meetings! Not all who made decisions kept the faith, but there were always some who became part of the church fellowship. Time and again we experienced that God's Word does not return empty!

Building relationships in the community was important. When I heard of eleven-year old Konomi Chan, the neighboring girl in the hospital with leukemia, I visited her every week. (In Japan children are addressed with the suffix Chan, and adults as San.) My Japanese was still limited, but I brought her interesting things from Canada to look at. Gradually her strength left her, and one day her bed was empty. I had prayed that I could be a good witness, but now my chest felt tight. My fear became reality. A nurse informed me, "Konomi Chan died yesterday. I'm sorry." With a heavy heart I returned home and cried that I hadn't been able to lead her to Jesus!

OUTREACH

The kindergarten provided many opportunities to reach out to parents and community. We started monthly meetings in our home for mothers and neighborhood women. Armed with invitations, I embarked on my exciting journey inviting every woman in the neighborhood. Sixty homes later, I rushed home to tell Peter the exciting news. Every woman had agreed to come!

Now I had another problem, a good one. How would they fit into our house! And how could I serve sixty women tea and refreshments? My worries soon dissipated. Six ladies showed up. What happened? Why did they say they would come and then not come? It was quite a learning experience when someone pointed out to me that their nod of assent and the "yes, yes," didn't mean "Yes, I will come," but "Yes, I understand."

It was a beginning, and gradually the group grew to twenty. We studied the Bible, had fellowship and teatime. Sometimes it was a cooking lesson. However, to teach baking was not practical, because most did not have ovens. In those days missionaries' ovens consisted of a metal box with a shelf placed over the gas burner.

Kindergarten children were a big asset to the church. They talked freely about Jesus and they insisted on praying before meals in their homes. A number of parents made decisions for Christ. One of the fathers, Hirakawa San, often came to the kindergarten and stood at the open windows listening to Bible stories. Then he went home to read the Bible, holding his "sake" bottle (alcohol)!

One day Hirakawa San came to our door asking where the pastor lived. A few hours later he was back, face radiant! Pastor Yamada had led him to a decision for Christ! His wife immediately noticed a big change. Now instead of consuming alcohol, he was consumed by the love of Christ! The whole family became Christians. Hirakawa San became a strong lay leader in the church, and later in the church conference.

The teachers worked hard to make the kindergarten programs exciting. The creation story was the most inspiring spring program. The fall undokai (field day) was a first for us. It was not only for the children, but the whole family was involved.

Christmas dramas were full-scale productions of the birth of Christ. This was all so new, and the auditorium was always packed to capacity. Kindergarten graduations often ended in tears, as parents realized that their little ones would now enter elementary school.

As Christians grew in their faith, they made life-changing decisions. Hiejima San, an elderly widow wanted to get rid of the god-shelf in her home. The church decided to have a bonfire on the kindergarten yard. She burned her god-shelf, and young people brought their "idols," unwholesome magazines and comic books. What a time of growth for the young church! We were reminded of what happened in Ephesus two thousand years ago (Acts 19:19-20).

Church choirs were something new for the Christians. Peter started a mixed choir that sang at special occasions. Twenty girls ages ten to seventeen followed my invitation for a youth choir.

Kitahara San, a nurse in the local hospital who was studying flower arranging, came to our home after each lesson. I watched, fascinated as she taught me the intricate art of flower arrangement. I studied with different teachers every time we moved. Unfortunately, each teacher taught a different school of arranging, of which there were dozens. My arrangements got kind of mixed up with three schools, which brought interesting comments. "What school of arranging do you follow?" I had no answer. They finally decided that I had my own unique Derksen school! Kitahara San was also our volunteer family nurse, bandaging our kids when they got hurt. She was a good friend and attended church frequently.

One day a beautiful young lady came to the door and asked, "Would you please buy my silk kimono? Mother bought it for my graduation, but she got very sick and we need the money." We never doubted her story, and since I wanted a kimono, bought hers. Later we discovered that she sold kimono to many gullible people like me at quite a nice profit. I also discovered that it was not silk. Oh, well, I had a kimono!

Snow was rare in southern Kyushu. When big white flakes drifted through the sky one memorable winter evening, the quiet was soon disrupted by laughter and squealing! The whole neighbourhood came out to enjoy this rare magical phenomenon even though it was far past bedtime for kids! Winter wonderland greeted us the next morning! However, the only snow that lasted more than one day were the snowmen families had made the night before!

CHILDREN'S EDUCATION

Our children's education was important! Our mission opened a school for missionary children and wanted us all to participate. However, we did not want to send our children to boarding school at such a young age. We also wanted to fit into our Japanese community, to belong! As far as we could see, the Japanese educational system seemed excellent. Was this how God wanted us to get involved in the community? We sent our children to Aburatsu Shogakko, the local Japanese elementary school, only a block away.

Vangy was in grade one with Chikako Chan, her best friend from kindergarten. Except for private schools, elementary school children do not wear uniforms so they were free to wear what they pleased. This sometimes caused friction because Vangy tried hard to fit in. Even on a sunny day, she sometimes insisted on wearing boots because all her friends were wearing boots.

The school boasted a modern auditorium, a beautiful new swimming pool built mostly by parent volunteers, and a new kitchen with facilities to make l,700 lunches for students and teachers every day. Each child received a daily pint of milk, plus rice, pickles and side dishes. Lunch was mandatory and the cost minimal so that even the poorest could afford it. With school lunch programs, Japan's children were well nurtured, and gradually the Japanese race began to grow taller.

As our children grew, Peter started a habit that lasted through most of our years in Japan. Japan had no central heating, perhaps due to earthquake dangers, so in winter he would get up first, light the portable heater, and then rouse us with "*Rise and shine!*" That greeting fit in with our purpose in Japan, to shine for Jesus in this land.

It was quite a novelty for the Japanese children to have a little blue-eyed blonde "gaijin" (foreigner) among the hundreds of black-eyed, black -haired children. Every morning our breakfast was disrupted by Vangy's guardian angels who called on her an hour before school started! "Banji!

Ikimasho!" (Let's go' Vangy!) There are no 'v' or 'th' sounds in the Japanese language.) However, this didn't last long. Soon they tired of waiting.

Japanese schooling not only gave our children an excellent education, but it proved to be an education for us as well. We struggled to decipher the many notes Vangy brought home several times a week, checked the behavior chart, helped with homework, and attended the monthly open house days, plus the PTA meetings. Sometimes it was overwhelming! We soon discovered the many differences in schooling between Japanese and western education. The school taught us how to train our children, when and how they should brush their teeth, how much money they could have for allowance, ad infinitum. However, having the children in the Japanese school helped us bond with our neighbors.

Homework took us by surprise. In grade one it was usually thirty minutes per day, including summer and winter vacations. The new school year began in April, and summer holidays began the last week of July. School commenced again in the beginning of September. In winter schools had two weeks of vacation beginning Dec. 24, ending after the first week in January. Since the school year ended in March, the two-week interval before the new school year was the only time of the year without homework. Yippee!

We felt the only drawback was that unless we taught them at home, our children would forget their English. We discovered BC's English correspondence course, free to BC residents except for postage. Vangy got excellent grades in math, science, and social studies in the Japanese school, so that I taught only English language related courses. Oh, me! How I regretted that I had been so stubborn when my father wanted me to be a schoolteacher. Now I had to be one! After school Vangy and I would sit at her desk upstairs and try to shut out distractions as we settled down to study English. Oh, oh! Distractions could not be shut out. School friends came to the door and shouted, "Banji, asobimasho!" (Vangy, let's play!) It was tough to keep going, but keep going we did!

UNDOKAI!

Many school functions happened on Sundays, so we usually missed them. We prayed that it would rain the Sunday of the "undokai," or field day, because that meant it would be postponed to a weekday. This was the biggest school event of the year. Mothers were up at the crack of dawn to fix fancy lunches for the whole family. The town was jolted awake with the school siren at 6 AM. Parents, grandparents and younger siblings all came to watch the highly organized races and games for the whole day. Someone from the family would go early to stake out their spot for the day with straw mats where they could sit and cheer for their children.

Our school was divided into four groups, all vying for first place throughout the day. After each race, the group standings were posted high on the school windows for everyone to see. It was hot, so there were tents for city officials and other special guests, for music bands and cheerleaders. Each group had either its own color of ribbon around participants' foreheads or colored caps. By the end of the day everyone was hoarse from cheering! These events were usually held in October in southern Japan. The kids practiced for months for this big event. If these events were held on Sunday, we went in the afternoon. We always thanked God when they happened on a weekday instead of Sunday so we could take part. Most schools had over 1,000 students, so it was a very lively, colorful, exciting day!

SUMMERS

Many missionaries went to cooler resorts for the summer months. During our first summer we rented a cabin for a few weeks in cool Karuizawa high in the central mountains and took Takumi San with us.

Our cabin was surrounded by woods and shady paths. In the morning the singing birds woke us. How refreshing after the hot busy hum of the city. It was wonderful to renew acquaintance with Seiko and her husband who came to visit for a few days. The inter-denominational missionary conferences were like a fresh breath from heaven. Language study was set aside as we enjoyed the many special speakers and singing groups in our native English. We had never heard of Corrie Ten Boom, author of ***The Hiding Place***, a story of her Dutch family who hid Jews during World War II. Now we not only heard her but met her. What a saint! We made many lasting friendships with missionaries from all over Japan. Japan's royal family also vacationed in Karuizawa, and we watched the crown prince play tennis with his girlfriend, a commoner who later became his wife!

In following years we wanted to express solidarity with the church people, and decided to forego the luxury of summer vacations. This allowed us to participate in various summer activities, including church camps at Aoidake in the mountains between Miyazaki and Miyakonojo.

Taking our family meant washing diapers by hand in cold water and sleeping on straw mat floors next to all the other campers. Twins did not deter us from camping. There were always eager babysitters wanting to play with the children and hold the babies. What a joy to see adults and children decide for Christ at these camps. The added bonus was bonding with people from different churches and cities.

When Rosie was still a baby, we took a train trip to visit missionaries in a neighboring city. In those days the trains belched black smoke and were not air-conditioned. Windows were open in the hot summer. On the train we met a group of high school students who immediately wanted to hold Rosie. When the train stopped at a station, they spied their friends on the platform. These kids screamed with excitement at the sight of a foreign baby, and before I knew it, the girls passed Rosie out of the window to their friends on the platform. The train whistle blew, and I began to panic. They passed Rosie back just before the train lurched forward, and I vowed that I would never let that happen again! What a scare!

Our children were always popular in the neighborhood, and young girls often came to play. One day when Rosie was about three, a friend took her outside to play. Usually the girls were very dependable and we never worried. But when I went out to check this time, Rosie was nowhere to be found. We searched for two hours, first at the kindergarten next door, and then knocked on all the neighbors' doors. Finally, we found her at a friend's house several blocks away. The girl who had taken her home thought nothing of our plight.

PREPARING FOR FURLOUGH

The mission board had changed our terms from seven to five years, so in 1959 we made plans to leave in summer. Vangy finished grade one in Japanese school in March, and in April she started grade two. Rickie entered grade one in Aburatsu Shogakko. They enjoyed their school, had many friends, and were fluent in Japanese children's language. They did not want to leave home! Neither did we. Our first five years had been a parallel of our first boat trip to Japan.

In our May,1959, prayer letter we wrote:

Calm and stormy days. Such has been our voyage in this land of our adoption. There have been times when Satan has attacked the church, Christians, and missionaries with relentless fury, seeking to devour and destroy! But the Captain of our ship never left the helm, and after every tempest, the glorious light of 'the Sun of Righteousness' pierced the darkness, filling our hearts with renewed strength and joy for the journey!

Now therefore stand still, that I may reason with you before the Lord of all the righteous acts of the Lord, which he did to you…(*I Samuel 12:7****).***

The time has come to stand still for a while, to leave the land of our adoption, to leave the Japanese whom we have learned to love. The Lord willing, we will be arriving in Canada in the beginning of July. We are looking forward to spiritual refreshment, and to have the opportunity of sharing what the Lord has done in the lives of many Japanese.

*And thus it was with us. We had survived five years of intense living in a new, hitherto unknown land, with a strange, difficult language, customs, and ways of thinking. We had experienced the joys of a new young church growing in maturity, with a pastor of their own, but also the devastation when some rejected the faith and left the church! We had seen parents of kindergarten children come to faith in Christ, but we longed for more to see the light of Christ. Such had been the voyage in our adopted country. This was home. We loved the people. We loved Japan! However, it was time to ...**stand still…** (I Sam. 12:7). It was time not only to share what the Lord had done, but also to find renewal, refreshment and energy to continue serving in Japan.*

Some time ago our church had hosted a wiener roast. This was something new. It was also a lot of work, since buns were not available in the stores and I had to bake my own. I made the relish. The wieners in the meat shops were a bit fishy tasting, but at least we didn't have to make them! The idea of a roast caught on. When the church had our farewell down at the beach, what a surprise when they treated us to a potato roast!

Packing consumed time and energy! Everything had to be stored under the eaves of the mission house. After furlough we would move to a different city, and Vorans would be back in Nichinan. We packed only necessities to take along such as clothes, including slides and items to "show and tell" at mission meetings.

We were looking forward to meeting our parents and siblings, friends and relatives again. We had missed several siblings' weddings during our first term in Japan, but just accepted that as part of missionary life.

DEPARTURE

The departure date arrived. About 100 Christians and friends walked to the train station to see us off. Vangy had spent much time with her friend, Chikako Chan, and cried, "I don't want to leave my friend!" She was inconsolable.

Mission policy told us to take the cheapest route to and from the mission field. That meant freighters and passenger ships in the early days. However, that changed when it became cheaper to fly. This day we boarded the train in Nichinan, which took us south to Kagoshima. There we took a ferry to Okinawa, where we would catch a flight to San Francisco and on to Vancouver.

When we walked out of the ferry in Okinawa, Peter carried our two huge suitcases (more like small trunks). I had one twin strapped to my back and carried the other, while the three oldest walked hand in hand between us. People stopped and stared with open mouths! Interesting family!

It was hot July, and we were taken to a third-floor room of the hotel which was paid for by the airline. We had to wait three days for the next flight. No fans or air-conditioning. Our twins were one year old. That meant two babies in diapers, and that also meant washing them by hand. The airlines promised us and all the other young missionary families on the same flight that they would supply disposable diapers, formula and whatever else we might need. They broke their promise.

At the hotel we could order anything we liked for meals. And what did our children want? Rice! Plain white rice! And ice cream! That was a rare treat in Japan, but Okinawa was still under American jurisdiction, so they had real ice-cream!

When we finally got on the plane three days later, dozens of missionaries with little children and babies joined us. We noticed that the plane had been in the war zone. The ceiling and walls were full of patched bullet holes! There were no disposable diapers or milk formula. Crying babies and little kids were more than the stewardesses could handle!

Our first stop was Guam Island. We arrived at midnight, and the children were sleeping. No matter. Everyone had to get out, so we sat on the grass with many other families. This stop was to be one and a half hours, but it was three hours before we could board again because of clogged toilets! We flew on to Wake, a small desert island with a large U.S. military base. Here we finally got the promised diapers! It was very hot, and the air-conditioned airport was a good respite. This stop was to be three hours, but by the time they repaired the toilets again, it was six hours! We landed in Honolulu, Hawaii, on July 4. The airport was packed. Our stop was to be six hours, but the hours dragged well past leaving time. In such cases the airlines put passengers in hotels, but because it was a holiday weekend, hotels were full.

TROUBLE IN THE AIR

Finally, we were on our way again. Those were the days of propeller planes. Fifteen minutes before the point of no return the pilot's voice came on the intercom. "Ladies and gentlemen, we will be returning to Honolulu because one propeller (out of four) has stopped!" We could see the idle propeller as we looked out the window.

A coast guard plane from Hawaii was flying out to guide us back in case we had to ditch into the Pacific Ocean! The pilot lowered the altitude and we could see the waves below as well as the coast guard plane flying off to one side. An elderly lady passenger sitting beside us was very worried. The Lord filled our hearts with His peace. Hadn't we dedicated ourselves to Him? If He wanted us to serve longer in Japan, He would protect us!

However, we had a problem. The annual Canadian Conference sessions were to convene in Abbotsford the day after our arrival. Peter was scheduled to speak at the morning session. It became obvious that we wouldn't make it because we were flying via San Francisco.

When we got back to Honolulu, Peter phoned home to let them know we would be late, so they rescheduled him for the evening meeting. At the busy airport we waited and waited. I finally took the children into the ladies' restroom where we lay down on couches. Peter began looking for direct flights to Vancouver. Our airline had a much bigger baggage allowance than regular airlines. He persuaded Canadian Pacific Airlines to let us transfer our baggage without extra charges. What a relief! We had spent nine hours in the Honolulu airport! This plane would fly directly to Vancouver. It was half empty, and the stewardesses eagerly took on our big family of seven! They put the twins into hammocks, and the other three each had three seats for sleeping. Peter and I could also spread out! What a change from the other airline! Nor did the plane have any patched bullet holes! Everything looked new and clean. We arrived at Vancouver International Airport at noon, in time for Peter to speak at the evening session of the Canadian Conference.

Mom Derksen had a long table loaded with delicious food set under their majestic pine trees. What a family reunion! Five years ago we had left for Japan with two children. Now we returned with five! Excitement filled the air! Yes, we were exhausted from our long flights. But it was good to be on solid ground again, surrounded by our loved ones in BC!

FIRST FURLOUGH

Now things were reversed. We eagerly looked forward to news from Japan. A kindergarten teacher wrote that when she had asked the children to what land Abraham had gone, the prompt reply was, "Canada!" Yes, we were indeed experiencing Canada, *the land flowing with milk and honey!*

Canadian supermarkets had a never-ending choice of breakfast cereals, ice-creams, and jello. However, we also discovered how rich our Canadian churches were in spiritual food. Church choirs! What a treat! Care groups and prayer meetings in English or German Languages we could fully understand!

Our parents had a small cabin moved to their property, and we moved in. There was barely room for beds for all of us plus a tiny kitchen and washroom. Oma said no need to set up housekeeping. She would cook our meals. Oma was in her glory! Five grandchildren living right on her yard!

Opa and Oma's farm was so much fun. The children watched fascinated as Oma milked the cow. Billy tagged along with Opa to the chicken barn to help take out eggs, helping Opa by pointing at the eggs. Wanda was weaker, and quite skinny. Oma had a great solution. She gave her rich creamy milk and lots of butter! They also had miniature chairs which the three oldest set up beside the road to watch the traffic go by on Marshall Road where we lived with Opa and Oma. They waved at everybody. But they spoke only Japanese! Suddenly they realized that people looked at them oddly when they heard chatter that no one could understand. After three weeks they abruptly stopped using Japanese!

We enrolled Vangy and Rickie in their dad's former school, North Poplar Elementary, diagonally across the street from the folks' farm. So convenient!

FURLOUGH ITINERARY

Interest in overseas missions was strong, and we had many invitations to speak in churches, women's meetings, and schools. Every weekend was booked. To churches close by, we often took the children.

Chilliwack Mennonite Church was one of our sending churches. We had worked hours for this presentation and were ready with our first slide showing. Just as the lights went out, Peter dropped the slide tray. Our slides lay in disarray on the floor. We picked them up and went on with the tattered show. Even a well written script would not have helped. It wasn't funny then, but I still laugh every time I think of it!

A church in Montana asked us to come for a week-end in October. Oma wanted to keep Vangy and Rickie, who were in school, and the twins, who were a year old. We decided to take Rosie with us and spent the first night of our trip in a motel. The next morning we awoke to a white world! Rosie had never seen snow and asked, "Mommie, can you buy some for me?"

Christmas was very special that first furlough as we celebrated with family and with our wonderful supporting West Abbotsford Church. The choir programs and the children's Christmas Eve program were not only a blessing but a challenge to improve our children's ministry in Japan!

After Christmas we left Vangy and Rickie with Oma and Opa again so they wouldn't miss school and took the three youngest on a cross-country trip by car to visit the Klassen side of the family. We spent New Year's with my brother Helmut, wife Laura and their son Jimmy in Regina, where they were pastoring a church. What fun for the kids to have a cousin to play with!

Next we drove to Steinbach to visit brother Walter and his wife Grace and baby Pearl. There were no freeways yet, and winter roads were treacherous. In Manitoba the roads were a sheet of ice, and we crawled along. After two days of visiting and resting, we headed for Virgil, Ontario, where Mom and Dad Klassen were waiting for us. A happy family reunion!

A Saskatoon Church had asked Peter to come for two weeks of evangelistic meetings in January. The children and I stayed home in Virgil. Alas, Bill and Rosie got the measles and Wanda had chicken pox during that time!

We had arranged for Vangy and Rickie to fly from Vancouver to Toronto on February 1, where they would meet their Daddy at the airport on his way to Saskatoon. Our good friends, Abe and Eleanore Epp from Niagara, had taken Peter to the airport and brought Vangy and Rickie home to our parents in Virgil where we were staying.

AMBS ELKHART

When Peter returned from Saskatoon, we left for Elkhart, Indiana. Peter was continuing his seminary education at AMBS (Associated Mennonite Biblical Seminary). The Pannabeckers, former missionaries in China, now teaching at the seminary, welcomed us into their home for the first ten days. Peter and I decided this would be a good time to begin morning exercises, and I went at it with great determination! Alas, the next morning I couldn't move! A visit to the chiropractor showed a vertebra out of joint. The doctor said it was big enough to hang a hat! He restored me partially, but I suffered pain for many years.

Moving was another huge upheaval. We had to register the children in a different school in a foreign country, the USA! Shortly after arriving, Billy broke out with chicken pox. Sunday I took the oldest three to church, while Peter stayed home with the twins. This was the first Sunday in a long time that he didn't have to preach, and he was restless! Then Rosie contacted chicken pox. Oh, well, better the children get it over with when young! It certainly was a rough beginning.

On Feb. 13, 1960, we moved to 600 Hubbard St., Elkhart, Indiana. The outside of the house was stark, white, and unattractive, and the inside was not much better! It was a mile from the seminary. This was not a happy place for us. I spent most of my time at home.

The twins were still in diapers, so laundry days came often. The washing machine was in a corner of the kitchen and was not working properly. There were always puddles on the floor. My eyes released almost as much water as the machine! The furnace came on with a blast and a shudder, and finally gave up the ghost in the middle of winter. Brrr! We froze! A repairman finally fixed it a few days later. Rickie and Rosie had the flu, and then I was sick for three weeks. Peter had his hands full with a sick family and seminary classes. Finally, we were all healthy once more. How wonderful to be alive!

Henry and Helga Dueck's family, on furlough from Paraguay, lived near us, but we mothers felt cut off from seminary. Mrs. Pannabecker, Mrs. Waltner, and Rosella Regier dropped in occasionally. They helped to keep me sane. I vowed that no one would ever drag me back to seminary, not even with a team of horses!

In March the seminary had special sessions, and pastors and guests came from all over the U.S. and Canada. Suddenly we were swamped with visitors for nights and meals. It was good training because we were learning to be hospitable even during sickness.

We were very excited as we drove home to Virgil for a weekend in March. On Sunday our family sang in my home church in Virgil, and Peter preached. That afternoon we headed back to Elkhart again.

My mother had been struggling with Parkinson's disease. In March of 1960, she had her first Parkinson's operation in New York City by Dr. Cooper. Our good friends George and Marion Hardy graciously hosted Dad during this time.

A month later we were able to go home for almost two weeks during Easter. It was so good to be with family, and especially with Mother. It seemed that every visit we were kept busy with sick children and speaking engagements! We were deeply touched by the caring of many friends. Our dear friends, Jess and Hardy Tiessen, insisted on giving us their station wagon for the rest of our time at seminary while they drove our older car!

In May the Ontario Mennonite Frauenkonferenz (women's conference) invited me as speaker. In those days the churches were still using the German language. We took every opportunity available to be with family again.

We left Elkhart in June, and stopped at the Ramseyer's, who were in Bluffton for their furlough. It was good to connect again, and the children had a great time! In Japan we had no physical family nearby, and so our fellow workers became family. All the missionary kids called our missionaries uncle and aunt.

FAMILY

Once more we spent time with our Klassen family in Virgil. Furlough was coming to a close! On our return trip to the west coast we had car trouble. However, the Lord kept the car moving, and we learned *in all circumstances to be content*. Along the way we served at a family Bible camp in Montana.

The day after arriving home to the Derksen family in Abbotsford, BC, we left our five children with Opa and Oma, and flew to Kansas for a missionary seminar at Bethel College in mid-July. Congo was in crisis, and we heard stories first hand. Both Sundays Peter and I were involved in different churches. We spent one Sunday in the Walton church where Peter had been assistant pastor during his year at Bethel College in 1951-52. On Monday July 27, we flew home in time for Vangy's eighth birthday, July 30.

August was a busy month with Missionsfest and other speaking engagements in B.C. churches. In between we packed for our return to Japan. Once again it was time to say good-bye. We left August 24 from Vancouver on the S.S. Orsova passenger liner.

This was quite a change from our first trip. There were about sixty missionaries on board besides more than a thousand other passengers! The ship had playrooms, a library, deck games and a swimming pool. No time for boredom. The ship docked in Honolulu for one day, so we rented a car to visit beautiful Hawaii, and even spent time at the beach. The ship left at midnight. The Lord had done marvelous things for us during our furlough. Now we were ready to return home to Japan!

We arrived in Yokohama on Sept. 6, 1960. Ferd Ediger met us at the airport. Edigers had moved from Hyuga to Tokyo during our absence. The next day we boarded the new bullet train, Kodama, for Kobe. The mission board allowed missionaries to enroll in language school for four months before beginning a second term of service. Our mission board was the best! So we were back in our first home in Japan, the Kobe mission house. We had come full circle! In my diary I wrote, *Yes, we belong here – home!*

Daytime tent meetings for children

Peter leading singing

Kindergarten class

Kindergarten teachers with the bride

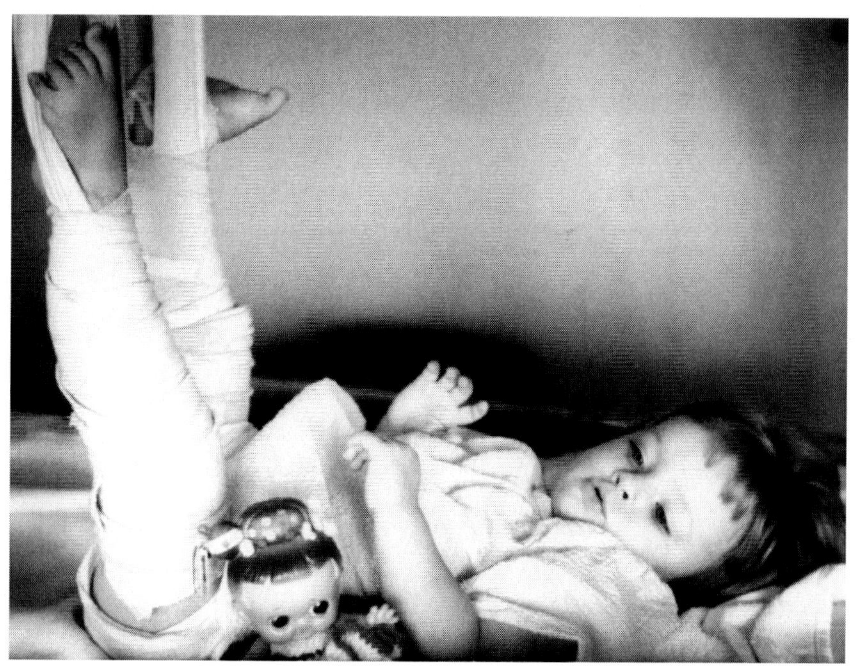

Rosie's broken leg

Vangy & Rickie on firewood for the ofuro

Higashiguchi plants a tree as a symbol of his faith

Kindergarten children and moms

Bicycle Ad

Peter, off to the villages

Home with the twins

Twins, Billie & Wanda

Vangy pulling for the team

Good-bye Nichinan

Good-bye Japan - first furlough

JAPAN FOR CHRIST

PETER AND MARY DERKSEN

Peter & Mary, Vangy, Rickie & Rosie, Wanda & Billie on laps,1960

Good-bye Japan - first furlough

Peter - Kindergarten principal

Chapter 4

Hyuga
1960~1965

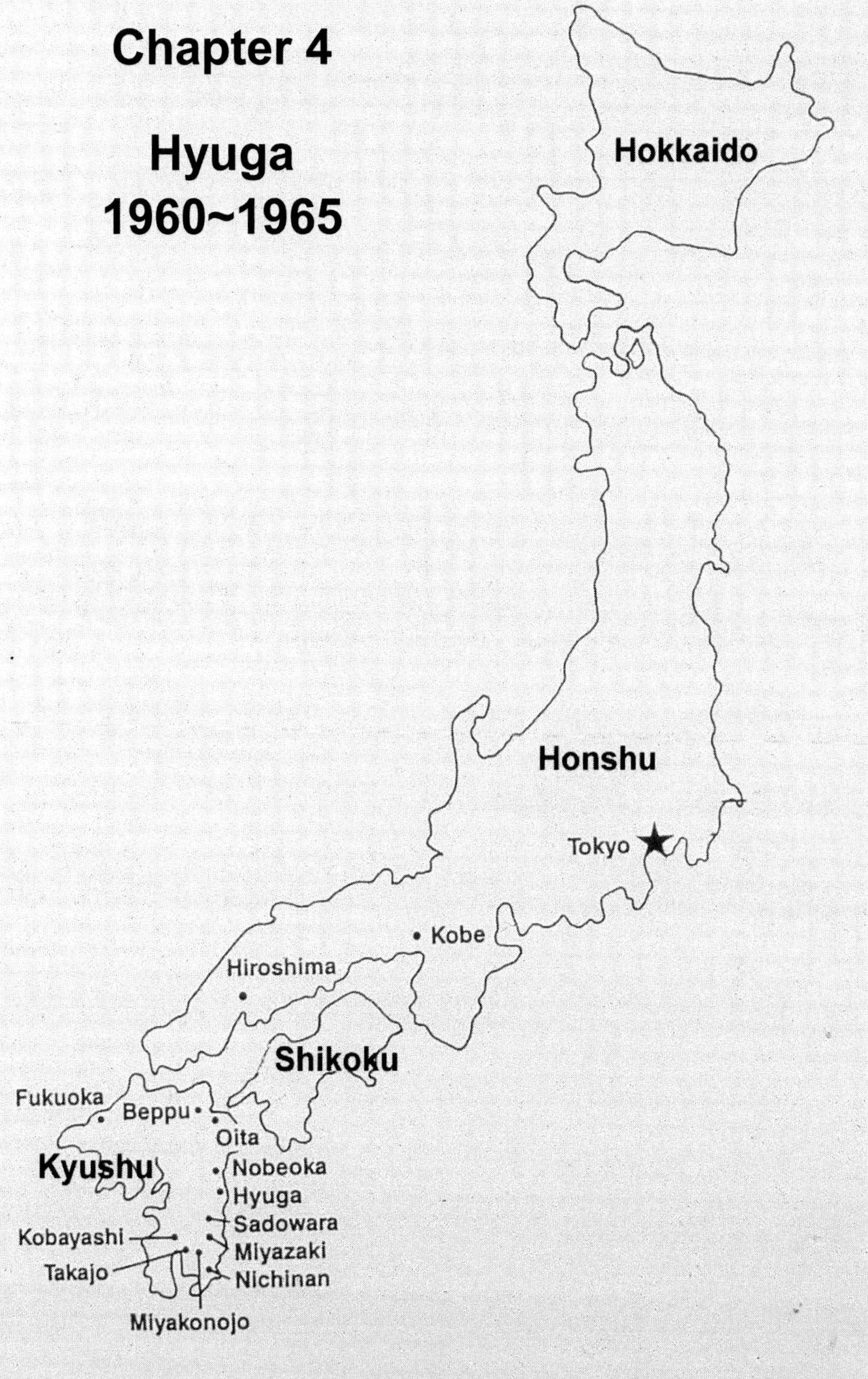

HOME AGAIN

Memories of life as it was in Japan flooded back. Once again we were home in Japan with our five young children. And once again we lived in the mission house on 122 Yamamoto Dori in the city of Kobe. Our mission board graciously allowed us a second time in language school for four months.

Kobe had many foreigners from around the world, business people, missionaries, and students. We enrolled Vangy and Rickie in Canadian Academy, a large school for foreign children in Kobe. The children took a bus to school each day, together with children of the Krause's and the Van Schooten's, missionaries attending language school in Kobe, all living in our mission house. Peter and I went to Japanese language school every morning and kept up with homework afternoons. Our children were happy for their new friends.

At the annual missionary conference in October, the mission decided that after language school, we would work in Hyuga where Ferd and Viola Ediger had started a church during their first term. After the Edigers left, Verney and Belva Unruh moved there for a year, and then Bob and Alice Ruth Ramseyer served for half a year. Now the church had to adapt to another missionary couple. Even though we were all in the same mission, each had different ways of working and "endearing" ourselves to the church. Hyuga City on the east coast of Kyushu Island, had a population of 50,000. Hyuga had three churches, Catholic, United, and Mennonite.

In the fall of that same year, 1961, we participated in the All-Mennonite conference that met every three years. Four Mennonite mission groups took turns hosting. One year the Brethren in Christ hosted us in a Japanese inn in Yamaguchi Prefecture. Yamaguchi is home to the largest caves in the country, so we toured the caves with their fabulous stalactites, cathedral-like caverns, underground ponds, and smaller tunnels where we had to bend to get from one cave to the next.

We stayed in a Japanese inn, and lived on the floor, meetings, meals and fellowship times, as well as sleeping. No chairs. Oh, did our legs get stiff! But that didn't rob us of wonderful blessings. It seemed as if the Lord himself was in our midst, as indeed He was. We had a glimpse of what glory awaits us in Heaven! Refreshed and energized, we returned home, ready to serve the Lord faithfully.

MOVING!

In January, 1961, we moved into the mission house in the city of Hyuga in Miyazaki Ken (prefecture). We had stored our things under the eaves of the Nichinan house where we had lived for three years after language school. We packed for hours. During this time the twins developed fevers, and I took them to a doctor. One thing was almost sure. If you went to a doctor for anything in Japan, you would get a shot, young or old!

The rental truck came at 4 PM the next day to load our belongings. We left at 6 PM, drove along the east coast of Kyushu, and arrived at our new home in Hyuga at 10 PM quite exhausted. We were happy that our three youngest were good all the way. The truck with our belongings arrived at noon the following day.

Later in the afternoon we went to the train station to get Vangy and Rickie when they came home from our mission boarding school in Miyakonojo for the weekend. This was their first train trip alone, and they were a bit frightened. They were also very excited about their new school. What a relief! We had worried about changing from a Japanese to a mission school.

NEW HOME IN HYUGA

In Japan a town with a population of 50,000 is a city, so Hyuga qualified. However, it was still like a small country town where the stores opened right onto narrow streets. Maneuvering through main street by car was no small feat. No sidewalks. People walked where they pleased. The mission house was also on a narrow, unpaved country road in a residential area.

The church met in the garage. It had been remodeled with a cross on the roof. In Japan the Christian Church is always associated with a cross. The entrance was welcoming, with glass windows in the doors.

We were immediately involved in preaching, teaching Sunday School, women's meetings, as well as meetings in surrounding villages. During the week, the pulpit and folding chairs were stored in a corner of the garage to make room for the car.

Our new home was surrounded by flower gardens and a gardenia hedge that spread its fragrance far and wide during blooming season. There was room for a large vegetable garden. I was especially fond of the sotetsu, a palm tree in front. Our neighbors were farmers. Having grown up on the farm, we loved it. One year we grew enough melons to supply our mission summer campers for quite a few meals. The children helped shell peanuts we had planted so we could make peanut butter. The children loved their pet goat, Snow White. In the distance we could see and hear the waves of the Pacific Ocean crash on the rocks. Alas, later factories and piers in the new industrial zone hid the ocean from view.

Our house was typical of early missionary homes and churches, made of cinder blocks. We had come to Japan wanting to live like the Japanese, but here we were in a western style bungalow. Because of much rain, homes in Japan do not have basements. A unique feature in our new home was a staircase into the attic that was excellent for storage, and in a pinch, for wall to wall floor sleeping space when the church billeted the guests who came during conferences. The stairway was stored in the ceiling of the hallway, and you just pulled it down when you needed it.

My fears of wild creatures surfaced unexpectedly one day when I bent to pick up a belt in our hallway, only to have it slither quickly away! Peter managed to find and dispose of it. Another day I was putting linens in a closet and found a snake coiled neatly between the sheets. That one got away!

SETTLING IN

The Japanese did not eat cereal for breakfast, but missionaries found rice poppers who made snacks. When the rice popper was in the neighborhood, I quickly took rice, white or brown, and some sugar, to the popper man. He had a long metal net like a big narrow burlap sack with a lid. A small machine with a container to hold rice was fastened to the top of the net. The man lit the fire in the machine, kept cranking the handle, and suddenly opened the lid of the machine. With a loud bang the rice popped into the wire mesh container. Our small bundle of rice had become a large plastic bag full of delicious puffed rice. However, like the Israelites, we got tired of the same breakfast all summer, and often longed for the flesh pots of Canada. What a treat when Mom sent a box of corn flakes for Christmas! During the winter months we ordered oatmeal from Tokyo.

Houses and schools in Japan were always built with the living rooms or classrooms facing south to utilize the winter warmth of the sun. There was no central heating, so we used small portable kerosene heaters. At 10 o'clock on a sunny day, we turned off the heaters and basked in the sun's warmth streaming through the windows. We lit the little heater at 4 PM.

We had three bedrooms, one for the boys, one for the girls, and one for us. The living room and study were separated by the genkan, a Japanese style entrance where you left your shoes before stepping up into the house. Slippers always stood ready for guests above the step. Japanese kitchens were in the darkest corner of their houses. Ours was bright, facing south.

This time we had brought a stove so I could bake properly. Baking was not part of Japanese culture, but they certainly enjoyed our cookies and cakes, and missionary ladies spent many happy hours teaching the ladies to bake.

Our washing machine had tipped on its side on the voyage, and as a result, all the oil leaked out, causing the gears to grind. When we checked the parts manual, it simply said, "Call the nearest service center." Right! Thousands of miles across the ocean! Peter and Franzie, a short- term worker, painstakingly took the machine apart, laying each piece on the attic floor in right order. They found the offending part and ordered another from the U.S. When it finally arrived weeks later, they had the fun of trying to put it together again. It worked! Peter learned to enjoy taking things apart when they weren't running properly, but I was afraid that one day he might electrocute himself!

I taught many English classes. We had so many guests, both Japanese and foreign, that I needed help in the home. At first we hired a pleasant young Christian girl. She also helped with Sunday School, but soon she left for Osaka for further education. Kuroki San, a neighbor, was happy for part-time work. Mornings when she came we would read the Bible together. Kuroki San was like a sister to me, and our family loved her.

One morning she came running breathlessly, "President Kennedy was shot!" We had rented a TV for the first time, and that was the first program we watched – news of the shooting. Some Japanese thought that we were Americans and spoke their condolences to us. It was indeed a sad day for us, even though we were not Americans.

EARTHQUAKE

The last weekend in February we had a terrifying experience - our first major earthquake. Missionaries took turns hosting a monthly fellowship. That Monday it was to be in Nichinan. Friday, instead of coming home after school, Vangy and Rickie took the train with the Voran boys to spend the weekend in Nichinan. Sunday afternoon I took Rosie, Billy and Wanda to Miyazaki by train to spend the night with Bernard and Ruby Thiessen. Monday morning we would all travel to Nichinan together by train. Peter stayed in Hyuga for the Sunday evening meeting. Thus our family was in three different cities that night.

I was sound asleep with our three youngest, Rosie, Billy and Wanda, and two Thiessen children upstairs. Suddenly I was jolted wide awake when the house began to jerk back and forth with loud cracking noises. A large picture in a glass frame hung above the heads of our sleeping children. It began to swing back and forth like a clock's pendulum. I jumped up and took it down.

Shaking, I wondered which child I should grab and run downstairs with? The house just kept on shaking. I was so terrified that I couldn't even pray, so I finally just sat down on the bed waiting for everything to collapse. Gradually the shaking eased, and I began to breathe again. The children were all sound asleep, and when I stepped to the top of the stairs, it was littered with broken plaster. I was glad that I hadn't tried to carry a child down. We would surely have fallen and broken bones. Bernard called from downstairs, "Are you o.k. Mary?" No more sleep for me that night. A whole wall of Bernard's books had crashed down in his study. Later we heard that one man had been killed by falling debris. The earthquake registered over five on the Richter scale.

Other missionaries told how they had stood in doorways during the worst of the shaking. The first impression was noise! Bookcases fell over. Dishes, trays and canned goods fell out of kitchen cupboards. Plaster cracked and crashed. A faucet snapped off. The new cement wall behind Thiessen's house fell, and nine feet of the stone wall ended in the neighbor's yard.

An hour north of Miyazaki in Hyuga Peter also felt the shaking and went outside to enjoy-his first earthquake! He took an early train Monday to join us as Thiessens and we boarded a bus for Nichinan. We didn't get very far. A huge rock slab from a mountain had slipped across the road during the earthquake. The bus coming from Nichinan was stopped on the other side. The bus drivers found a unique solution. Passengers walked around the fallen rocks and just exchanged buses.

That earthquake began my season of fear. I shook for days. At nights I would suddenly sit upright, and in the dimness watch the light hanging from the ceiling. If it was not moving, I lay down again. We often had minor quakes, and each time I would be terrified. Peter slept undisturbed. Finally I shared my fear with Bob and Alice Ruth. Bob read Psalm 46, *God is our refuge and strength, an ever-present help in trouble. Therefore we will not fear, though the earth give way and the mountains fall into the heart of the sea..."* They prayed for me, and I was finally able to yield my fears to the Lord. What a relief!

OUR CHILDREN

Vangy and Rickie attended our mission school in Miyakonojo, two hours by train from Hyuga. Vangy was in grade 3 and Rickie in grade 2. On Monday afternoon they took the train to school, and returned home Friday after school. Peter kept Friday evenings free for family time. In nice weather we played outside, and in winter we had cozy times reading books or playing games. Our kids used to say, "When our family is together, what we lack in time we make up in quality."

Peter's call, "Rise and shine!" roused us. The little ones grabbed their clothes and rushed to the warm room Daddy had prepared for us. Before breakfast we read a chapter in *Little Visits with God,* and held hands for prayer and a song.

Hair needed attention. One of my monthly jobs was haircuts for the boys, and the girls if they needed it! Looking at pictures years later, the girls laughed at their very straight bangs. I braided Rosie's thick hair, which grew almost long enough to sit on.

Our children were an important part of our work. Week-ends they helped distribute tracts. Rick went with Dad on house visitation. Vangy helped with her younger siblings, telling them Bible stories with flannel-graph. They helped clean, wash dishes, and weeded our small yard in summer. There were no lawn mowers, as the grass stayed short. But oh, the weeds! In our tiny yard we were very close to each other doing that job!

The children never lacked friends, even though often they were a bit older. Vangy had a host of junior high school friends when she was twelve. This lively group came to Sunday School. Some were from problem homes. In Japanese culture, when there is a problem, friends first report to the teacher, who is responsible for her students even out of school hours. Vangy's friends told us that Makiko Chan had run away from home, apparently taking the train to Tokyo, a 24-hour train ride away. They had already told the teacher, who had to let the parents know that their daughter was missing. It was the teacher's business to help trace the runaway. It took several days to find her and bring her home.

RICKIE

Rickie started violin lessons with a Japanese teacher in Miyazaki, which was halfway to their school in Miyakonojo. The first few times I took him to Miyazaki by train. From there we boarded a bus to his lesson. After the lesson, we took another bus to our mission friends who lived on the other side of the city. Our friends took him to the train station and put him on the same train that Vangy had boarded in Hyuga. After two or three times, he managed the trip without my help.

Rosie was five and ready for kindergarten, or so we thought. We enrolled her in the local Japanese kindergarten. I took her by bike to get her settled – oops, not so fast. As soon as I turned to leave, she began screaming. Next morning the same thing happened. After a week of trying, I couldn't stand her screams as I drove away. We decided to keep her home longer.

In a few months we tried again, this time successfully. We never had trouble finding her among the hundreds of children. She was a head taller than all the rest! One thing she did not like was the obento lunch that I packed for her. I tried to make it as much like the Japanese lunches as possible – rice, pickles, some vegetables. Billy and Wanda wanted to attend kindergarten, too, but they were still too young. In the meantime, they amused passers-by, bowing and greeting, their only vocabulary so far. They spent much time playing church and did all their singing and praying in a make-belief Japanese language! This was shortly after furlough. When Rosie came home from kindergarten, two eager little students were waiting to learn what she had learned that day.

Rickie was a people person. He made many friends on the trains, including the conductor, who would treat him special and take him into first class. Once he locked himself into the bathroom on the train and couldn't get out. He pounded and pounded, but nobody heard him. Finally, Vangy found him and notified the conductor who helped him out!

One Friday Peter went to the station as usual to pick up the kids. I had a phone call from Rickie at the station. "Mom," he said, "we met two German university students on the train. Can we bring them home for the week-end?"

His dad had told him, "I think you should call Mom and ask her permission before bringing your new friends home." Of course, Mom said yes! What an interesting week-end!

Weeks later we received a letter from one of the students. He wrote, “After that week-end with you, I decided to attend church in Germany again.” During family devotions he had realized how far he had strayed from God, and now he wanted Christ's power in his life as he prepared for the medical profession. Just an unplanned week-end, used by God to draw a wandering sheep back into the fold!

The following year Rosie joined Vangy and Rickie for the two-hour train ride every Monday afternoon to our mission school in Miyakonojo. Vangy and Rickie were always happy to return to school. Not so Rosie. Invariably, she would be sick before train time, either with a stomachache or a bad headache. I found it more and more difficult to send the children back to school. Some times after they left, I cried. How could I be a good mother to our children when they were gone more than they were at home?

On the way home one weekend, Rickie fell asleep in first class. When the train arrived in Hyuga, Daddy, Mommy, and the twins, Billy and Wanda were at the station to welcome Vangy and Rosie home. But where was Rickie? The whistle blew, and the train began to move. Suddenly a surprised little face popped up at a window, and Rickie just glided by! We hurried to the stationmaster and had him inform the conductor to have the little blonde boy get off at the next station, Nobeoka, half an hour north of us. Then we phoned George and Martha, our missionaries in Nobeoka, and asked them to meet the train and take Rickie home with them. The rest of us quickly piled into the car, and in less than an hour we met a teary-eyed little boy who was very happy to be with his family again!

FAMILY TIMES

Our family loved singing. At the breakfast table and evenings we sang. Sometimes Peter would sing bass. One evening Billy piped up, "Daddy needs a new battery in his tummy!"

Occasionally we returned home quite late from a trip. After one such trip, I checked on the girls, and found Vangy had the light on and was reading her Bible. I scolded her, because it was far past bedtime. She began to sob, and told me, "Mommy, when I gave my heart to Jesus, I promised that I would read my Bible every night!" Oh, the example of a child!

Our children were getting free piano lessons at school, but they could not practice at home, since we didn't have a piano, a costly luxury in Japan. After a family discussion, the children decided to add their allowance to a piano fund. What a day when we finally had our own piano! We bought one that didn't have a full keyboard, but that didn't matter. Now the children could practice at home.

Our children were the only foreigners in town, so they caused quite a stir when people saw them for the first time. When Billy was four, I took him to a neighbor's house. Teen-agers spied the little blonde, pointed and said, "Isn't he cute?"

He pointed his finger at them and repeated, "Aren't you cute?" In Japanese, of course! We all laughed at his quick response.

When he came home with a dirty face one day, I asked him, "Who made your face so dirty?"

Solemnly he answered, "God."

Often Billy amused us by shinnying up the sides of the living room doorpost. When his head touched the top, he called out, "Here's the sun shining!" Or he called, "I'm going to fly!" Well, he did fly when he returned to Japan as a missionary years later! He was a happy little boy, the family entertainer! In boarding school he was an early riser, and always started his day with a loud "It's a great day today!"

We were sad to lose our view of waves crashing on the rocks when a new industrial zone developed along the coast. Foreign ships began entering Hyuga. On weekends Rickie rode his bike to the harbor and made friends with captains and crews.

One Saturday he returned home at noon unannounced with a captain and several crew members for lunch! He also began collecting coins from other countries. But he wasn't the only one to get involved. When an American mine sweeper came to port, the mayor asked Peter to help with translating. How exciting to have the mayor's luxury car come to our gate to take Peter to the ship! Of course, he also got to dine with the mayor and the captain. The next day the city office delivered an extravagant fruit basket to our home as a thank you gift.

One morning we awoke to strange sounds coming from beneath our bedroom floor. The whole family went out to investigate, and found a stray dog had squeezed through the air vents and had a litter of puppies right under our bedroom. The kids were jubilant! “Can we keep them? Can we keep them?” they begged.

“Yes, you may keep one,” we said. Once the pups were old enough to be weaned from their mother, we found homes for them among friends and neighbors. The children named their new pet Jingle. No one was more excited than Billy. He loved to crawl into the doghouse with the dog and both stuck their heads through the small door. It was hard to tell which one was happier, the boy or the dog!

In those days spanking was still the normal punishment for misdeeds. One day I found the children in a close circle on the yard. When I bent down to see what they were doing, I was shocked! They were pulling a daddy long-leg spider apart. Years later Wanda told us, “Mom, we deserved that spanking!”

Since none of the missionaries had family nearby, the children suddenly had more aunts and uncles than ever, for each missionary was either one or the other. When parents of missionaries visited, they made the rounds. Our parents never came, so when other grandparents visited, the children asked, “Can we call you Grandma and Grandpa?”

Some Japan missionaries leaving for furlough chose a roundabout way home so they could attend the Mennonite World Conference in Europe. After all, they might never have the opportunity again. Our children complained, “How come everybody can go around the world except us?” We never did travel around the world, but later some of our children did as they served in various countries. Zaire, Africa, became home to Rick and Marilyn; Taiwan to Wanda and Bruno; and Nepal to Vangy and Ernie.

MIYAZAKI CHRISTIAN SCHOOL

Schooling. What a difficult decision! Our dream was to send our children to local Japanese schools. Vangy took grade one in the local elementary school. After school hours I taught Vangy the BC English correspondence course. Since we would be going on furlough in time for Rickie to enter grade one in Canada, we didn’t have to worry about him. Much as we wanted to be part of the Japanese school system, we did not want our children to lose their English.

We had three younger ones, so even with help in the home, I didn’t see how I could manage to teach English if they all attended Japanese school too. The homework load in Japanese schools was heavy. In grade one the children had a half hour of homework every day. That escalated until in high school the students studied four or five hours a night. Sadly, but out of necessity and with quite a bit of coercion from fellow missionaries, we sent the children to our mission school, Miyazaki Christian School.

In 1959 the mission had built a one-room school in Miyakonojo. It was across the street from the Miyakonojo Mennonite Christian Church, next door to the mission house where The Unruh’s lived. Verney and Belva became the first house parents for the two-story dormitory that was added to their Japanese style house. By late September of the same year, Miyazaki Christian School opened its doors to twelve pupils from grades one to eight.

Virginia Claassen from Whitewater, Kansas was the first teacher. Miss Claassen had a big job teaching eight grades. However, the highest enrollment never exceeded nineteen, so there were always one or two grades without students. The children loved Uncle Verney and Aunt

Belva. However, two full-time jobs were too much for any missionary couple and the mission asked for short-term house parents.

Every three years the children had to adjust to new house parents. Esther Patkau taught German and a local Japanese lady taught the Japanese language. Thus the children had full schedules. They helped with dishes and other chores, but also found time to play.

Miss Claassen agreed to stay two additional years after her three-year term. Agnes Dueck, the second teacher, arrived in the summer of 1964 and taught for three years. Then Miss Claassen returned and taught until the school closed in I971. By that time most of the missionary children had graduated from grade eight.

When they were fourteen, Rickie and Mark Ramseyer decided to bike around Kyushu! It was not without deep concern that we parents finally gave permission for such a venture!

SCHOOL PROGRAMS

Our teachers made sure that the children were introduced to music and the arts. They prepared special programs for Christmas, Easter, and Valentine's day. Five different missions had children in the Miyazaki Christian School, and all came from different directions, some traveling by train for two or three hours, boarding for the week.

Amazing what the teachers could do with so few kids. Their enthusiasm made up for lack of numbers. Our mission was blessed with several musical short termers who not only taught English in the schools and in the community but gave missionary children free piano lessons and helped the teacher with programs.

The Christmas program was the highlight of the year. The children learned many new Christmas carols. The nativity story never lost its glory and was presented in different forms each year.

Hansel and Gretel, **Seven at one Blow**, **Johnny Appleseed**, and **Tom Sawyer**, were some of the captivating dramas they presented. Who can forget the bent old lady (Vangy) who bewitched Hansel and Gretel? Or the big little giant, (Billy) who killed seven at one blow, (which were actually flies,) or Tom Sawyer kissing Betty (Billy and Wanda), and Rosie as Tom Sawyer's mother? Rick was none other than the famous Jean Valjean in another drama. We were all very proud of our "professional" actors and actresses! What a bonus that every child could be involved in the performances. After the programs it was fellowship time with potluck meals before all headed home again.

In summer we worked with other mission groups for a camp for the children at the Baptist mission campgrounds, and another summer at the Mennonite mission campgrounds. Parents took charge of cooking, programs, sports, and Bible dramas. I don't think the kids will ever forget little David killing the giant Goliath, the tallest of the missionaries! Most missionary families also took part in Japanese church camps.

MEDICAL SCARE

One day I discovered a small lump in my breast, and immediately went to our family doctor. Yes, it was there. I needed a biopsy, but that was difficult in Hyuga. The doctor would have to send the biopsy to a big city. The results would come in weeks later. We decided I would go to the city of Osaka, to the Presbyterian mission hospital, which meant an overnight train trip. After making arrangements with the hospital, I took a sleeper train to Osaka.

At the hospital they gave me anesthesia for a major operation, in case the biopsy proved positive. The worst scenario would be a major operation with immediate removal of the offending breast. It was a comfort to have Christian missionary doctors and nurses praying with me. When I finally awoke after the anesthesia wore off, a smiling nurse was bending over me, saying, "You're OK!" The lump was benign. What a relief!

BACKWARD EIGHT

In the early years when most of us were still in language school, the mission had a van to take us to classes every day. No seat belts in those days, so we could pile in as many as needed a ride. When missionaries moved to the cities in Kyushu, the need for cars was obvious, and the mission supplied them. During our years in Nichinan Peter was happy to use only a motorcycle. When we needed a vehicle, we could borrow a mission car or van from the other missionaries.

Before leaving Canada, we knew that we wouldn't have a vehicle, so I returned my license to the BC license bureau for a $5 refund, much to my regret later. We finally acquired a Toyota car big enough for our family of seven. However, we heard criticism about missionaries driving luxury cars, so we exchanged it for a smaller car.

Peter had to leave for Tokyo to attend committee meetings. When it was time for the children to come home Friday after school, there was no driver to get them from the station. That's when I realized that I needed a license!

It would have been a simple matter to exchange my Canadian license for a Japanese license. Now I had to take a driving test in a Japanese driving school with one of their vehicles. That would be costly, but even worse, I had to take the test on their driving range, with its narrow, paved roads, mock railway crossings (Japan's law is that every vehicle has to stop, look and listen before crossing a railway track), and oh, joy, a small paved figure eight which you were required to back around! Each narrow road was raised a few inches. If you slipped off the narrow ledges during the exam, even when backing around the eight, you were waved off. Next try? Next month!

Besides the driving test, you also had to pass the physical tests (vision and hearing), and a written test on rules and regulations, the makings of engines, ad infinitum! And all this in the Japanese language at which I was still very poor. Oh, what I wouldn't give to have my license back from Canada!

The driving school gave me a booklet to study, and for a month I spent my recuperating time from the mini operation, studying a booklet morning, noon, and night, in Japanese, about road rules and engines.

Peter and I rented the driving range by the hour several times. We had to pay an instructor, but since Peter was an excellent driver, we decided not to hire one. We were also allowed to use our own car for practicing. The first time I was in the driver's seat with Peter beside me, a small wiry man who had been watching me drive, came up to us, waved Peter out of the car, and sat down beside me. Then he taught me how to drive!

DRIVING TESTS

For the driving exam, I would have to use one of their vehicles. Those were supposed to be for rent, but they only had the Toyota pick-up available, and no one knew whether they would be driving that one or the Prince pick-up for the exam. The vehicles were quite different. One had the gears at the steering wheel, while the other was a standard. However, the driving school had no Prince on the premises. The closer it got to exam time, the more people waited in line for a chance to rent the Toyota. I took my turn, too, but found it hard to steer. How could I ever back around an eight?

On the exam morning almost eighty people signed up for the driving test, only four were women! That morning I got to practice on the Prince for fifteen minutes before exams started, and each time I ground the gears. I made a mental note that I didn't dare do that during the exam, or I would be out for another month. Each person received a number, the even ones driving the Prince, and the uneven ones the Toyota. I was quite relieved, because I decided that trying to steer around the eight would be worse than grinding the gears!

I was number 74, so I had the advantage of watching 73 people ahead of me making it or being waved off for their mistakes! It was pretty scary to see a mechanic fail because he slipped off the track. Finally, my turn came, and I did a great job, except oops! The gears started to grind. I quickly caught my mistake and the examiner let it go. Maybe he was just as scared of this foreign woman as I was of him! Anyway, I passed!

Next was phase two, the physical test. At one point the examiner asked those who were left, (all four women made the driving test!) to close our eyes as he tested our hearing. I closed my eyes and kept them shut. The examiner was saying something out loud, and suddenly it dawned on me that he was calling my number, 74. I jumped and opened my eyes. Everyone started laughing. I never caught on to when it was okay to open my eyes again, but I did pass the physical exam.

Now for the worst! We sat at tables with a sheaf of papers about driving rules and engines. We had fifteen minutes to answer multiple choice questions. I stared at the papers, unable to read most of them. Everyone was finished. I was left sitting alone. Finally, an examiner came out of the office waving his arms. I knew I had failed. But no, he came and sat beside me and read each question. Ah, that was better. At least I could understand him. To make matters even easier, he pointed to the answers that I should circle! I passed with flying colors! We had prayed much about this, and God had answered in a way that I hadn't expected, but I accepted with thanks!

CHURCH GROWTH

Church growth was slow. One Sunday I wrote: "*Eighteen. Record attendance!*" Masao Miyazaki, a young seminary student, was helping. After several years he moved to Tokyo to continue studies while working. He married a lovely Christian girl. They started a small church on the outskirts of Tokyo which gradually grew to become one of the largest churches in our conference. Miyazaki Sensei had blossomed and become a very capable and respected pastor of the Misato Mennonite Christian Church in Tokyo. Pastor Miyazaki has retired, passing the baton on to his son, a graduate of the seminary AMBS in Elkhart.

A teacher in the local high school made a decision for Christ shortly before his wedding. He brought his wife to church faithfully, and she became a Christian. Christian homes were few in Japan. The couple invited us to start a Bible study in their home in the neighboring village of Mimitsu. We discovered that the older sister was a Christian. The Lord uses many links to draw unsaved family members to himself.

The Hyuga church planned special meetings throughout the year. Often, we used Christian films like ***Martin Luther***. The church put up posters announcing meetings weeks in advance, and distributed invitations and Christian literature door to door. At one of these meetings the attendance was only sixty. We tried not to show our disappointment. Surely more would come the second night. But it rained, and attendance dropped. We were discouraged, but God in His great love and mercy forgave us and showed us in the following nights that to make His power manifest He depends neither on crowds nor certain individuals who we had prayed would come. Several new people made decisions for Christ, and some Christians who had become lax renewed their faith in God.

I started a prayer book, writing names of believers and seekers in the first column along with a prayer request, and recorded answers in the second column in red. Whenever we got discouraged, I would check my prayer book, and see the encouraging red notes, answers to prayers! We relied on God's promise in Mark 11:24: *Therefore, whatever you ask for in prayer, believe that you have received it, and it will be yours.*

I took private Japanese language lessons from Endo Sensei (a retired teacher). One day I asked God for an opportunity to read the Bible with him. Endo Sensei began talking about a famous Japanese Christian, and it was just natural to open the Bible and answer some of his questions. Another day I went to visit and found him very sick. He recovered, and he and his wife invited our family to a birthday celebration. He said God gave him life again. Both confessed faith in the living God.

Vangy had many junior high school friends. We prayed for their salvation. The following year two of her friends were baptized. Takahashi San stayed faithful, and Vangy kept up contact. When Vangy visited us in Japan many years later, Takahashi San came to see her. Vangy was worried because she had almost forgotten Japanese. They connected instantly. What a joy to hear them laughing as they tried to carry on a conversation.

Higashiguchi San had made a decision for the Lord in Nichinan but had become lax in his faith. We asked the Lord for a definite step of faith and commitment. He immigrated to Canada with his family, and there, in a Japanese church, he renewed his faith. His wife also made a decision for Christ. When Higashiguchi's father became sick, they returned to Japan.

Some days when I was discouraged, I just needed a promise. One discouraging day I was reading Habakkuk 3:17~18: *Though the fig tree does not bud ... yet I will rejoice in the Lord.* Once I simply asked for victory in my own life. The Lord replaced my bitterness and desire for justification with a deep desire to understand and love those who were causing difficulty.

MEETINGS

Peter and several of the Christians had meetings in surrounding villages. What a challenge to share the gospel with people who had never heard of Jesus Christ. Nakada San, an elderly Christian, lived in a mountain village, a two-hour drive away on narrow winding roads. Once a month we gathered for a meeting in the couple's home. At Christmas they invited the village children. With shiny black hair, sparkling eyes, and glowing faces, they sat crowded, legs tucked under, on the straw mat floor. I told them the story of Jesus' birth with pictures. Their eyes grew wide in astonishment and asked, "Honto?" (Really?) Yes! We brought Christmas treats, which was a first for them. Our hearts were warm all the way home! What a joy when Nakada's wife accepted Christ as her Savior.

We had monthly meetings in another village in a Christian home. The roads to these mountain villages were bumpy and muddy on rainy days and dusty on dry days. Through the testimony of Fujimura San, convalescing in the same sanitarium as Fujimoto San, Fujimoto San, in whose home we met, had also become a Christian.

INDIVIDUALS

After his recovery, Fujimoto San returned to his mountain home where he and his wife had a small farm. The kitchen floor was dirt, and the living area was on a raised floor with straw tatami mats. In the center of the floor was a square fire pit, with a water pot hanging from a metal hook in the ceiling. That was their only heat in winter. Chickens scratched in the dirt floor of the lower level. Smoke from the fire pit burned our eyes as we huddled near the fire. The Lord filled us with great joy in sharing the gospel with his wife and neighbors. We often took Christians along to share their testimonies.

A neighbor who taught private English lessons often dropped in for a visit. One day he invited me to speak to 150 high school students in a country school. We drove through the narrow main street of Hyuga, lined with storefronts on both sides. No sidewalks! Suddenly he sideswiped a student. She twirled around but managed to keep her balance as the car bumped her school bag out of her hand. He didn't even stop, just laughed it off.

After my talk, students asked me to sign my name in text books or on scraps of paper. On the way home we landed in a rice paddy. I walked home, because I couldn't really help him out of his predicament!

The Hyuga Church experienced many blessings. Christians who had become believers during the Edigers' time were growing in their faith. However, some dropped out, and others moved away. We were often discouraged. How we thanked God for faithful prayer partners back home.

Sato San, a neighboring farmer, had become a Christian because of Ferd's help. When Sato San's sow refused to feed her baby pigs, Ferd took a plier and pulled out a few of the piglets' teeth. Problem solved. Ferd Ediger won the respect of farmers.

After we had been in Hyuga for a while, Sato San, the farmer, stopped coming. He became very ill with cancer and spent several months in the hospital. The Lord spoke to him during this time, and he told us he wanted to make a new start in his faith when he came home from the hospital. Later his cancer surfaced again. During his last weeks at home, we often ran across the road to visit him. The end was near. He had no pain but was unable to speak.

One evening I found the family and many relatives gathered in his room where he lay on his futon on the floor. When he opened his eyes, I started reciting Psalm 23. Slowly he began to repeat each word. The family was shocked. He had not spoken for weeks, and now he spoke plainly. I prayed with him and went home. The next day he went to be with the Lord.

The family had promised to have a Christian funeral, but as soon as he died, they changed their minds. It would never do to have a Christian funeral for the father of the city's mayor! About 2000 people attended the Buddhist funeral. We were disappointed. However, most of the family, including the mayor, came to a memorial service in church the following Sunday. Slowly we realized that if we only had victories and great stories to share, Christians in the homeland might stop praying for us. Now we tell our friends that their prayers are what kept us going.

MORE CHRISTIANS

Fujimura San, one of the early Christians in the Hyuga Church, who was in the hospital for TB, suddenly took a turn for the worse and the family was called. Peter was with the family when he passed away. Many times even when the deceased was a Christian, non-Christian family members would take over and arrange for a Buddhist funeral. His wife was also a Christian and was thankful that the family respected her wishes for a Christian funeral. Non-Christians noticed the difference. The Christian faith offered hope. Life after death!

The Yamada sisters who had been baptized earlier lived just a five -minute walk from the church in a Korean community. Korea and Japan were not on friendly terms. Many Koreans living in Japan changed their names to Japanese names in order to avoid the stigmatism Koreans experienced. Even though many were born in Japan, legally they could not become Japanese citizens, and always had to be fingerprinted. Many who had been born in Korea were brought to Japan by the Japanese army to work. Most of them lived in poorer communities exclusively for Koreans, called boraku. They were excluded from professions. Thus they responded with great relief to find welcome and acceptance in the church.

Christians who moved to Hyuga from other cities found our small church. Aiko San had a drug store in town. Her husband was not a Christian, but she prayed faithfully for years and was able to lead him to Christ before he died. What a victory!

Nagatomo San lived in an old folks home and walked an hour to church every Sunday. In those days only people who had no family lived in old folks homes. The church became his family. He made a decision for Christ after hearing the Gospel. Nagatomo San was such a man of faith that we called him our Abraham.

Occasionally a new Christian would surprise us with a dedication that reached far beyond the local community. A student in the local high school began attending English classes in our home. Soon she made a decision for Christ. She trained as a nurse and got a job in Miyazaki. Friends often accompanied her to church. She studied midwifery in Osaka; there she heard about MCC and applied for ministry. MCC sent her to Vietnam for three years. We were thrilled to have a witness from our church working overseas!

A widow came to church with her three young children. She had aborted her last child and was overcome with guilt and sorrow. What joy when she found forgiveness in Christ! Then she asked for baptism. Since she would be moving to a town where there was only a Baptist church, she wanted immersion. The ocean nearby was too cold; so the church rented a community bathhouse. After her testimony, she was baptized in the big warm public tub!

PROBLEMS

One day a mother asked us to take in her wayward daughter. The parents had put her in a private school, but she kept running away. Should they put her in a Catholic convent? They decided they would ask us first. Peter could never turn people away. If God sent them to us, God would give us the strength to help. Well, guess who spent the most time with her? Sewing, cooking, shopping, talking, and witnessing. And what happened? She ran away from us, too. What a shock! I like to believe that God started the process of wooing her, and we were just one link. When the chain of links is complete, God will have the victory in her life!

One day a very angry man came to our door! He was angry about the war Japan lost to these hated Americans! Peter invited him in, and just listened to his long rant. Then Peter shared about our Mennonite peace position. Finally, he told him that we were Canadians. Well, that brought quite a change in his attitude. However, he never came again. Another link in a chain?

A handsome young man stood at our door one spring day. Before he was even inside, he shared that he had just received Christ as his Savior. Kashiwada San was a university student in Tokyo, and had been attending Bible studies at a Christian student center. He came under such deep conviction of sin that he could not eat or sleep. While reading the Bible on the train, the Spirit of God revealed the way of salvation to him. He was burning with zeal for his new-found Lord and wanted to tell the whole world about Christ. His family lived in Hyuga, so he was home for the holidays.

After returning to university, he spent much time studying the Bible. The Lord brought him through a dark time of his life. In Tokyo he found and married a lovely Christian girl. They came to visit us on their honeymoon! The Kashiwadas eventually returned to Hyuga and became pillars in the church.

Drinking was a major problem, particularly for men. One teacher, a new Christian, liked to drink at school parties. However, at a New Year's party he stood aside and watched his fellow teachers drink. As he listened to the raucous laughter, lewd jokes and smelled the foul air, he rushed outside. He drank in the crisp air and fell to his knees, thanking God for saving him from such a life. Soon he emerged as a strong lay leader and began preaching once a month.

Christian homes are rare in Japan. Most believers are the only Christian in their family. What a joyous celebration when the Ueno's, Nakada's, and the widow, Kawagoe San, dedicated their babies to the Lord.

Two young working men began coming to meetings. One dropped out, saying he would like to become a Christian, but salvation was not for him. He tried to commit suicide but failed. His friend, Aratake San, worked for the city offices. He lived far away in the mountains, so often spent weekends with us, and became part of our family. Aratake San became a Christian, felt God's call upon his life, and enrolled in a Bible College in Tokyo. During his last year in college he became quite sick.

He never married but remained faithful to the Lord and helped where he could in the church. In September, 2008 the Lord called him to his eternal home.

Every year the church planned evangelistic meetings. Now instead of tents, we rented halls. Young people in Bible schools served enthusiastically in the churches during vacations. These were the future pastors for our churches!

After months of planning and praying, the Christians decided to invite one of these students to be our evangelist for the spring meetings! It was 7:30, and time to start. Our hearts sank as we looked over the rows of mostly empty chairs in our small garage church. Five Sundays preceding the meetings the Christians had distributed tracts house to house in town. Each Sunday we took a different tract to the homes. We distributed hundreds of invitations. Why so many empty chairs? However, gradually people filtered in, increasing every evening, until on Easter Sunday evening our small church was packed. At the end of the meetings, the people were reluctant to go home, so they sat and listened to our student evangelist share and answer questions.

In those days the common saying was that for every 5,000 tracts or pieces of literature you distribute, you can expect one seeker. That was the average. Gradually attendance grew as people accepted Christ. One couple wondered, "Why have we never heard the gospel until now?" What joy to also see church members renew their faith in the Lord.

CHRISTMAS

Christmas day is not a holiday in Japan. However, Christmas is good for sales, so department stores and malls decorate with fancy garlands, Christmas trees and Santa Claus. Christmas carols peal from loud speakers. The outward forms of Christmas are all quite visible, but many do not know the meaning of the celebration.

When I asked our non-Christian English students what Christmas meant to them, they said, "Oh, it's just like another day at our house. Father goes to work as usual, but he brings home a big Christmas cake to celebrate." Christmas is a time for parties and sales. Famous hotels advertise big Christmas dinners and shows, so "be sure to get your reservation in early!" Newspapers and TV stations often sought out the missionaries and asked them to share the meaning of Christmas. What a thrill to see a newspaper headline on Christmas morning: ***JESUS CHRIST IS BORN IN BETHLEHEM!***

Schools want their students to know the meaning of Christmas. Many churches have a Christmas Eve candlelight service. City churches organize joint citywide Christmas celebrations in large halls. In large cities choral societies sing ***The Messiah*** to capacity audiences.

CHRISTMAS IN HEAVEN

The Hyuga church had dedicated Christian young people willing to teach Sunday School, even though they had no training. Sunday School peaked during the Christmas season, and the little garage church was filled to capacity. The kids loved practicing for the Christmas program. Tomomi, a mentally challenged girl, was one of the most faithful. She always brought her Bible and loved to sing the songs of Jesus and hear Bible stories. The children's Christmas program was to be the Sunday before Christmas. Tomomi had her Bible and Sunday School attendance card ready hours before bedtime. Her father had promised to attend the program, and her excitement knew no bounds! Suddenly Tomomi became very sick. They called a doctor, but Tomomi died. The family was devastated!

Her aunt, a Sunday School teacher, came running and asked us to come. Peter was gone, so I went and sat with the family. In Japan the funeral is the day following death. Since the family was Buddhist, we had no other expectations. However, the father suddenly turned to me and asked, "Will the church have the funeral?" When Peter returned, he made arrangements with the family. The funeral would be in our small garage chapel.

The next day, Sunday, instead of the children's Christmas program, we had a funeral for Tomomi. The Sunday School children sang, and we were reminded that Tomomi was celebrating Christmas in heaven with Jesus whom she loved so much. Many neighbors attended the touching service. Those who couldn't get in, stood outside. One elderly lady who was not a Christian said, "I want a Christian funeral too! The Christian funeral is full of hope and of meeting again!" Tomomi's father began attending church.

Other funeral customs included memorials one week after death, one month after death, and one year after death. The family asked Peter to officiate at each memorial. They invited extended family and neighbors. What wonderful opportunities to share the hope we have as children of the living God!

RADIO EVANGELISM

Japan was very favorable to missionaries, and opportunities for evangelism abounded. The Pacific Broadcasting Association began broadcasting the Gospel throughout Japan. Our mission decided to sponsor the ***Good News*** and ***Light of the World*** programs on local radio stations.

Rev. Akira Hatori, the radio pastor, a graduate of Fuller Seminary in California, returned to Japan burdened for his people. A talented choir and organist assisted in the broadcasts. Many subscribed to the Bible correspondence course.

In rural communities, homes were connected by radio transmitters called "yusen hoso." It was the only station available, and they could have transmission on or off. Those who subscribed had daily local and national news, as well as music. Churches signed up and paid for broadcasts, using Rev. Hatori's programs. Thus the Gospel was reaching into countless communities which could not be reached otherwise.

There was no way anyone could know the far-reaching effects. How could we connect the listeners to the local churches? Why not try a radio rally? The response was overwhelming. Much prayer and planning went into preparations. The first big rally was held in Miyazaki city, the capital of Miyazaki Prefecture, on Nov. 5, 1961. Rev. Hatori was the guest speaker. Approximately 200 people attended. Many were Christians from the new churches, but there were also people who had come as a result of announcements from the radio program and through pamphlet distribution.

Smiles and a feeling of warmth spread through the audience as Rev. Hatori announced himself in the same way as he did in every broadcast. Although his voice was familiar, most were seeing him for the first time. His inspiring messages touched all. He shared experiences of his recent trip to the US and Brazil where he met people who had heard him over the air while in Japan. Indeed far-reaching results! Several in the audience shared testimonies of how they had come to know Christ through these radio broadcasts. To God be the glory!

NEW ERA

Our mission had made a conscious decision to start indigenous churches that would not depend on the mission for finances. Each church called a pastor when they were able to support one. After a pastor came, the missionary moved on to start a church in a new area.

By 1961 the missionary was not alone any more. In each church younger and older Christians were eager to witness, teach Sunday School, and help with village meetings.

During spring vacation, the mission held a retreat. Seventeen pastors, Bible school students, mission kindergarten teachers, Sunday School teachers, and ten missionaries attended.

A heavy downpour did not dampen the first Sunday School teachers' seminar. Thirty-six eager teachers crowded a missionary home in Miyazaki and drank in what the experienced Japanese evangelist had to say. Some of their comments were: *All I've done in Sunday School was wrong! I am determined to spend more time in preparation. I'm going to try to do better this coming Sunday*. Needless to say, the churches benefited!

The new Christians also caught a vision of *the regions beyond Japan* when Pastor Takashi Yamada received an invitation to serve in Taiwan for a series of meetings. The churches raised funds to help with travel expenses, and to help support his family during his absence.

In September 1961, the General Conference Mennonite Mission celebrated ten years of missionary work in Japan. We met in Miyazaki city, where the first missionaries, William and Matilda Voth, who had been missionaries in China, planted the first Mennonite church in Kyushu. Christians from all the churches gathered for this special celebration. Each church had a representative who gave a brief outline of the history of the church in their city. How could they share all the blessings in the five minutes allotted to each church? Impossible! Everyone went overtime! Dr. S.F. Pannabecker, retired missionary from China representing the mission board, was guest speaker. This was a day of remembering that *The Lord has done great things for us, and we are glad.*

- Ten years ago: our mission started work in Japan

- Today: seven organized churches
- Ten years ago: most of these people did not know Christ.
- Today: many in Christian service, and a number of young people in Bible Schools or Bible College preparing for Christian service
- Ten years ago: no Sunday Schools
- Today: weekly children's meetings in all churches,
- Two churches have part-time pastors, while others still rely on missionaries.

The following year four churches had full-time Japanese pastors. Some of the pastors received full support from their congregations, and others received financial help from the mission, as the churches needed it.

A NATION OF STUDENTS

Spring in Japan! Thoughts inevitably turned to students! The school year ended in March and the new school year began two weeks later in April. Those were the only weeks of the year that students did not have homework. Schools took treks in spring, chartering trains and buses for sightseeing trips. Class excursions began with grade 6, which was usually one overnight trip. The junior highs ventured farther for two or three nights, and the senior highs had four or five days. In recent years schools discovered that it cost no more to take their students to the US or Canada than to the ends of Japan, so trips changed drastically. This was not just one small classroom of 30 to 50 students, but as many as ten classrooms of 40 students each! In other words, approximately 400 per school!

What a sight to see teachers leading their well-organized student groups in uniform to famous sight-seeing spots. These included Buddhist temples and Shinto shrines. Hiroshima and Nagasaki atomic bomb historic sites were on top of the list. Castle fortresses where their forebears faced battles that finally brought them together as a nation were important. Of course, each student was expected to bring omiyage, gifts for family and friends, and each souvenir shop was well prepared for the surge of lively giggling shoppers.

DID WE PASS?

Before the school year ended, students studied feverishly to pass exams. Only the best would make it into a good high school which had room for 600 new students. However, 1000 applied. That meant that 400 would fail. Results were announced on a huge billboard outside each school. Students, parents and friends crowded around to see if they made it. As they scanned the huge poster for their names, there was a burst of screaming, laughing and hugging when they spotted the name they were searching for. Others kept on scanning, hoping against hope that they had somehow missed it, and then looked again. The result? Heads hanging, crying, they dragged themselves home. It is a season of jubilation for parents and students who passed, and devastation for those who did not.

Every spring we saw trains packed with thousands of junior high school graduates who had failed high school entrance exams. They were sent to work in factories in the large industrial cities of Osaka and Nagoya every spring. They lived in dormitories and worked during the day, with the opportunity to study evenings.

What daily sad farewells at train stations in many cities along the train route! By the time the train reached Hyuga, it was quite crowded. Parents and friends filled the station platforms, cries mingling with "Sayonara!" as their fourteen-year-olds boarded the train, many not to return home for a year.

High school graduates, who passed exams for only low-class schools or whose families could not afford more schooling, searched for employment which was scarce in their hometown. This meant that they had to leave for the large cities for employment. The better students went off to university. The capital city of every prefecture (province) had at least one public university.

A new young Christian high school student in Hyuga felt God wanted him to be a doctor. He failed the exam and went to preparatory school in Tokyo. The next year he tried and failed again. He finally made it the seventh year! For many years now, he has been a devoted Christian doctor in Tokyo.

Bob and Alice Ruth Ramseyer had a burden for university students. Thus the mission built a student center near the Miyayazaki University. Students came to study the Bible, to read Christian literature, to find a quiet place to study, to get personal counseling, to study English, or to get fellowship and recreation. Here their faith could be nurtured. The center was also used for church conferences and seminars, and thus served the larger church community.

The Pax (a peace program) workers our mission board sent out taught English in churches and at the student center. During an English Bible class, the students would ask the typical questions. *Why are you here? What do you believe? Do you go to church? Are all the people in America Christians?* These questions opened the doors for witness. Pax couples taught English in different cities. What a big help for evangelism and church planting ministries.

CONSOLIDATING

Every New Year churches took turns hosting a Christian retreat. Participants loved the fellowship with so many Christians, and the special speakers challenged them to grow in their Christian life. Most of the churches were small, and many believers were the only Christian in their family or work place. Some years over 100 attended these meetings. If the church had a building, they would sleep there, or Christian families billeted them. Each hosting church fixed meals for the crowd. For the Christians this was a great opportunity to realize they were not just from a small church in their town or city but were part of a larger fellowship of churches. Our hearts burst with joy! This was not just another meeting of Japanese Christians and missionaries, but of heavenly citizens, a seikai, or holy meeting!

One year the Hyuga Church hosted. It was bitterly cold that New Year and we huddled in our coats in the city auditorium which had been rented for the occasion. Our attic became a wall to wall bed. Guests slept on rented padded mats on the floor.

Two weeks later the city auditorium burned to the ground on a freezing cold night. With the fire raging out of control in the howling wind, 184 people were left homeless as the fire spread to near-by apartments and homes. The church had their first experience of collecting clothes and necessary items for fire victims.

BOOKSTORES

Japan is 99% literate, and bookstores are popular places where people stand and read. However, there were no Christian bookstores in any of the cities where we had churches. There were other Christian denominations in our area, too. Churches need Bibles, songbooks, Christian literature for distribution, and books to help pastors, Sunday School teachers, and lay people. Each church had to order what they needed from Tokyo. The mission decided to open a Christian bookstore in Miyazaki city. Esther Patkau, missionary, was the first bookstore worker. Then the mission opened two more Christian bookstores, in Nobeoka and Miyakonojo. Many churches distributed tracts regularly. How good to have them available in our own bookstores.

Ogawa San, an older Christian woman in Hyuga, was very zealous for the Lord. She lived with her mentally challenged son in a ramshackle home beside the main railway crossing. It was the main railway track for trains going north and south on the east side of Kyushu Island. Ogawa San never missed a church meeting. She loved the Lord Jesus and wanted to be involved in the work of the church. But what could she do? She had never attended school. One day she came to the church with a unique idea. Even though she couldn't read or write, she knew the importance of Bibles and Christian literature. Thousands of people passed by her plot beside the railway every day, not only people in cars, but students, workers, and shoppers who walked across the tracks. Everyone had to stop right beside her house when the railway arms came down to wait for the trains to pass.

Gradually a vision took shape. Why not have a Christian bookstore on her property? Her present home was certainly not functional. No problem. If she sold part of her land, there would be enough money to build a modest new home with a bookstore facing the road where everyone waited for the trains. The church was thrilled with her idea!

However, she could not afford to stock the store with Bibles and Christian books. Would the mission be willing to take on this part of the project? The answer was yes! The mission also decided to pay a bookstore worker.

Ogawa San's building was demolished. There was a small shed at the back of her lot where she and her son slept. As for the kitchen? She just moved it outside. Trains passed slowly, because the station was just a few feet from her place. Passengers curiously watched this woman cooking in her open-air kitchen surrounded by pots and pans!

When the new building was finished, the Christians from the Hyuga Church and other churches, and missionaries gathered for the dedication service on February 9, 1964. It was a small, beautiful little bookstore. The pastor of the Hyuga church could augment income for his growing family by working in the bookstore. The Christians were thrilled to have Christian books and literature in their own city. No one was more thrilled than Ogawa San, who saw her vision come true!

God's challenge in Malachi 3:10 *Test me in this,* says the Lord Almighty, *and see if I will not throw open the floodgates of heaven and pour out so much blessing that you will not have room enough for it...* was fulfilled in the life of Ogawa San who had built the Christian bookstore. Her cruse of oil was overflowing, and so was her joy!

PRAYER PARTNERS

In the meantime, the church continued reaching out in tract distribution, special evangelistic meetings, Sunday School, English classes, women's meetings, and personal witnessing. When attendance reached 40, the garage church was crowded.

We had our ups and downs during these days as well. At the end of a long day I wrote in my diary: *Discouraged! No fruit visible. Self-pity is the road to defeat!* There was a constant stream of guests. Our children were sick. When we were at our lowest, the Lord encouraged us through friends like Mrs. Neufeldt in Rosthern, Canada, and Mrs. Kaufman in the US who prayed for us daily.

One day Peter and I just sat down wondering what we were here for anyway. What were we accomplishing? On that day it seemed like nothing was being accomplished. We felt as if nobody cared whether we were there or not. A dull despair settled over us like a dark cloud.

And then the mailman brought a letter from a dear old friend, Mr. Rempel. We sat down amidst our bleak thoughts to read the letter. The peace of God passed from his lines and seeped slowly into our hearts. Here was a man who practiced the presence of God in his daily life. He found great joy in his daily communion with his Savior. Many happy hours were spent in his intercession for missionaries. God's Spirit touched us. God understands. God cares. He sent that letter into our hands in our darkest hour of need.

A NEW BUILDING

The Christians had begun a church building fund. However, the government had designated an area in our city as a new subsidized industrial zone. This caused land prices to double. Purchasing affordable land in any city was expensive. It was common practice that on paper you would cheat in order to keep taxes down for the selling agents. That was not an acceptable solution for Christians. Thus we ended up paying more than the asking price to offset the taxes for the seller.

Encouraged by gifts from Christians in NA, the Christians became enthusiastic. When it seemed that we might finally be able to buy land and begin building, some gave more than anyone thought possible. A 10,000 yen bill in the collection plate was a miracle! One lady brought her entire bank savings. A poor Christian, whose husband was in the hospital with TB, brought 10,000 yen. One afternoon a high school student slipped an envelope into the church building fund box. He had skipped school lunches for a month in order to share in the building of the new church! A high school teacher and his wife brought a generous gift. The Christians were blessed by their own sacrifices, and we felt deeply humbled.

What a contrast to one Christian who regretfully quit church rather than contribute because he was building a new house for his family. Sometimes we felt like the words in Habakkuk 3:17-18, *Even though the fig trees are all destroyed, and there is neither blossom left nor fruit; and though the olive crops all fail, and the fields lie barren; even if the flocks die in the fields and the cattle barns are empty, yet I will rejoice in the Lord; I will be happy in the God of my salvation.*

In March 1964 the Hyuga church bought a small plot of land 60 feet by 40 feet near the train station. Paid in full! The church was very thankful for the contributions of Canadian friends, which amounted to approximately half the cost.

In August 1964, building was begun. A Christian man from our area, Nakada San, had helped with the mission kindergarten construction in Nichinan years before. He and one son had become Christians during that time. The church now enlisted him. Nakada San and Peter spent many days getting estimates for building materials. What a big help to have a Christian with his expertise. After the workers had built the foundation (there are no basements in Japan because of much rain), the beautiful laminated plywood arched frames were raised. The church building was taking shape!

Excitement grew with each passing week as we squeezed into the little garage chapel. In February of the same year, the church called a young dedicated Christian from the Nichinan church attending Bible School, to become pastor of the Hyuga church. The pastor's family moved into a rental home in the neighboring town of Kadogawa, an outreach of the Hyuga church. Thus the young pastor took care of the meetings there and also helped with the church in Hyuga. The pastor's family increased from two to five boys. They ran circles around their father while he was preaching!

EMPTY NEST

What a busy year for all of us! Agnes Dueck from our home church in Abbotsford came in August, 1964, for a 3-year teaching assignment in the school for missionary children in Miyakonojo. We had known Agnes for years and were thrilled to have her join the missionary team. This meant helping her adjust and get settled. I sewed curtains for her apartment and helped with shopping. It was also the end of summer vacation for our children, and Aug. 31 I took all five to Miyazaki Christian School to get settled in their dormitory. Rickie, grade 5, and Billy, grade 1, were roommates. Vangy, grade 6, Rosie, grade 3, and Wanda, grade 1, were in a room with Nancy. Tuesday, September 1, the children started school, and I had to go back to our lonely home with only Peter and me.

Peter had to make a business trip with George Janzen to Kobe to sell the mission house where we had all lived while attending Japanese language school on Yamamoto Dori. The Mikimoto Pearl Company bought the house for ten times the original price! The mission bought a house in another part of the city for the Kobe Mennonite Church.

Then Peter made a business trip to Hokkaido. I often found myself at home alone during the week, and very lonely. I couldn't even listen to records, because soon I would be in tears. What an empty home!

The Hyuga Church was having special meetings in the garage

chapel, and I arrived home from taking the children to school in time to sing a solo the first night. Thirty-five attended and forty came the second night. We were quite excited that my language teacher, Mr. Endo and his wife came.

THE WORLD IS ONE

Another big excitement grabbed our attention in October, 1964. Japan, a sports-loving country, was host to the Olympics. Thousands were on hand to welcome the Olympic torch with fanfare, waving the rising sun flag as it arrived in southern Japan. Miyazaki city had colorful events of ancient dances, a 13-stringed Japanese koto (harp) orchestra and a mass choir. Then the "Sacred Flame," as they called it, was relayed north to Tokyo along the east coast of Kyushu. One of the Christian high school boys from the Hyuga church was chosen as the local relay runner. Hyuga's population was out enforce cheering the runners on.

Of course, we would love to see the Olympics, but that was out of the question because of time and expense. So we did the next best thing. We rented a TV, and for the first time in our life could watch the Olympics from our free front seats in our living room! What a grand event! Certainly, the world seemed to be ONE during those weeks of intense competition.

That same year, on October 31, Peter complained of chest pains. He was 36 years old. Was this a harbinger of complications in years to come? However, the pains disappeared, and were forgotten. The next attack didn't come until after we had moved to the city of Beppu in Oita many years later.

MIXED UP FAMILY TRIP

In 1964 when Billy and Wanda were six, we planned a family trip to visit some of Japan's famous places: Hiroshima, where the first atom bomb was dropped during World War II, Himeji Castle, Kyoto, Nikko, and Tokyo. Peter made train reservations through Japan's top travel agency, to make sure we would have seats on the trains and hotel rooms for nights. A few days before leaving, he checked with the travel agent, only to be told that we had no reservations! What a blow! What should we do? Postpone our trip for another year, or go without knowing what we were in for?

We bravely went ahead with our plans. Without reservations we might have to stand for hours in the non-reserved train cars. That's exactly what happened for part of our trip. The cars were full, so our family of seven stood in the hot vestibule. No air-conditioning! The kids were good sports. We did have reservations for a night in Hiroshima at the Friendship House, and in the Kobe Mennonite Church.

At the Peace Park in Hiroshima, we stood around a huge display depicting in 3-D how the city looked after the bombing. Silence, until Billy suddenly said, "But where are all the people?" No one had an appetite for lunch that day! It was just too horrible!

This was the busy tourist season. One night we could not find lodging. Finally, we begged a Japanese inn to let us sleep in one of their big meeting rooms, and they gave in to this desperate, needy family!

CHURCH BUILDING DEDICATION

The church building was taking shape and was completed in November 1964. Nine years ago Ferd and Viola Ediger had begun evangelism in the city of Hyuga. After several years of contributing to the building fund, the church could finally experience the fruit of their labor of love. On November 29, the new Hyuga Christian Church building was filled to overflowing with 120 people who came for the dedication. Present were the mayor and other city dignitaries as well as pastors, Christians and missionaries from other cities. All came to share in this joyous celebration to the Lord!

Our children's friends in the community also came to Sunday School. I had practised music with them, and at the dedication they filled our church with joyful song.

At long last the Hyuga Christian Church had a large, bright building. The garage had outgrown its purpose! Our hearts were filled with joy for what God was doing in our midst and we had great anticipation for the future of the church.

In our home we experienced great joy when Rosie gave her heart to Jesus. Her younger sister asked, "When can I be a Christian?" What a thrill to see our children accept Christ, and one by one ask for baptism.

Through the years, Peter had the joy of baptizing each of our six children.

1964! A RICH YEAR

February:	celebrate the dedication of Ogawa San's bookstore in Hyuga
March:	the church buys a plot of land, and welcomes new pastor Nakazaki Sensei (term used for teacher or pastor) with his wife and two small boys
April:	many new students seek English instruction
August:	Agnes Dueck from Canada arrives to teach in the mission school
September:	Billy and Wanda enter grade one
September:	radio evangelist Hatori Akira Sensei is here for three days of meetings in the Hyuga garage church
November:	dedication of the new church building, hearts overflowing with gratitude, we could only say, "Our cup runneth over!"

A VISION

On our monthly trips into the mountains, we always drove through numerous villages. Who would ever reach the thousands of isolated homes up on the mountainsides? During one summer vacation, we packed our five children and boxes of tracts into the car. Every Home Crusade provided tracts for all the churches who joined the distribution program. Our destination: Shiba Dam, four hours into the mountains. Purpose: to begin house to house tract distribution in these remote mountain areas. But how would we get to those homes? "Only by foot-path," was our answer!

We began in the farthest inland village, and slowly worked our way back. People were friendly, and most eagerly accepted tracts. There were also those who said, "We have our own religion and don't need another." After the first surprise of seeing foreigners at their door, several children ventured to make friends with ours.

At one small village we quickly made the rounds of six or seven homes. "Is this all?" we asked.

"Oh no! There are many more up the mountain." So we climbed up and up, until each home had been contacted.

One of the Christians from the Hyuga Church had been transferred to a mountain village to teach. One day she met a group of school girls skipping along singing snatches of *Jesus Loves Me*! They recognized the new junior high school teacher, "She might know this song that the missionary taught us a month ago," they said. And she did!

Three days later we returned home with mixed emotions. We were very thankful for the many homes reached, but also burdened for the many still unreached. In most of these places the name of Christ had never been heard.

We prayed much, and felt God calling us to live in Tashiro, a small mountain town, after our next furlough. This was the hub of a circle of five towns and many villages with a combined population of 45,000.

The final decision for our placement after furlough would be made by the Japanese Mennonite Church Conference. We let them know of our desire to move into the mountains to share the Good News with the thousands who had never heard the name of Jesus!

SECOND FURLOUGH (1965)

In late spring of 1965 we began packing for our second furlough, amidst children's school functions in Miyakonojo, lessons, and English classes. Then the last good-byes before leaving for Canada.

Our life was divided into predictable segments. Five years in Japan and a one-year furlough. Furloughs were supposed to be for deputation, study, relaxation, and family. We looked forward to living together as a family again.

AMBULANCE RIDE

We had left Hyuga by train on June 30 and transferred to Japan's famous bullet train in Kokura City. It hurt our eyes to watch the countryside hurtling by. Of course, there was no opening of windows! Somehow a fleck of something lodged in Rickie's eye.

In Tokyo we settled into our hotel, where Peter stayed with the younger three, while Wanda, Vangy, Rickie and I went shopping on Tokyo's famous Ginza Street. Rickie's eye became increasingly painful. We stopped at a fire station, and they immediately took us to a hospital. We laughed as the ambulance went tearing through Tokyo's streets stopping all the traffic with screaming sirens! The doctor found a small irritating speck of soot in his eye. Did we ever have a story to tell when we returned to the hotel! What an exciting end to our second term of service in Japan.

Hyuga Church (garage)

Child dedication

Wanda, Billie, Rosie, Rickie & Vangy

Lunch time with Wanda & Billie

High school English class

Harp orchestra welcomes the Olympic torch

Good-bye junior highs

Earthquake

Bill in the dog house

Mary's teacher

Hyuga Sunday School

Dendo with Hatori Sensei

Japan All-Mennonite Conference, 1960s

Chapter 5

Hyuga 1966~1967

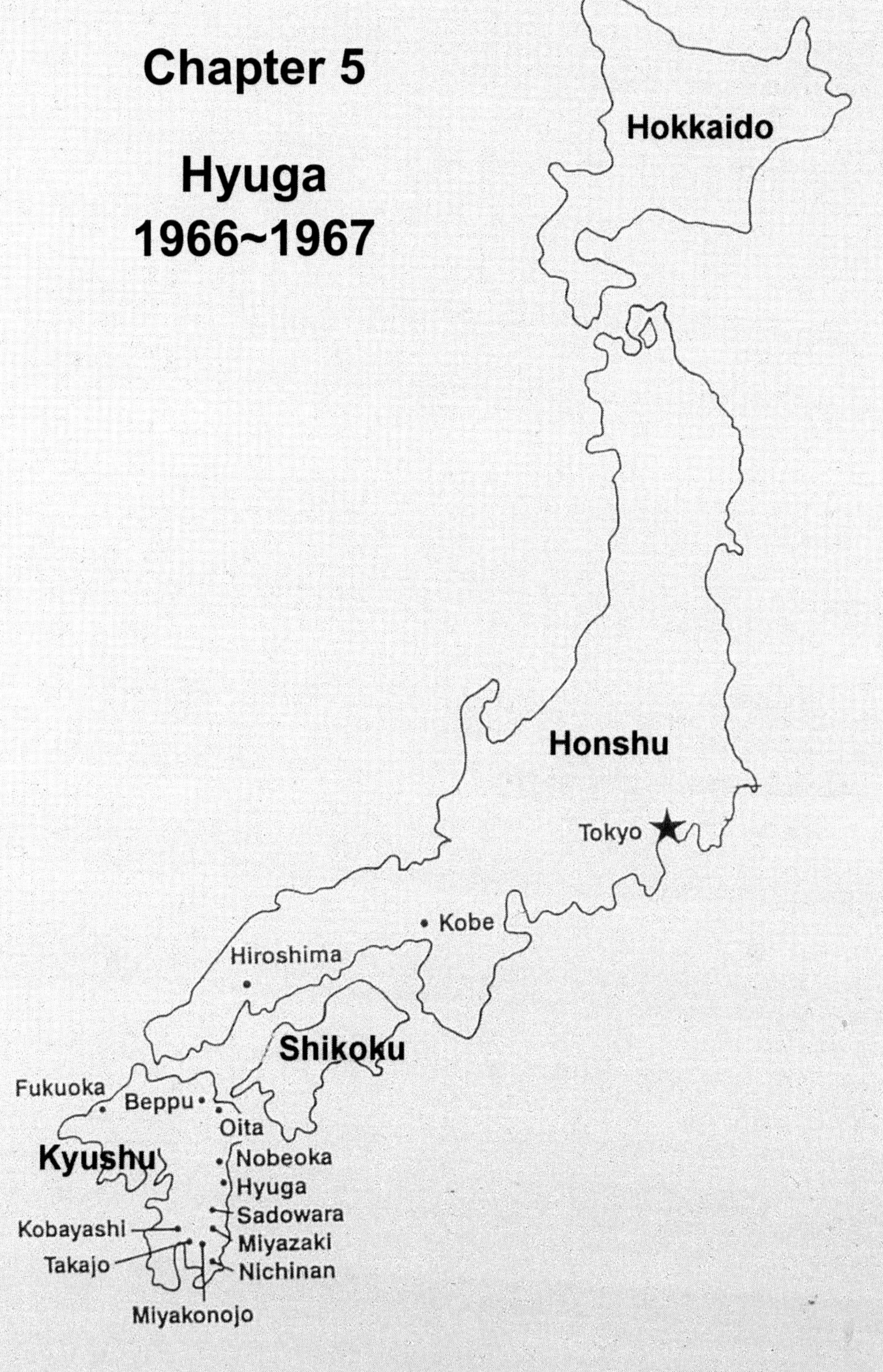

RETURN TO CANADA

Decisions! Where would we live? Where would the children attend school? Where would Peter be able to continue his seminary education? I had promised my sister Hilda that we would take care of Mother during that year. Living in Abbotsford, BC, seemed the best solution. My sister Martha and family lived in Abbotsford, so she would be able to help. We would live close to Peter's family. His parents had found a small house for us on Hillcrest Street.

On July 1 our flight left Japan at 6:30 PM. Since Japan was sixteen hours ahead of Canada's west coast, we arrived in Vancouver July 1 at 11:30 AM! Of course, Mom Derksen had a huge meal ready, not quite aware of the fact that we had already eaten three meals that day! A long table laden with our favorite foods was laid out under the pine trees on this beautiful sunny BC day, with all the extended family present.

There was not much rest. The first Sunday, July 5, Peter spoke in our home church, West Abbotsford. That afternoon we attended a Billy Graham rally in Vancouver with 30,000 people. Our hearts throbbed to see the stadium filled with searching people.

The triennial sessions of the General Conference Mennonite Church, NA took place in Estes Park, Colorado that same summer. Friends loaned us a Chevy, and our family of seven headed for the beautiful mountains of Colorado. The clear mountain air, beautiful scenery, and reunion with many friends were so refreshing.

After our mountaintop experiences, it was back to the hot plains, driving for days until we finally reached Virgil, ON, on July 24 for time with my family. The month in Ontario fled by with family fun, shopping, birthday parties, and many speaking engagements. One week while traveling from church to church in Ontario, Wanda became quite sick with a fever. We moved her from one bed to another wherever we happened to have a speaking engagement. Those were times when it was no fun to be on the road with the kids.

DEPUTATION

We never made just a trip. Deputation was important, and we spoke in churches every Sunday and even during the week on our way back to BC. When we travelled Sundays, we always stopped for a worship service along the way. We were a bit late for the service in Rosemary, Alberta, so we tried to slip into a back bench without attracting attention. As if that were possible with a family of seven! Someone immediately recognized us and took a note to the worship leader. Peter was asked to give the morning message. We had a very warm welcome from the congregation, many of whom we knew. One family invited our big family for lunch before sending us on our way.

In Abbotsford we enrolled Vangy and Rickie in Mennonite Educational Institute about a ten- minute walk from home. Both did well in their studies, and Rickie was quite proud to come in second in a class of twenty-four. Rosie, Billy and Wanda had a longer walk to North Poplar Elementary, which was across the road from Oma and Opa Derksen on Marshall Road. Peter had attended both schools, so it was special for the kids to be enrolled in their dad's former schools.

Peter only had one year of seminary before we went to Japan the first time, and another semester during the latter half of our first furlough. Furloughs would never be long enough to finish seminary, so he had to study piecemeal. He enrolled at Western Evangelical Seminary in Portland, Oregon for five months. Once a month Peter came home to Abbotsford for the weekend and was always booked for Sunday meetings. I marvel that we ever had time for family, because I was always either preparing for, or speaking at various meetings, including the BC Women's Conference. During this time the children and I took turns having flu.

LIFE WITH MOTHER

Mother Klassen had suffered a stroke after her second Parkinson's operation. She also had a bad fall, breaking her hip, so now she could neither talk, nor walk alone. My sister Hilda had taken on the responsibility of caring for Mom. During the day when she was teaching, and Dad was working, they hired help. This double duty life was becoming increasingly difficult, and I had promised my sister that if she could just keep on until our furlough, we would take Mom for a year. The problem was, my parents lived in Ontario, and we were planning to live in BC. After we settled, Hilda and Mom flew to BC. My sister, Martha, helped with Mom when I had speaking engagements for women's groups or schools in BC.

Our kids accepted Grandma Klassen as part of our family. The first night we all crowded into her bedroom to say good-night. Her false teeth were in a glass of water on the bedside table. This was strange! They had never seen anything like that! Billy, six, said, "Whose were they before?" That broke the ice! Grandma laughed with us!

Having an invalid living with us was not always easy, but it was a great experience. Sometimes Billy would sit on Grandma's lap facing her, pinching her cheeks and prodding her to say, "Ja!" (Yes in German.) Grandma would laugh and laugh, and finally blurted out a loud "Ja!"

Sundays I would lift the wheel chair into the trunk, walk her down the stairs and into the car. As soon as we pulled up to the church, several men would rush down to help Mom into the wheelchair and carry her up the steps. Many Christians came to visit Mom, and sometimes well-meaning people told her, "If you only have enough faith, the Lord will heal you." Mom cried, and I was upset.

God did a miracle for me that year. I had been concerned that my back would not hold out. Mother needed complete care, dressing, bathing, and moving from room to room. She could still feed herself and she could read. One day as she was sitting at the kitchen table reading ***Die Rundschau,*** a German Christian paper, Mom began to cry. "Mama, what's wrong?" I asked concerned. She pointed to an article she had been reading. Albert Schweitzer had died!

BACHELOR DADDY

We looked forward to the monthly visits from Daddy. Batching was no fun, although he managed cereal for breakfast and a chocolate bar for lunch! Peter did learn to fry an egg. I sent along as much food as possible. A few times I took the kids to Oma Derksen, took Grandma Klassen to my sister Martha, and then took the bus to Portland to spend a week-end with Peter.

At home Peter and I slept on a three quarter-sized hard sofa in the small living room. Grandma and the three girls had the two upstairs bedrooms, while the boys slept in the basement. Oma Derksen had worked hard to supply necessary furniture, dishes, bedding, and whatever we needed for one year. However, sometimes my proud heart had trouble with the people who had donated an ugly chair. Fortunately, we didn't know who did so. We finally moved it to the basement, so I could have peace! The Lord had much to teach me that year.

My youngest sister, Frieda, came for Easter. She stayed with Mom while our family drove to Portland by car to show the kids where Daddy was staying, and where he was going to school. It was fun to go shopping in the big mall, and the children even went skating with some friends. Peter fell behind in his studies with us around for several days. On a Friday night, we drove home to Abbotsford. Saturday Peter performed his first wedding ceremony for relatives Mary and Jack on April 16, 1966.

LONELY DAYS

One day when the children were all off to school and Peter was back in Portland, I sat and sat on the front steps. The neighbors were friendly, but there really was no time in my life for cultivating friendships. Years later after retirement, I was a hospice volunteer in Abbotsford, BC, partnering with a 90-year old cancer patient, Mrs. Loewen. She looked at me strangely, and then asked, "Did you ever live on Hillcrest Street in Abbotsford?"

"Why yes," I replied. Then she told me her story. She and her four children lived across the street. One day she had seen me sitting on the steps outside. God was nudging her to visit me, but she felt inadequate.

"How can I visit a missionary?" she argued with God. She never went. "I have asked God many times to forgive me, and now I can ask you, too," she said. She discovered that we were ordinary people after all. We had wonderful times of fellowship before she died.

One week-end I complained to Peter. Taking care of Mom was taking its toll. He tried to encourage me that I would receive my reward someday. I responded, "I don't want a reward by and by! I want relief now!" However, at the end of the year, I was thankful for the privilege we had of caring for Mother in our home.

My dad was working on a fruit farm in Niagara all winter, living with my sister in their home in Virgil, ON. They searched the area for care homes for Mother but found nothing suitable. Finally Dad decided to move to BC so that Mother could enter Menno Home. He would have to live in BC for a year first.

Dad asked me to buy a house for him. Peter wasn't home, so I asked my sister and her husband to help. We found a comfortable home on Autumn Street, bought it, and moved in with Mom May 25. Peter was finally finished with his semester at seminary and came home May 26. Our family was together again. It was good to have more room in Dad's spacious new house.

Hilda from Ontario joined us for May and June. She took over care of the family while I had a varicose vein operation. Dad moved to BC in July and tried to take care of Mom again. Dad was not well, so it was difficult to leave him and Mom alone in their Autumn Street house. After dad had lived in BC for a year, Mom was finally admitted to the Menno Hospital in Abbotsford where she spent the next five years of her life.

END OF SECOND FURLOUGH

Vangy and Rickie had both studied well throughout the year and were exempt from MEI's year-end examinations. But Rickie was disappointed that he ranked only third in his class! He also continued violin lessons with Walter Neufeld in Abbotsford, and in June went to New Westminster for a Toronto Royal Conservatory examination.

A former classmate of Peter's invited us for a meal. He had prepared a steak barbeque, and asked Peter whether he liked his well done or rare, not knowing Peter was a vegetarian. The kids and I had a hard time not to burst out laughing. Without batting an eye, he said, "Well done!" and ate what was set before him!

Time was closing in on us. We packed for Japan when we had time. Our calendar was filled with meetings, so friends helped us by taking Grandma Klassen for a few days at a time. In July we drove to The Canadian Conference in Winnipeg. We loved to stay with Tante Anna in Winnipeg. She had a small house. Whether we were two or seven, she welcomed us warmly, and always treated us like family. She knew our favorite foods and we ate like royalty.

My brother Helmut had come to Abbotsford to visit, and he took

Mom and Dad Klassen home to Prince George with him. Tears flowed often that day after saying good-bye to my parents. It was hard to leave. Even though we had not been able to communicate verbally, our family had bonded with our invalid Mom and Grandma.

HOME TO JAPAN

Good-bye Mom and Dad! Good-bye family and friends! Good-by Canada! On August 16 many followed us across the border to Bellingham where we boarded the train for San Francisco. There we stayed at The Home of Peace, a place for missionaries returning to their respective countries. Peter and Rick even went to a baseball game at Candlestick Park!

Two days later, on August 18, our 16th wedding anniversary, we boarded the President Cleveland passenger liner in San Francisco, bound for Japan. We were not happy that our family was divided into two 8-bunk cabins, one for females and one for males. However, this big boat was an exciting place, with a swimming pool, games, festivities, and lots of friends. Almost two weeks of fun! On Sunday the Baptist missionaries, who were housed in first class, arranged for Sunday School for the children and a worship service for the rest. We docked in Hawaii for a day and night. Of course, we had no friends there, so we bought our own leis, and then rented a car to see a bit of this beautiful island, enjoying several hours at the beach.

The morning of September 1 dawned bright and clear. A sweltering heat swathed the passengers pressed against the rails. Japan's famous symbol, Mt. Fuji, raised its majestic peak high above the surrounding mountains, as if welcoming us with open arms. Even the stifling heat could not dampen our joy at being home in Japan once more! Ferd was there to help us through customs and took us to their home.

The next day we had our biggest and most difficult good-bye ever when we took Vangy to CAJ (Christian Academy in Japan), and left her in the dormitory among strangers! She would not come home until Christmas, and that seemed a long way off!

The following day we boarded an overnight train to our home in Hyuga, arriving the next afternoon. Martha Janzen and the Hyuga Christians had cleaned our house. What a happy welcome!

WE BELONG

Our family was happy to be back in Japan. Rickie said, "I feel as if I'm where I belong!" Instead of moving to a new place after furlough, we would spend the first year of our third term in Hyuga. The kids could enjoy their friends again.

Peter and I talked and prayed much about working in the mountain villages and began looking for a house to buy or rent in the village of Tashiro, where we had distributed tracts the previous year. However, we found nothing. The Hyuga Christians wanted us to stay longer to help with the church. God gave us peace, and we stayed, assured that the Lord would open doors at the right time. Church leaders and other missionaries were suggesting that maybe we should think of going to a large city rather than working in the mountains.

There are two schools of thought in Japan: The future of the church lies in the cities and if the rural areas are not evangelized, the church in Japan will never become strong.

During that year several pastors from the church conference, George Janzen and Peter investigated both Kagoshima to the south and Oita to the north to seek a location for a new church. Was the Lord closing one door and opening another?

Pastors in our conference felt it was more important to work in the larger areas of population, so we redirected our thinking. We chose to begin a new church in Oita city which was driving three hours north of Hyuga, on the east coast of Kyushu Island. Until now, we had worked in rural areas of southern Japan. We felt at home in the farming community on the outskirts of Hyuga. We wondered how we would we fit into a large city like Oita.

In the meantime, we continued with meetings in Hyuga and surrounding villages. Our children were very happy with many good friends. The church had become independent. They had their own church building and a pastor. This year of interval in Hyuga was a time of reflection and changes in our life. Starting over was not easy for the family, but we knew it was time to move on.

Thirteen years ago we first arrived in Japan. The beginning was a time of adjusting to our new country, Japan, learning a new language, a new culture, making new friends, and getting used to being far away from our own families.

We made many mistakes in those early years. We were gradually learning to understand and appreciate the Japanese culture, and language was coming easier. Until now we had stepped in when missionaries went on furlough and continued the work the Lord had begun through them. Now we were to start a new church. Even though we were excited at the prospect of working in a mega city, we were shaking in our boots.

CHANGING VISION

A few days later, Rickie, Rosie, Billy and Wanda left by train for our mission boarding school in Miyakonojo, a two-hour trip. When they came home for the first week-end, a typhoon had just passed through, and their train didn't arrive until 10:30 PM The children were tired and starved!

Typhoons were common in fall, and even if you weren't in the path of the storm, there was always lots of rain. It was so humid that rivulets ran down our inside walls. There was always the danger of landslides. We knew a typhoon was heading our way when we heard neighbors boarding up windows and securing whatever was loose. It was scary and very hot inside, since we couldn't open windows. No air conditioning! In fact, electricity would often go out with the strong gusts of wind and rain. After a typhoon, the sun always shone and the skies were clear blue.

When it was time for the children to return to school, I stopped to inspect Billy, and asked, "How did your neck and arms get so dirty?"

"Mommie," he scolded, "That's not dirt! Those are freckles!"

We discovered that the church conference was discouraging us from moving into the mountains. The pastors felt it would be easier to establish churches in the cities, because most of the young people from the country go to the city after high school, either for work or further schooling. However, the church conference left the decision up to us.

Early in 1967, Yanada Sensei from Miyazaki, George Janzen and Peter made survey trips to Kagoshima in southern Kyushu and Oita to the north. We were amazed at how clearly God showed us that we should begin evangelism in the city of Oita. The men visited pastors of several other churches, and all were very welcoming. The Lutheran pastor said, "No problem even if you locate next door to us!" Both church conference and the missionaries gave their approval to begin church planting in Oita, and the Lord helped us to shift our vision.

Packing was always a big job, especially since we had been in Hyuga for so many years. I also found packing difficult due to my pregnancy. Friends invited us for meals. Some brought sushi and we enjoyed eating together. Good-byes were difficult, but the time came to say: We'd love to stay longer. We love you. Sayonara!

On moving day, July the 5th, 1967, we prayed desperately that the Lord would hold off the rain until the truck we had hired was packed. God heard our prayers. Our fellow missionary, Ray Reimer, drove the girls and me to our new home in Oita, while Peter and the boys followed the truck with our car.

PARENTS WITHOUT KIDS

During the week I kept busy visiting the seniors and the sick but felt so bereft of our children. When a very lonely Vangy wrote letters from CAJ in Tokyo, my heart would ache and the tears rolled. I tried to find comfort in listening to records while I worked, but that just brought more tears.

Instead of giving in to sadness, I signed up for a writers' correspondence course from the US. I wrote letters to family, churches, and articles for church papers in NA.

My part-time Japanese language teacher, Endo Sensei, was in his 80's. Formerly a teacher, he was also an artist, and I learned much about Japanese poetry in our hymnals. Singing the hymns in church began to make sense! What a thrill when our conversation turned to religion, and we read the Bible together. He contributed his long life to God's goodness.

My attitudes needed changing, and I prayed that God would give me a gentle tongue, and commit our work to Him so He could establish His plans for us. The Lord replaced my relationship problems in the church with a tranquil mind and inner joy and peace.

God gave me wonderful promises. *From this day on I will bless you,* Haggai 2:19. *The Lord, your God, is in your midst...he will rejoice over you with gladness!* Zephaniah 3:17. *Though the fig tree does not blossom...yet I will rejoice in the Lord...in the God of my salvation,* Habbakuk 3:18. In times of testing and trouble I found comfort and joy in God's Word.

In March of 1967 a widow and a young working woman were baptized. This was the first baptism in over two years. How the church rejoiced! Matsubara San, the widow, had become a Christian thirty years ago, but lost contact with Christians when she moved to Manchuria during the war. After returning to Japan, she heard a Christian radio broadcast and came to the gospel bookstore to buy a hymnal. There she met the pastor and began coming to the Hyuga church. She remained a loyal, radiant, faithful Christian.

Easter Sunday was special that year. Vangy, fifteen, our eldest, was baptized. Her faith has often put us to shame. A week after her baptism we were surprised to find this announcement in our home church, West Abbotsford Mennonite Church, B.C. bulletin: "Today Evangeline Derksen is baptized in Japan. We herewith welcome her as a member of our church." What a happy surprise!

ACCIDENT

Would you know what to do if you are first at the scene of an accident? One night when we were returning from a meeting in the mountains, a truck sped past us on a short stretch of pavement. We were shocked to see this truck lying on its side where the pavement ended and the rough wet road began again. The driver was already tugging at the occupant inside. He had a gash on his head and was moaning. We rushed back to the village we had just passed to call the police. It took time for the police to come.

In the mean time other cars arrived at the scene. The main concern was to get the man to a hospital. With our background that you don't move the injured, we hesitated. But they picked him up, none too gently, so we offered our car. The police arrived and said, "Onegai shimasu!" (please take him), so we hurried off. It turned out that his injuries were not serious. The truck driver, who was uninjured, called the next day to apologize and express his thanks. He had taken a radio Bible correspondence course at one time, and now he was reflecting seriously on his deeds.

SURPRISE AT 40

Another baby? Surely not! I had many conversations with God! The twins were long out of diapers. Could I handle baby life again? We were in the midst of making big decisions about our future. How could we possibly concentrate on new church planting with a new baby? Just thinking about all the changes – well, it was quite obvious that we were not 26 anymore! The baby was due in December, 1967. I would be 39!

Gradually God changed my thinking. Look at all the mistakes I made raising the first five! Now God is giving me a chance to start over. Wow! We made many blunders as new missionaries doing church work in a country we still knew little about. God seemed to tell us, *I'm giving you a new challenge. A chance to begin again. A brand new start! And as a seal of my guidance I am giving you a new child to raise for my glory!*

My first four months of pregnancy were always difficult, but now my attitude changed, and I looked forward to our new beginnings. We focused on Oita City in Oita Prefecture, three hours north of Hyuga. At the same time, meetings in Hyuga church and in mountain villages kept us busy.

We shared the news of our baby with the children when they came home one week-end, and they were overjoyed! Rickie, fourteen at the time, asked, "Is it okay to tell my school friends? Life was busy. New life was on the horizon! God is good!

OUR CHILDREN'S MEMORIES OF HYUGA

Hyuga Memories from Vangy

- I loved my kid goat
- growing peanuts
- Isegahama picnics
- birthday parties with Japanese friends, Hisayo and Nobuko and others
- chirashisushi on Saturdays
- hamburger gravy and lettuce salad on Fridays
- coming home to you at the train station!
- leaving on Mondays
- bringing you driftwood

- church in the garage
- polishing the floors in our house
- our old-fashioned ofuro, bathtub, with the wooden platform, heating water with wood, so relaxing and warm (hot!)
- the excitement over the new Christian bookstore by the train tracks
- carolling on Christmas Eve
- the new church building
- my baptism (14)
- making a swing for my doll
- puppies under the house
- our obachans, Japanese aunties
- Christmas projects as a family
- puffed rice
- corn-flakes for Christmas from Oma
- Christmas parcels all sewn so carefully with lists of the contents on the outside
- special gifts: a mini sewing machine, a camera
- New Year's omochi, rice balls
- my long hair cut short, all my new curls!
- drives into the inaka, country, where I hoped to live
- Aratake san/sensei

Hyuga Memories from Rick

- I remember going to boarding school alone by train. First I had to get off in Miyazaki, and take the bus to my violin lesson. My teacher was very good, but much too strict. He pushed me hard and was not encouraging.
- After my lesson I took another bus to the Liechty's for supper (my own lunch), and then they took me to the station again to join my other siblings on the train to school in Miyakonojo.
- I have many good memories of Japanese friends. One of these was a neighbor, Nobuo Kuroki.
- Tohara San was an older church friend, and we had lots of fun together. Dad took me along to the village of Mimitsu for the weekly meetings in Ueno Sensei's home. He also took me along to Kadogawa for home meetings and to the TB

hospital there. The village of Mikado far into the mountains was another one of my favorite places to go with Dad.

- I remember the delicious panshoku (bread meals) in the Hyuga church. Then there was our first Christmas in the new church building in Hyuga with a special visiting singing group. Mom criticized the group because there was no Christian content.
- Our favorite family get away was Isegahama Beach close to home. We kids would explore the beach and surrounding rocky shore.
- Often on week-ends I went to the new harbor, where I met ships from Cuba, Russia and other countries. I made friends with the sailors and was invited for meals on board. Once I took the captain and other top officials of a ship home for lunch. Mom and Dad were quite surprised when we showed up at the door! I also started a coin collection when sailors gave me coins from their countries.
- A high school friend had a scooter, and he let me drive. We went to the big wide road by the new harbour to drive. A policeman stopped me, but I pretended I didn't understand Japanese!
- At Ayabe Tsutsuji Park we played samurai ninja (black hoods).
- On furlough I had saved for a bike back in Japan and rode it to Miyazaki (a two hour drive by car).
- In boarding school in Miyakonojo we boys went for milk every morning at 6:30 AM before breakfast. School rules set limits to how far we could explore, but.... In our dorm we were divided into teams. We would hide plastic “gold" bags and try to find the other teams' bags (steal!)
- With Brian Oxley, who was older, we played Sugar Creek Gangs, and climbed into the garage at night.
- We had good teachers at Miyakonojo Christian School. We were amazed that they were able to teach so many grades at once. Our programs were great. We did ***Hansel and Gretel***, ***Seven at One Blow***, ***Jack and the Beanstalk***, and many others.

- Recess in the playground was fun, and also lunch time. The giant stride was our favorite equipment - dangerous fun!

Hyuga Memories from Rose

- First and foremost, I remember the house. I think my favorite memory of living in Hyuga was the ofuro, that amazing iron-cast tub with a slated wood floor. We'd fire up the wood from the outside underneath the tub, and by the time we got in, it was piping hot. Wanda, Bill, and I would all squeeze into that bowl-shaped thing, being so careful not to touch the curved sides. When we got out, we'd always have hot water marks on our skin, bright pink below, white above.
- And then there were the spiders. Every night, I'd get up to go to the bathroom, and go across the hall to wake Mom to go with me. There were always several spiders in there, maybe four or five inches in diameter. Every time a spider story is told now, I proudly say, "Oh, that's nothing! You should have seen the spiders in the house where I grew up!"
- I also remember headaches, and Mom sitting by the bed, stroking my forehead. She would often also rub Wanda's legs with liniment to ease the cramps.
- And then I have this picture of us all kneeling on the wood floor in the living room saying our evening prayers, taking turns. We blessed a lot of folks, and it always took a while to get through all seven, Dad being the last to pray.
- There were the wonderful swings in the yard, the puppies that were born under the house, the goat in the back-field, the fragrant gardenia bushes behind the house that bloomed and smelled so wonderful; the Halloween party we had for missionary kids; the huge snake we found in the gutter by the road; walks to Kuroki obachan's house through the rice fields; coming home from boarding school and having snacks around the kitchen table Friday nights; going to church in the garage; and of course Isegahama, the beach where we spent hours looking in the rocky tide pools for sea creatures, and changing into our swimming suits in the big cave.

Hyuga Memories from Bill

- playing with the Nakazaki boys, catching tadpoles in the culverts at the construction site of the new church building
- visiting Ogawa San at the bookstore by the tracks, hoping a train would go by so that we could see the gate being pulled down and up with that huge wheel
- finding snakes in our yard, and getting a shovel to cut the heads off, and throwing the snakes in the field across the road pulling the attic staircase down so that we could play in the big space on the old tatami floor
- Finding the twelve pups under our house and having to choose two of them to keep; we chose the skinniest and named it fudge because of its brown color, and chose the plumpest one and named it roly-poly; fudge died a short while later and we had a burial ceremony in our back yard.
- Nakada San's hearty laugh and cheerful spirit; the big bump on his head was always a point of curiosity for me.

Hyuga Memories from Wanda

- the warm and tender face of Kuroki Obachan
- the fragrance of the gardenia bushes (the Body Shop had gardenia perfume for sale a few years ago and it immediately 'took me back' to Hyuga)
- the iron 'kettle' ofuro, bathtub
- the puffed rice man and the yaki-imo man, baked sweet potatoes
- the wonderful exploration picnics with Mom to Isegahama beach and all the beautiful fish, the waves, the matsu, pine trees
- the seven puppies under the house and keeping two of them
- the goat and all its dung
- the snakes, especially the big one
- the swing
- the train station and trains

Billie & Wanda off to Kindergarten

Welcome

Rosie in Kindergarten

Annual fellowship of Mennonite churches

New church dedication

Ogawa's outdoor kitchen

Hyuga church

Ogawa's bookstore

Adeline Kaufmann prayed for us daily for 40 years

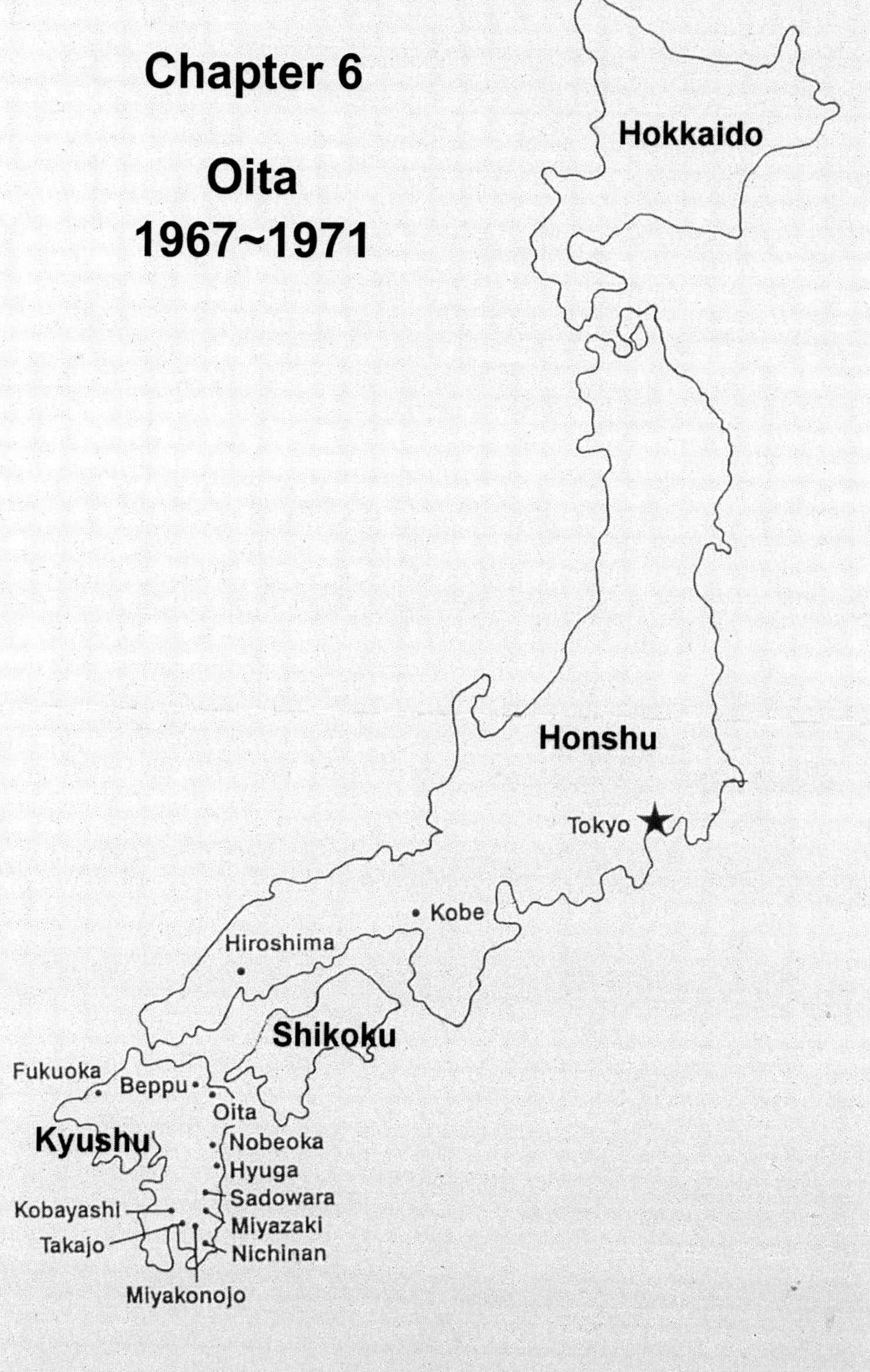
Chapter 6
Oita
1967~1971
Hokkaido
Honshu
Tokyo
Kobe
Hiroshima
Shikoku
Fukuoka
Beppu
Oita
Kyushu
Nobeoka
Hyuga
Sadowara
Kobayashi
Miyazaki
Takajo
Nichinan
Miyakonojo

COUNTRY TO CITY

Until now we had worked in rural areas of southern Japan. Oita seemed like a very large city with a population of 230,000. Since it was the capital of Oita Prefecture, it had a university and several colleges. Oita was also a growing industrial city. Japan Steel, the second largest steel company in the world, built a large factory along Oita's Pacific Ocean coast. This brought an influx of leaders and their families of the steel company to Oita where a new housing unit of private homes was built for them.

Oita was the least evangelized city on Kyushu Island. The Protestant churches were small, each with approximately one Christian per year of existence. A tourist pamphlet of Oita city calls this area the "Mecca of Christian Culture in Japan." The center of town boasts a statue of Francis Xavier, holding a Bible in one outstretched hand, and reaching his other hand to the world in a half circular cement relief wall map of Japan. Xavier spent several years evangelizing Oita in 1551. Xavier's ministry was the first Christian influence in Japan.

A Christian Martyr's Memorial Park reminded us of the two hundred Catholics who died for their faith during severe persecutions after Xavier left. A huge cement relief wall in the park showed a young person kneeling in front of a cross. Two men with raised swords stand behind the cross, ready to kill unless the youth recants his or her faith.

A restaurant along the main highway on the west coast of Kyushu had "Christian" in its name. "Why do you use the name Christian?" we asked.

"The original owner had a relative who was a Christian," they told us.

There were no foreign missionaries in Oita when we moved there. The Southern Baptists who formerly had missionaries in Oita, had a large empty house. The Baptist church started by missionaries had a Japanese pastor. Our mission was planning to buy land and build a house as soon as possible. In the meantime, the Baptists agreed to rent us their house.

Moving was not easy because of my pregnancy. I was thirty-nine. Our children all pitched in with a will. Friends and missionaries from other churches came to help. That summer of 1967, God was giving us two new opportunities: beginning a new church, and as if that wasn't enough of a challenge, a new baby was on the way. The first five were in schools far away from home. We were starting all over!

ADJUSTING TO OITA

The main highway on the east side of the island was only partially paved, so after a bumpy three-hour drive, we finally arrived at the gate of our new home, the Baptist mission house. The front of the yard had a rock wall topped with a row of azaleas. A beautiful old-fashioned Japanese gate with double wooden lattice sliding doors welcomed us into the spacious yard. The kids loved the huge enclosed yard that was mostly lawn. However, the house was completely western, and we wanted to live like the Japanese. We had a rental contract for the Baptist Mission house for four months, and four months to the exact day we moved into our new Japanese style home.

We did not have to look for new contacts. While we were unpacking the truck, two college girls came to the door asking for English lessons. A few days later they brought a high school English teacher who asked if Peter would teach an English Bible class. However, where could they meet, since we were not to have meetings in the Baptist house because their church was in the same community?

Just a few days later a city employee paid us a friendly visit. Through him we were able to rent a room for classes in the new ultra-modern concert hall within the moat, all that was left of the castle that used to be in the heart of the city. A group of junior high school teachers asked for English. After the second class, they suggested fifteen minutes of Bible study after each class. Soon they changed it to half and half! Then several medical doctors wanted an English class. English? But our purpose was to make Christ known and to build His church! That was our goal. However, we also wanted to use every available means to reach out to people and build relationships. A junior college asked Peter to teach English. He declined, so then they asked him to teach the Bible!

God used English contacts for another lifelong benefit. Dr. Tachibana, one of the dentists, offered to take care of Peter's dental needs free. Dr. Kono took on my dental cleaning and work for only one third of the regular cost. This included partial dentures for Peter and bridges for me. They did this for us as long as we lived in Japan. God took care of our big and little needs.

During our first month we spent much time searching for suitable land and planning the new house. We found a perfect southwest corner lot in a fast-growing residential area without a church. Facing south was important, because there is no central heating in homes. Windows facing south absorb the sun's warmth during the day.

One day we asked God to give us a lot that day. At noon we had a phone call telling us the lot we had wished for was available. Peter made the first down payment the same day!

It was great to have the family together for the summer. We explored our new city with interest. There were several department stores, a large train station, many narrow, crowded shopping streets, and many wide roads crisscrossing the city. Sundays we were warmly welcomed in each of the Protestant churches we visited. We realized how difficult church planting is in Japan. The combined number of Christians in the Oita Protestant churches was approximately three hundred.

I was having difficulty due to varicose veins. The pain was so severe that I was afraid I would have to stay in bed for the rest of my pregnancy. One night as I was asking the Lord for healing, He put it on my heart to have our family participate in a healing prayer. Peter and the children agreed. We read James 5, *the prayer offered in faith will make the sick person well; the Lord will raise him up.* God answered our prayers! I was able to stay up every day and the pain gradually subsided.

BACK TO SCHOOL

Separation was part of our chosen lot, and it was time for Vangy and Rickie to leave for Christian Academy in Japan a thousand miles away in Tokyo, entering grades 10 and 9 respectively. However, they were not the only ones traveling to school. Thousands of university students were returning to their schools after the summer vacation and getting train tickets was a challenge.

Peter and Rick went to the train station at 6 AM a week before the trip, and after standing in line for hours, they managed to get two reserved seat tickets. Otherwise the kids would have to stand in the train for hours, maybe the whole trip. The next day we said a sad good-bye to Vangy and Rickie as they left for Tokyo on Japan's famous bullet train, the Shinkansen.

Christian Academy had students from kindergarten through grade 12. Many were missionary and business people's children and internationals. Some were children of Japanese diplomats who had been stationed abroad. These students would be behind in kanji in a Japanese school, so it was easier to attend an English-speaking school.

Our children were in separate dormitories for boys and girls. They were soon involved in sports and music besides their regular studies. Vangy had already distinguished herself in her studies by being on the honor roll. They sang in the school choir. We had enrolled Vangy for piano lessons and Rickie for violin lessons. When they came home for Christmas we naturally asked how the music lessons were going. Rickie said he quit violin lessons. Shocked, we asked, "Why? We paid for the whole year already!"

His answer? "I was better than my teacher!"

Travelling to Tokyo was expensive, so we seldom attended sports or music events at CAJ. As representative of our mission, Peter had to attend committee meetings in Tokyo once a year, and then he spent time with the kids.

Soon the younger three had to return to the mission school in the two-hour train trip they had until now, it was four hours. But at least we could drive to special events. The music recitals at school were *a joyful noise unto the Lord!*

We were thankful for Christian house-parents who felt called to the difficult task of caring for missionary kids away from home. House-parents changed every three years, so that meant readjustment for the kids.

OUR DREAM HOME

Before coming to Japan, we had decided to live like the Japanese as much as possible. It was disappointing at first to live in western houses. Now we would finally be able to live in our dream house, much smaller, but Japanese style. Planning together was exciting! We tried to keep the size to a minimum, but there had to be three bedrooms, one for the boys, one for the girls, and one for us. The children's rooms were upstairs. We all slept on mats on the tatami floor. During the day the mats were folded in three to store in special closets that fit the folded mats.

The main floor had two tatami, soft straw mat, rooms downstairs, separated by paper sliding doors. The six mat room was our bedroom. We slept on the floor. When we removed the dividing sliding doors, our six mat and the eight mat rooms became a spacious meeting room. Our bedding was neatly tucked away in the closet. Everyone sat on cushions on the floor, legs tucked under, Japanese style. When Japanese guests first came into our home, especially the older folks, they were pleasantly surprised, and felt at ease sitting on Japanese floors.

The eight mat room also served as an English classroom and a guest bed-room. Oh, yes, our guests and we could hear each other breathe, and occasionally snore. The kitchen did double duty as the dining room. The study was beside the front entrance. The very best part of our new house was a Japanese ofuro, bath. Our washing machine was in the back entrance, and we hung laundry on the back covered patio. The garage was a prefab structure. I loved our small yard where I could plant a few trees and flowers.

We had not brought beds to Japan, believing that the Japanese slept, and so would we. However, the first years we lived in western houses with hardwood floors instead of soft tatami. So we bought beds from missionaries going on furlough. Now all our rooms except the kitchen and study had tatami floors. Peter promised faithfully to fold the bedding and put it into the closet every day! He kept his promise. We had two small easy chairs that could easily be moved out of the way during meetings.

SUMMER DAZE!

The Aoidake Mennonite Church Camp was situated high in the mountains between the cities of Miyazaki and Miyakonojo. As we wound up the narrow mountain dirt roads, we hoped no one would be coming down, or one vehicle would have to back up to a wide spot for passing. The fresh mountain air energized us. We could hardly wait to meet Christians and seekers from the other churches. Camp was for bonding.

Recently a Japanese man from Vancouver, who came to the Surrey Mennonite Church (Japanese) in Surrey, BC, where we were serving after our retirement, surprised us. He remembered that he had attended a Japanese Mennonite Church camp in Japan one summer. He even remembered the theme of Peter's message at that camp forty years ago.

The first summer in Oita our family spent two weeks at Aoidake camp. Reunion with friends from the churches in Hyuga and Nichinan where we had worked was the highlight! Oita City was still too new and strange, but here we felt at home. The mountains were a wonderful retreat from the heat of the cities. Missionaries and pastors had put a lot of work into the campgrounds. Here we could focus on our great Creator and His creation through nature hikes, Bible studies, singing, prayer, food and fellowship.

Peter and I took turns driving kids to Aoidake camp. One summer he took a carload to junior camp, including Rosie, Billy and Wanda. I took a carload to the adult camp. That still did not solve the problem for kids who couldn't go to camp, so we had an overnight camp right in our home. We started with a wiener roast, something quite new. We rented futon, mattresses, for ten campers. A room without furniture is versatile, changing from living room to meeting room to bedroom with the slightest of ease.

There were extras like summer camp for missionary kids. Most of them knew each other from the mission school in Miyakonojo. No one will forget the camp where they dramatized ***David and Goliath***. David was one of the smaller boys at camp, and Goliath was a six-foot-plus father! Another camp was held at the Oxley's Baptist Camp in the neighboring prefecture of Kumamoto. It was situated along a tributary of the famous Kuma River where long boats took tourists through the river rapids.

One summer our family camped at the Baptist camp beside the Kuma River for a few days. It was between camp sessions, so we were the only ones there. The children spent much of the day in the water and loved to swim the short distance out to the raft. I decided that I could manage that short swim, too, so I bravely jumped in. All was well, until I reached the raft. Suddenly the current pulled me under. Wanda grabbed my hand and hung on, screaming. In God's marvelous timing, Dale Oxley, the Baptist missionary who had built the camp, had come for a relaxing afternoon. When he heard and saw what was happening, he jumped in, clothes and shoes, and swiftly swam to me. He managed to get me onto the raft, where I lay sputtering water for some time. How we thanked God for sparing my life! I awoke in the middle of the night, and began to sing in my heart, "Thank you, Jesus. Thank you, Jesus!" over and over. I will never forget Dale Oxley who saved my life.

Several excellent beaches were within an hour's drive from our home in Oita, and we went to a beach every summer. The kids loved to swim in the ocean, but they could also swim in the local sports centers and pools.

We made trips into the mountains to escape Oita's oppressive summer heat. Mount Aso, the world's largest active volcano, was a favorite and only two hours away by car. We could drive right up to the crater's rim when the volcano was not active and wander around peering into the fearful sizzling, smoking depths! Numerous cement shelters surround the area in case of a sudden eruption.

Soon we were back in the almost unbearable heat. For months the temperature stayed above ninety day and night. No air-conditioning in those days, so we just wilted! We barely managed the basic necessities, cooking, laundry, cleaning, shopping. And guests. What a relief when September brought cooler nights.

Hot or not, the kids had summer jobs. Rose enjoyed working at Elle, a clothing store in the covered mall. Bill and Wanda had jobs at Mister Donuts. We all liked that, because they brought free donuts home at the end of the day. When we went to our family camp, a healthy menu was almost destroyed by donuts, donuts, donuts!

FLOATING SCHEDULES

Many missionary families, some from India and some from Taiwan, came to visit the Japan missionaries on their way to the US for furlough. The MCC director from NA and his family came for an overnight visit. Our Japan missionary families and friends from other missions also came. There was a constant flow of guests. Now I wonder how I managed to get sheets washed and dried between guests without a drier.

After our older two left for school in Tokyo, we took Rosie, grade six, and Billy and Wanda, grade four, back to our mission boarding school in Miyakonojo. Our missionary Anna Dyck lived next door to the school dormitory. Anna was a nurse, so she took care of missionary family shots through the years.

That day we got typhoid shots. Around 10 PM. Peter began to shiver and shake. We piled blankets on him, but nothing helped. His severe reaction gave him chills, high fever, nausea, and a terrible headache. We thought we were losing him. At 1:30 AM Anna tried to call a doctor, but no response. In the morning a doctor finally came. Peter got the typical Japanese treatment, a shot. A night long to be remembered! How we thanked God for restoring Peter. The next day we said goodbye to our youngest three and returned home.

One day several junior high English teachers came to ask if Peter would teach English in their school. One teacher told us that he read the Bible every day. We had contact with him throughout our years in Japan. "I am Japanese. I can never become a Christian," he told us. The teachers requested Bible lessons for the last twenty minutes of the class. However, when the daughter of a teacher married a young man preparing for Christian ministry, he was quite proud.

Every morning before breakfast we read a chapter in ***Little Visits with God***, and then held hands for prayer and a song. We ordered English materials from the US and had SS with our kids. Flannelgraph Bible stories, singing, memorizing Bible verses. What a blessing as each of our children made a decision to follow Christ. We had our times of troubles but trusted God to finish what He had begun in our family.

Sometimes I wondered how we accomplished anything. Guests kept coming. This was part of our ministry. We called it our "floating schedule." The blessings increased as we made new friends from around the world. Parents of our missionaries came. My parents came, as well as my sister Hilda and family. Peter's sister Melita was the only one of his family to visit.

Many years later we also had the privilege of visiting our children in their various countries of service: Rick & Marilyn and family in Zaire with AIMM, and Vangy and Ernie and family in Nepal with MCC.

MUNEAGE

September 16, 1967. What an exciting day! Muneage means raising the house. Neighbors, kids and adults gather when they see the frame with a flag flying on the rafters. A family member throws rice cakes and coins into the crowd. What a scramble as kids try to get as many as possible! We prepared gift fruit baskets and a New Testament for each of the workers. What excitement to see the house taking shape! A few days later it rained, but the roof was on and the workers could proceed.

Our new mission house was finished in the beginning of November, 1967, and on November 5 we moved in. Peter had to judge a junior high English contest that morning, and I went to the bank for money for the movers. New friends, wives of two English teachers, came to help with cleaning.

Our rental contract with the Baptist mission was over after four months. Four months to the day we were able to move into our new house. God is faithful.

When you move to a new neighborhood in Japan, it is custom to call on each of the neighbors, introduce yourself, and give a small gift. I bought seventeen hand soap boxes to bring each home. What a friendly, welcoming neighborhood. We also discovered that I made a mistake by starting out by myself. I didn't know that the han-cho, neighbor representative, was to introduce me to our new neighbors. A new han-cho was chosen at a general meeting every year. One year it was my turn, and I wondered if I would be able to fulfill my duties. A few times a year the han-cho had to go around the neighborhood with a two-wheeled cart collecting newspapers and bottles for recycling. Our back porch was full of sake bottles during collection time!

THE MESSIAH

Eighteen came to the first English Bible class in our new home. The same day I attended a friend's music concert. New friends had stage jobs for our beautiful cultural concert hall, and they often gave us tickets for special events. One was a choir of eighty-five junior college women in long white gowns singing two numbers from ***Handel's Messiah***, "Surely" and the "Hallelujah Chorus" Another special gift was tickets for the Vienna Boys' Choir.

When a community choir presented Handel's Messiah, it was a first for Oita. A missionary friend and I were the only two foreigners. Part way through, tears stung my eyes as I realized that they were singing in English without books! Later I asked a friend how they accomplished that.

She said, "We slept with the Messiah tape playing under our pillows for weeks!"

The Japanese have no "th" or "l" sounds, so "the mouth of the Lord" became "za mouse of za Rorudo" When they sang the Hallelujah Chorus, my friend and I stood up. We were the only ones! In following years Japanese audiences also began to stand.

KENDOSHIKI

Rain did not dampen the big day on Sunday, November 19, Kendoshiki, Dedication Day, for our new home and church. In the morning we had a quiet worship time and Sunday School with our children. Vangy and Rick had come home for Thanksgiving school vacation. In the afternoon 50 neighbors, English class members, and friends managed to squeeze into our double meeting room for dedication day. They were squished side by side. A representative from each of the homes in our kumi came. Cities are divided into sections called kumi. Every kumi had 30 or 40 homes. For most of these neighbors this was the first time they had ever attended a Christian meeting. Christians and pastors from other churches joined us.

We sat on zabuton, cushions on the floor, feet tucked under us. In Japan shoes are always taken off in the genkan, or entrance, so if you want to know how many people are inside, just count the shoes. After the service, a guest's shoe was missing! A search revealed nothing, until we found out a dog, not ours, had carried it off through the open door. After teatime, the young people stayed to sing. What a wonderful day of blessing!

The following Sunday we started the first regular morning worship service with eight Japanese present. Neighbors brought fruit and flowers. We felt accepted. Some even asked for Sunday School for their children. The Lord opened doors wide. What a tremendous challenge lay before us!

OUR NEW BABY

The next weeks were busy shopping for curtain material to sew drapes for the meeting room, and preparing for the new baby. A minor earthquake shook us up a bit!

Peter had to drive to Kobayashi on Monday, Dec. 5. Since the mission school was along the way, he took the children with him. The next day I phoned Peter to come home, my pains had begun. However, I managed to finish the drapes. When Peter got home, we hung them up. I was happy for the privacy our new drapes afforded!

Our youngest three were born in the Osaka Presbyterian hospital with American missionary doctors and nurses in attendance. This time our baby would be born in Oita. At 10 PM Peter took me to Urata Sanfujinka, the small local maternity hospital, and stayed with me through the long difficult night. I finally asked the midwife for some pain killer. She said, "You've managed this far, why not have it the Japanese way?" A painful "yes!"

With the dawn of a new day, Lillian Ruth arrived at 5:18 AM on December 7, 1967. She weighed 8 pounds 4 ounces, had dark hair, and was perfect. Peter phoned the exiting news to our five children. I had survived nine long months of pregnancy and a long painful night of birth. But oh, the joy of a tiny babe in my arms!

Just at that time, some Japanese maternity hospitals were having a rash of baby mix-ups! Lily's hair was so dark, I asked Peter, "What if they mix her up with Japanese babies?" He laughed. When I was able, we walked to the baby room together. Would she look like the other babies? Could they possibly mix her up with another mother's little one? Then I saw her beside the dark Japanese babies. The little black-haired ones all had flat spaces between their eyes, until the little noses peeked out a bit lower! Lily's hair didn't look dark compared to the others. And her nose? Like no other! The little pug nose stood out on her fair face like a beacon on a hill. No chance of a mix-up! We laughed. Now I could rest in peace!

Lily and I returned to our sunny home on Dec. 16, nine days after she was born. The kids came home for the weekend, but they all had runny noses, not good for a new baby!

In Japanese culture, the oyome san, literally, the bride daughter-in-law belongs to the husband's family. Where families adhere strictly to culture, she could not return to her parental home unless she was expecting a baby. Then she was allowed to go home for a month before the scheduled birth and could stay a month after birth.

We didn't have either mother anywhere near us. But our dear friend,

Alice Ruth came for the weekend. Streams of visitors brought flowers and gifts. The hospital mid-wife came to bathe Lily. Guests at the Sunday service stayed for lunch. What a boon for our family to have Alice Ruth helping us through those first hectic days. Monday, the eighteenth, she left with the same train that took our children back to school for the coming week. I was worn out from the many guests who dropped by and others who came for night.

With a new baby in the family, it was easy to make friends in our new neighborhood. Six mothers on our short street had babies within a few months of each other. Often three or four of us would be visiting on the street, babes in arms. A few years later these same kids started kindergarten together and were in the same class in elementary school. What a natural way of becoming part of the neighborhood.

Usually at the end of September or the beginning of October we had a sudden cold spell, a timely warning. Then I hustled to dig warm clothes and bedding out of our barrels where we had stored them for the summer. The warm days returned, but the days gradually turned colder, with occasional snow in winter.

CHRISTMAS IN OITA

This was our first Christmas in Oita, and the first with baby Lily. December 22, we drove five hours to Miyakonojo for the children's Christmas program. Lily was the centre of attraction!

Shopping centers and schools ring with *Silent Night* and other carols on the radio and TV. Even though Christmas is not a holiday, schools close for the winter vacation on December 24. In Japanese homes the father brings home a beautifully decorated Christmas cake on Christmas Eve. That is their celebration.

Christmas Eve was on a Sunday that year. Seven people, besides our family, were in the morning service. In the afternoon 27 celebrated, and 19 attended the evening candlelight service. For most, it was their first real Christmas experience. The Christmas story took on new meaning as we shared it with those hearing it for the first time. We interspersed the biblical Christmas story with carols. One elderly lady who attended a Christmas service for the first time was quite surprised. "Oh, do they sing *Silent Night* in church, too?" she asked.

DAD COMES FOR CHRISTMAS

What a special Christmas when Grandpa Klassen joined us. This was our first Christmas in Oita. We were busy with English classes, decorating, baking, and practicing with SS kids. Grandpa enjoyed time with Lily. She took her first steps Dec. 2, just short of her first birthday.

We took Dad along to Miyakonojo for the children's school Christmas program. Lily was sick, throwing up in the car. No fun! But the Christmas pageant was great, and we realized what an advantage our children had in a small school, 12 to 19 students at the peak of school years. Each one could take part, and sometimes they even had to double up. After the program and potluck Christmas dinner, it was a long five hour's drive home.

The mailman had bought presents from grandparents, uncles and aunts in Canada. Rickie and Vangy had learned some German and wrote their thank-you letters to Oma and Opa Derksen in a funny mix of German and English.

Church young people helped with Christmas preparations. Many of the 31 children in the pageant had been coming since the beginning. Parents thought Christmas programs were just for kids, so only ten adults came the first year. However, every year more parents and neighbors attended, until we were crowded out with over one hundred. Eventually we had to rent a community hall for the Christmas programs. At the close of the program each child received a treat and a gift.

Mayumi was gifted in music, and also knew English well. I had brought the musical, ***Mary Had a Little Lamb*** from Canada, which she translated. A sixth grade pianist did an excellent job of playing, but I was having trouble with the jazzy beat. I practiced in front of the mirror until I caught on.

For Christmas Eve we had prepared for 40 people. The previous year there had been 20, so we thought doubling the number was good. People kept coming, and finally 60 people, besides our family, managed to crowd into the meeting room and halls of our home. Last year's candle stubs had to be recycled. Women and young girls had eagerly helped bake and decorate cupcakes. After cake and tea, 30 young people went Christmas caroling on the streets. This was a first experience for them.

NEW YEAR IN JAPAN

New Year is Japan's biggest celebration of the year. Each person turns a year older. Thus a baby born December 31 turns two on New Year's day. Families go to Shinto shrines to seek blessings for the coming year. Mothers are busy for days preparing special New Year's food, and arranging them in exquisite three or four tiered lacquer boxes, the contents too beautiful to eat! Dozens of rice dishes, each prepared differently, dozens of pickles, seafood, and vegetables. If you have no time to cook, or didn't know how (like me), you can buy it prepared in supermarkets or in stalls that line the streets.

Dust flies as tatami straw mats are dragged out for a good beating and sunning. The house must be spic and span. Young women and girls dress in their best kimono call on relatives and friends on New Year's Day. Peter and I made calls to close neighbors and church families. We made sure to be home part of the day to welcome callers.

Dad was enjoying Japan and even liked many different foods. We introduced him to a favorite, omochi. Cooked rice is pounded into a thick paste, rolled into small round balls in rice flour, then roasted over a fire until it doubles in size. Dad's comment, "It's good, but one end is already in the stomach while the other is still in the mouth!" A very good description of sticky rice balls.

Two of Vangy's close friends from Hyuga came for a few days at the beginning of the New Year. A happy time. Night guests seemed to multiply over the holidays.

A week before the children had to return to Tokyo, Peter and Rick spent a night waiting in line at the train station for train tickets, along with many Japanese students and workers who had come home for the New Year holiday. They took along blankets and a portable heater to keep them warm through the cold night. That was the only way to ensure tickets for the return trip.

Worshipping with new believers on the first day of the year became a very special experience. We served the traditional sweet bean soup, omochi, grilled pounded rice cakes, and a taste of our Russian New Year raisin yeast fritters, Portzelky.

SPECIAL DAYS

January was the coldest time of the year. There was no central heating in Japanese homes. We moved small kerosene space heaters to whichever room we wanted warm! In our halls the temperature plunged to 3 degrees Celsius. Getting up nights was no fun. You just ran the hallways shivering and quickly jumped into your warm bed again. At least the cockroaches left us alone in winter!

By mid-February 19 children were attending Sunday School. Attendance varied with the weather. We enlisted two young people who were attending worship services to help, even though they were not Christians yet. What better way to train them in the Christian faith? Soon both became Christians and were baptized!

In Japan every age group has a special day. Children's Day May 5, Seniors September 15, and Young Adults January 15, are all national holidays. On Young Adult Day every person who turned twenty within the last year officially becomes an adult. Young women wear beautiful new kimono for the occasion. On the streets and in the meeting place a rainbow of vibrant colors and hairstyles to match the traditional clothes meets the eye. One feels sorry for the girl in a modern suit who probably can't afford a kimono. Most young men wear western suits with an occasional brave one wearing the traditional men's kimono, quite drab compared to the ladies! Every city and town has a special meeting for new adults, informing them of their rights and responsibilities, including the right to vote. From that day on they can drink liquor since they are adults now.

Our missionaries had monthly fellowships, taking turns hosting. A day after one of our meetings, we made 16 stops on our way home. Then I forgot my purse at a rest stop, and by the time I remembered, we had to backtrack for over an hour of winding mountain roads with a baby in the car!

We lived a five-minute drive to the Oita airport. It was very convenient for Vangy and Rick to come home standby as students from Tokyo. This was much faster and cheaper than by train, because students got a discount.

Three friends from Chilliwack, BC, were our first foreign guests visiting us in Oita. It was a cold February! We sat on the floor wrapped in blankets, shivering and chatting.

HIGASHIGUCHI FAMILY

We tried to keep in contact with many friends in places where we had served. Seiko Higashiguchi used to come to English Bible class when we lived in Nichinan. He had been employed there by a large pulp company immediately after graduating from university. One day he had come with a small evergreen tree and planted it beside our house as a symbol of his new faith in Christ. That tree grew strong and tall in the years to come! When Seiko was transferred back to his hometown of Miyakonojo, he gradually drifted away from his faith. However, we kept up contact. His work took him to different cities in Kyushu, so he would often drop by for a visit and for night.

One day Seiko surprised us with a request. "Would you please help me find a sponsor so my family can immigrate to Canada?" He thought that their children would have a better future in Canada. Even though he had a good job, he knew that with the strong competition in Japan, his children would struggle to get into good schools and good jobs. In May of 1968 Seiko migrated to Canada. His plan was to find a job and a place to live first, and then send for his wife and children to follow a year later.

Living alone was a struggle, but Seiko found a small Japanese Christian Church in Vancouver. There he committed his life to the Lord once more. A year later he sent for his wife Junko and two young children to join him in Vancouver. When Honda Sensei, Japan's "Billy Graham," held evangelistic services for the Japanese population in Vancouver, Junko made a decision for Christ. What joy!

While they lived in Vancouver, we returned to Canada for furlough, and had good times of fellowship. That year our Canadian Conference had its annual sessions in Vancouver. Seiko was full of the joy of the Lord and gave his testimony at the assembly with Peter interpreting. Our hearts were bursting with joy!

When Vangy was a first year student at UBC, University of British Columbia, in Vancouver, the Higashiguchi's often invited her to their home for delicious Japanese food! The bonds with our family grew. They came to the airport to see us off to Japan. This was the first time we were leaving children in North America. The Higashiguchi's saw the tears and heart-rending farewells. Seiko thanked us for the sacrifices we made leaving family in order to share the Gospel of Christ in his country.

When they had been in Canada for five years, they were ready to become Canadian citizens. A son, Masaki, was born in Vancouver. Then they received the news that Seiko's father had cancer. Seiko was the only son, so they returned to their hometown of Miyakonojo to help care for his ailing father. Thus we had contact with the family again in Japan. The father passed away, and now he had his mother to care for.

Several years after we retired to Canada in 1999, we heard that Seiko had cancer. This prompted them to make one more visit to Canada while he was still able. What a privilege to have them visit us in Abbotsford!

In the fall of 2002, we made our first visit to Japan after retirement. We visited Seiko in the hospice in Miyakonojo. In the lovely lounge we sang Gospel songs, and Seiko even found energy to play his harmonica. Our farewell was mixed with emotions, sad that this would likely be the last time we would meet on earth but rejoicing that we could look forward to spending eternity together! Thus we could say, "See you again!" A few months later the Lord took him home! On our second visit to Japan in fall 2007, Junko, Seiko's wife and her children rented a small restaurant in Miyakonojo for an evening together. What a joyous time with the Higashiguchi family!

GROWTH IN OITA

Life became busy as more requests came for English. Four girls came to the first high school English class. Oita Junior College asked Peter to teach a class. Attendance grew to 30 in the English Bible class that Hideshi Nakano had asked for. Sunday mornings worship attendance in our home increased to 20.

It is important for new churches to get involved in giving, so we initiated offerings and a giving project. If there was a local disaster such as a fire or flood, the church helped. Often the church sent Christmas project offerings to MCC. Offerings also went into a church building fund.

The number of children kept increasing, and so did Sunday School teachers. One Easter the SS held a parade around the neighborhood, singing and carrying placards made by the children. The Pied Piper of Hamlin would have been envious; 80 children followed the parade back to the church for a Christian children's movie and treats.

Was Sunday School worthwhile? Only eternity will tell. Imagine a lively group of youngsters aged five to twelve. Try to make the Bible come alive by a tongue which still gets tangled in a foreign language. An impossible situation, but God specializes in the impossible! Imagine the thrill when eleven-year-old Ikuko Chan chooses SS instead of joining her family on a trip to a famous amusement park, or twelve-year-old Masahiro Kun's glowing face as he brings two new friends to SS (for boys the suffix kun is used instead of chan).

A LIFE SAVED

One Sunday evening the doorbell rang. A shivering high school student stood there. I invited her in. She sat quietly for a long time. There was no response to questions. An hour later she left. Suddenly a light flashed! "Peter, she's planning suicide!" I cried out. We grabbed our jackets and ran in various directions, but she had disappeared. We begged God to intervene.

An hour later Mitsuko (pseudonym) appeared at the door again. This time she began to share. She had gone to the river this cold night, intending to jump in. Her parents were wealthy, but the pressure to stay home and study was so strong that life seemed meaningless. As she stood on the bridge looking down into the swirling cold water, she remembered something that she had learned in S.S. Committing suicide was wrong, so she had come to church for help. She slept beside me on the floor that night. After she was asleep, I checked her coat that she had kept neatly on her lap. One pocket was full of rat poison. She had an alternative! The next morning she allowed us to call her parents, who had been searching for her with the police all night. She began attending church and gave her heart to Jesus Christ. A life saved! Thank you, Lord. When Mitsuko and her husband, also a Christian, came to visit us in Canada after our retirement, we fell into each other's arms crying. What a joyous reunion!

A CHURCH IS BORN

Nakano had been coming faithfully. One Sunday he announced that he would be leaving for Hawaii for a year of study on a scholarship. What a disappointment! However, we began to pray earnestly that he would make a decision for Christ before he left. The Lord began answering our prayers before we even prayed. The next Sunday 29 people in church had a farewell for him. The following day he called; he had received word that his trip had been postponed until September! During the June 9 worship service Peter gave an opportunity for participation in prayer. The silence was suddenly broken by Nakano's clear voice: "Lord God, I here and now give my life to you. I know Satan will do his best to hinder me, but give me strength to follow and serve you, Amen." A sacred moment! We sang *O Happy Day that fixed my choice on Thee, my Savior and my God.* Later he shared his desire for baptism!

August 4, 1968, Nakano and our son Rick, fifteen, were baptized. This was the beginning of the Oita Mennonite Christian Church! Vangy had been baptized in Hyuga when she was fourteen, so now we were five members! Rosie, Billy, Wanda and Lily were baptized in following years. How we rejoiced for each one as they took this step of faith. We serve an awesome God!

The following June we celebrated another happy day when two students, Utsunomiya and Yamada were baptized. A few weeks later we celebrated when Takakura and the Kudo sisters, one a high school student and the other in junior high, were baptized. Two of these young people were already helping with SS. This contributed to their Christian growth. They attended weekly Bible studies and prayer meetings. However, after several months, Utsunomiya came to the door and said, "I have come to return the baptism certificate. I don't want to be a Christian any longer." What a shock!

Sumiko (pseudonym) had become a Christian during high school days in Hyuga. She took nurses' training, and then went to midwifery school. This involved many moves to different cities. In each place she was a strong support in the local church. She came for a visit once more before going on a three-year assignment with MCC to Vietnam, our first "missionary" from the Mennonite churches in Japan!

INTRUDER

Our oldest five children were all in boarding school, so we moved upstairs. We always locked our doors for night. I don't know what woke me, but as I lay there wondering, I heard heavy breathing, and it wasn't Peter. I listened a bit longer, then woke Peter and said, "Someone is in our house." He heard the breathing, too. We moved quietly to the top of the stairs. The stairs took a turn after the first two steps, and a wall was at the bottom. We saw nothing, but we heard it. We bravely started down. A man was sprawled along the length of our hallway. No movement, just deep breathing. Then the smell hit us. Whoever it was, was quite drunk! Well, he could sleep it off in church.

We laid a futon on the church room floor and lifted him onto it. He kept on sleeping. When we turned him around, we were shocked. It was one of the young men attending church. We checked our door. It was unlatched. I guess we didn't latch it completely. Peter and I went back to bed upstairs.

In the morning a very embarrassed young man faced us. We never scolded. After breakfast he took leave. We were sad that he never came to church again, a link that we leave for the Lord to follow.

VISITORS

I love surprises! But when three couples, elementary school friends from my home village of Virgil, Ontario, showed up unannounced at the door one Saturday morning, I was not pleased! Of course, I was happy to see them, but my hair was in curlers, and I did not have a drier. So we just sat on the floor Japanese style in our living/church room and reminisced until my hair was dry. Then they took us to a fancy restaurant for lunch.

Guests were a constant during the summer months. Nakada San from the Hyuga church brought his granddaughter along for the night. They were on their way to Expo'70 in Osaka. Sometimes when guests surprised us, we just served a simple meal. Once I wrote "…hot dogs and slushy watermelon…" in my diary. One day, not knowing about our visitors, a neighbor brought a big plate of sushi, just in time for lunch with our guests.

Another day a Catholic priest called on Peter. The topic turned to speaking in tongues without interpretation. The priest said, "The Catholic Church has been using a foreign language for 2,000 years without interpretation. How unscriptural can we get?"

Peter invited a German man and his wife whom he had met in town for dinner the next day. Imagine our surprise during the course of the evening to discover that they were very dedicated Communists from

East Germany! America got the blame for all the woes of the world! We ended the evening reading the German Bible and praying. They thanked us when they left.

We were excited about Expo 70, too. This was our chance to see the world. We took an overnight ferry to Osaka and stayed in a missionary guest house. Hundreds of countries displayed the best and most unique aspects of their country. Fascinating! On our last day we were tired and ready to go home. Suddenly I asked, "Where's Billy?" Twelve-year-old Billy was missing. We returned to the last venues where we had been, but no Billy. Finally, we contacted the police. Guess who was enjoying a visit with the police? Billy! He gave us such a scare, but we were thankful that he was safe.

When we returned to Oita, we discovered that Annie and Adolph Ens, who had been working with MCC in Indonesia, had dropped in unexpectedly. Virginia Claassen hosted them, and we missed them. That was quite disappointing.

SCHOOL'S OUT

In mid-June Vangy and Rickie came home from Tokyo on stand-by plane for the summer. This was very convenient since the Oita Airport was only a five-minute drive from home. At the end of June, the five of us went to Miyakonojo for the mission school closing program. These trips meant an overnight stay with fellow missionaries. On our return trip, we stopped to see friends in Hyuga where we had lived for seven years.

Summer vacation was here. The children visited their former mission school friends. Rick spent a weekend with the Ramseyers in Miyazaki and shocked us by hitchhiking home!

Cooking for eight was a challenge. Young people dropped in, often just before mealtime, so our table extended to as many as came. Days were busy shopping, cooking, and all that keeps a household running! However, just having the children home energized me tremendously! The kids helped with chores. Their least favorite task was weeding our small yard!

This was also the best time of year to make friends with Japanese children, although the Japanese schools weren't out until the end of July. When the children were home, S.S. attendance increased. Vangy helped with SS and taught English classes. Rick found a summer job with Pepsi Cola. The Kihara family invited the kids for summer evenings catching fireflies by the river. Their grandparents lived with the family. When Billy came home from those visits he said, "They're lucky! They can have their grandparents with them all the time!"

We usually took guests to Marine Palace, a famous aquarium full of strange fish and sea life from around the world. Across the road wild monkeys roamed Monkey Mountain. When the caretakers called during feeding time, monkeys came running from every direction until it was wall to wall monkey!

MOVING SCHOOL

We were thankful for Christian schools. In September 1968, Vangy and Rick returned to boarding school in Tokyo, and Rosie, Billy and Wanda to our mission school in Miyakonojo. Oita was two hours north of Hyuga, so now instead of a two-hour train trip to school, it was four hours. Lily always went wild with excitement when Rosie, Billy and Wanda came home for the week-end.

Most of the children from the Miyakonojo mission school had graduated and were in high school in Tokyo. Our youngest three were the only ones left from our mission, and it didn't make sense to have them traveling eight hours by train on weekends.

In March, 1969, our faithful teacher, Virginia Claassen, spent a week -end with us "spying out the land." Would it be possible to move our school to Oita? The Baptists, from whom we had rented the house when we first moved to Oita, agreed to rent it to us again, this time for a school and a home for the teacher. July 22, 1969, Miss Claassen and the school moved from Miyakonojo to the Oita Baptist house. What a blessing to have Rosie, Billy and Wanda going to school from home every day.

Sundays when Miss Claassen came for faspa, an ethnic light meal, Lily, now two, would run to the door with open arms calling, "Virginia!" When Virginia was on a trip, and we told her Virginia was coming back the next day, she shouted "Banzai!" Super!

ETHEL

Ethel Kambs and Virginia Claassen met in Indiana. Ethel was organist at the Presbyterian church in Elkhart, and Virginia was studying at AMBS, Mennonite seminary during her leave of absence from Japan. They became friends. We met Ethel in Elkhart, too. I'll never forget the chills that ran up and down my spine when Ethel played the pipe organ at her church Christmas concert.

Years later Ethel wrote of her experiences: "I was greatly impressed with the sense of deep commitment and the life-style of the Mennonites. *Go ye into all the world* was taken seriously by even ordinary people like me."

After the death of her husband, Ethel checked out COM. She overcame family problems to follow her new calling. "I have put my hand to the plow," she wrote. Could there be a place for her in missions? Yes, Virginia, the Oita Christian School teacher, was back and would be happy to have her, and so would the Oita Mennonite Church.

During the school year of 1970-71 Ethel moved to Oita, and joined her good friend, Virginia in the Baptist house, now the school for our kids.

"People scratched their heads," she wrote, "a Presbyterian with a Lutheran background doing voluntary service work in a Mennonite Mission?" Ethel was a perfect fit! It was almost unbelievable how Virginia and Ethel presented ***Amahl and the Night Visitors*** with only four students in school. They doubled parts and borrowed one girl who was home-schooled that Christmas.

Ethel had a full schedule, English Bible classes, free music lessons for our school kids, helping the Adam and Eve Club at church, and playing for church. "After the first few weeks, I began to know the exhilaration of introducing Christ to my students through their study of the Bible," she wrote.

Of the five children left in our one-room school, three were ours. Kathy from an independent mission, would commute the same distance if we changed location, so now she boarded with us during the week. Kathy and Rosie, good friends, were both in grade eight. What a relief that our kids didn't have to take long train rides any more.

Since the mission family was so small now, we invited Japanese neighbors for school functions. Miss Claassen and her small school put on wonderful programs for parents and the community. Mark Twain's ***Tom Sawyer*** drama was unforgettable! Who could be better suited to play Tom and Betsy than the twins, Billy and Wanda? Adult thinking! They did not like to kiss in public or in private! Kathy and Rosie graduated from grade eight at the end of the school year.

Kerry, another missionary kid, lived with us during the week the following school year of 1970-71. Mari from South Africa, whose parents were missionaries in Oita, commuted to school every day. What an international school, two Canadians, one South African, one American and, of course, our American school teacher!

Ethel organized special music groups for evangelistic meetings and Christmas meetings. She was a real go-getter and gathered a community choir from different churches to sing at the joint Easter service in Oita. No language barrier could stop her. Virginia and Ethel became part of our family. We loved Ethel and Virginia! Lily did her Banzai for Ethel, too.

When we went on our next furlough in 1971, our twins were in their last year of elementary school, and so our little mission school closed its doors for good. The school had served us and many missionary families well. It would be a long time before Lily was ready for school!

In the meantime, our toddler Lily seemed to have decided on a singing career. She practiced from morning till night, sometimes with the needle stuck, but no one minded. She was the sunshine of our home!

NEW

It is quite natural that when missionaries move, the first people they want to meet are their new neighbors. Virginia lost no time in becoming friends with her new neighbor, Tomoko. Soon she was bringing her to church. They had twins, a boy, Tetsuya, and a girl, Mari, the same age as our twins, Billy and Wanda.

The children came to Sunday School occasionally. When we had school programs, Tomoko and her children were there. She also attended cooking classes in our home. When our school closed, Tomoko and her family also moved. We were sad, because we had become good friends. Many years later our paths with Tomoko would cross again.

Occasionally Japanese strangers stopped by. One Sunday Hanza, a man from Osaka, came early for worship service. He told us his sad story, and was seemingly in such pain, that my eyes filled with tears. Hanza stayed for most of the day, and then late in the afternoon Peter took him to the train station. We had decided to help him out financially.

As Peter waved good-bye, he detected a look of satisfaction on his face! A few weeks later at a missionary fellowship, we discovered that the same man had visited others, and they helped him, too. Each one had bought him a train ticket, which he turned in at the next stop. He got off and cashed in the unused portion of his ticket! The story of his calamities was slightly different in each case, but we all recognized that this was the same man!

MONTHLY FELLOWSHIPS

One fall when we hosted the missionary fellowship in Oita, we were in the path of a typhoon. Then the rains came tumbling down. We were all safe and snug in "the ark." We couldn't even get across the bridge to Virginia's house, so all 22 spent the night in our home! We were wall to wall people sleeping on the floors of each room! It was one of the most relaxing fellowships ever, since we had to wait for the storm to pass. Our Typhoon Fellowship saw that everyone was brave about stiff legs from sitting on the floor. After all were gone, Lily was happy to have our undivided attention again.

We looked forward to the missionary conferences in spring and fall. Early years we met in our homes for conferences, but as our numbers increased, we went to Japanese inns. Sometimes we sat on the floor there, too, so we were always happy for meeting rooms with chairs! Guest speakers inspired us to keep on even when we saw little fruit for our labors. What a relief to sing in English and understand what we were singing!

Our whole mission attended the All-Mennonite Conference once in three years. The four Mennonite missions in Japan took turns hosting, so we had the privilege of visiting each area of work: the Old (as they used to be called) Mennonite Mission in Hokkaido, Japan's most northern island; the Mennonite Brethren in the Osaka area, central Japan; the Brethren in Christ in southwest Honshu; and the General Conference Mennonite in Kyushu, southern Japan. Sometimes we were 40 or more. Mountain peak experiences!

TESTIMONIES

Oita was beginning to feel like home! Better yet, individuals were responding to the Gospel. A high school senior handed us an English letter one day. In it he wrote: "A few days I don't feel lonesome. Rather my heart is calm. The sky and mountains that are seen through the windows of the school bring me some meaning that I have never found. I had not been able to believe in God and His miracles. I don't know how faith to God and the miracles harmonize with scientific knowledge. But I want to believe it! And you said with such confidence, 'God is! What the Bible says is true.' Those words went to my heart. I will try to gain faith more and more. Please help me to do so."

Once a month we showed Christian films. After seeing ***King of Kings***, Setsuko wrote: "Thank you so much for letting me see such a wonderful film. To tell the truth, before I met you I was indifferent towards Christianity. However, after hearing much from you I came to believe, although still vaguely. Through the film I really understood how much Jesus suffered in bearing our sins and dying for us. I am grateful to God and also want to thank you for leading me to the joy of faith."

MACHIKO

My faith often lagged, and sometimes I just begged God, "Lord, give me compassion for the lost." That's when He sent Machiko!

The family was at the supper table. We looked at each other in surprise when we heard our piano tinkling in the living room. Who was in our house? We found a girl of about nine playing the piano. "What's your name?" we asked.

"Machiko," she said, but that was the only information she could give. She spoke with difficulty and did not know where she lived. Machiko left, but came back the next day, and the next. She spent many hours in our home that summer. Vangy, who wanted to work with challenged children, loved her. We were amazed that Machiko knew so much about God.

One evening when the children were playing catch outside, a car stopped. "Thank you for playing with Machiko," the driver said. "I am her father." He started attending church services. We discovered that the family had recently moved to our community. He told us about Machiko.

“When Machiko was little, she wasn't speaking like children her age. We began reading Bible stories to her every night and were touched by the miracles of Jesus. Soon the miracle came to life in our home. Machiko began to talk!”

Machiko’s father made a decision to follow Christ. Both parents came to share one evening. They fought often. He came to church regularly and was soon baptized. He became a strong support in the church. One Sunday he left with an armful of Gospels to share with neighbors and friends. However, his wife showed no interest.

The mother had a small corner store where she sold groceries and other necessities. She also had a shelf of tabloids and magazines at the entrance. Their home and store was opposite a small community park where children played. I began to pray that the Lord would remove that store because of the negative influence on children. One day I asked her if she felt good about having these magazines displayed so all the children could view them. She said, "No, but it brings in good money." I kept praying, and several months later when I walked past the store, the magazine shelf was gone!

We had prayed much for this family and said that if Machiko’s mother ever became a Christian, that would be a miracle!" When Machiko was 15, the miracle happened. She and her mother were baptized. What a happy day!

VANGY'S LAST SUMMER IN JAPAN

Vangy's four years at CAJ were complete. She had enjoyed school and studied well. Peter was able to attend the school program where Vangy had dramatized the poem, ***Creation***. I had sewn her navy dress for the occasion. She had made many friends at CAJ but had also kept up with her Japanese friends in the different cities where we had worked. Her faith was strengthened in the Christian environment of CAJ, and also in her dorm, where a girl from another denomination had challenged her faith because of a different mode of baptism. The time had come for a big change.

When Vangy graduated from CAJ on June 12, 1970, Lily was two and a half years old. We took her to Tokyo for the graduation. What a special time of bonding for our oldest and youngest. Vangy had applied to UBC, University of British Columbia, and was accepted. When we questioned why she wanted to attend a secular school instead of a Christian college, she told us, “Mom and Dad. I've been in a sheltered Christian home and Christian school all my life. Now it's time to try my wings of faith!” And she did!

The morning after graduation Peter, Lily and I boarded the train for Oita. Since it was cheaper for students to fly, Vangy and Rick flew home by plane that afternoon. Overnight guests arrived the same day, so it was back to our busy floating schedule.

The kids found summer jobs again. In July the girls had an amazing experience when they volunteered at a camp for physically challenged children. Rose said, "At first it feels weird to hold hands with a child who just has a stub hand, but after playing with them for a while, it seems normal." There were several who had no arms, just a short hand at the shoulder, due to the thalidomide drug their mothers had taken during pregnancy.

Lily received many dolls for Christmas and birthdays. We decided to recycle some of these dolls. Lily could choose her favorites to keep. The church ladies made new clothes for the rest, which we gave to the hospital for sick children in Beppu, our neighboring city just half an hour north of Oita.

Missionary kids and Japanese friends came for weekends. Once it was ten missionary kids from around the island. It's so easy to have night guests. Just roll out the mats on the floor and you have wall to wall kids, and a noisy night! Fellow missionaries dropped by for visits, as well as parents of missionaries.

The church youth had started their own club, called **Adam & Eve**. It was great to have our children involved with the local church.

VANGY TO CANADA

Thursday, August 27, 1970, we sent Vangy to a foreign country! Sending our first child to fend for herself in Canada, which was like a foreign country to her, was heart-rending! A large group of church people, neighbors and friends were at the Oita airport to see her off. This would be the first long separation for our family. Peter flew to Tokyo with her and they said their good-byes at the Tokyo airport. Our comfort was that the following year we would be leaving for a year of furlough, so we would be together for the summer months again.

Sending our children off to schools overseas was like cutting our last ties. I never expected it to be so hard. They feel like gaijin all over again. What do you do when your daughter writes she is so lonely that she goes to the cemetery across the street to cry at night? The dead do not comfort. Or when one “hates” Canada as soon as she gets there? We had to miss all their dating friends. Then came their engagements to total strangers. As I was struggling, God showed me Ephesians 3:20, *Now to him who is able to do immeasurably more than we ask or imagine, according to his power that is at work within us, to him be glory…* More than I can ask or imagine? I could finally release the choices to Him and the children, and my peace was restored.

The year 1970 had brought many new experiences to our family. Rosie was eagerly looking forward to joining Rick in Tokyo at CAJ. It was a sad day when she asked me to cut off her two beautiful brown thick braids that hung down to her waist.

Our home seemed so empty without Vangy, but we didn't have time to sit around. Twins from an orphanage came for the weekend. Missionary friends dropped in on their way home. Kerry, our new boarder for the school year, arrived. Her parents brought the mayor and his wife from their town. During that week Shirley, a friend from Taiwan, came for a visit. Ethel had arrived for a year of volunteering with our mission. We were thirteen for lunch. Rick and Rosie left for school in Tokyo that evening.

It was Rosie's turn to experience Tokyo. She felt as if she was walking in the shadow of her older sister! Students would stop and say, "You must be Vangy's sister." She joined the pep club and glee club and fitted into her new life in Tokyo. We thanked God for house parents who followed God's call for ministry to missionary kids. Occasionally the children had problems, but often that could be attributed to the fact that some house parents had never had children of their own. The children also learned many valuable life lessons. Not everything will turn out the way we would like. We prayed much and trusted the Lord to help them face both good and bad experiences.

How thankful we were that Vangy was boarding in a Christian home in Vancouver! Weekends she went to Oma and Opa Derksen in Abbotsford. She participated in the church choir, and made friends among the youth of the church. She also discovered that grandparents could be quite possessive. They were happy to finally have the oldest grandchild with them after all these years of absence, the one they had welcomed into the world so joyfully eighteen years ago!

At UBC Vangy found the Intervarsity Christian Fellowship and joined. There she met a young man, Ernest Thiessen, who became a special friend. It was during the Jesus People movement, and students were sharing their faith in Christ on the streets of Vancouver. Before the end of the school year, Vangy wrote that she wanted to quit university and join the new Christian youth movement. Jesus was coming soon. Their mandate was to win people for God's kingdom now.

Furlough was God's perfect timing! This gave us the opportunity to encourage her to stay in school. When we told her that we could not have become missionaries to Japan if we hadn't gone to school, she was touched. Vangy became a schoolteacher, a profession she followed all her life. During two terms with MCC in Nepal, Vangy taught their children and the other missionary children in their area.

CHURCH GROWTH

In 1970 a junior high boy was baptized. His older brother had been baptized earlier. Their mother came to church occasionally. In May 1971, on Pentecost Sunday, our little church grew again, when Akio, a high school student, and a student in a vocational school, were baptized. Our ties with Akio grew when her mother, a schoolteacher, could not attend her daughter's graduation ceremony. Akio asked me to substitute for her mother. What an honor! She was a close friend of Vangy's, and when we wrote Vangy about Akio's baptism, she cried for joy! When we visited Japan in 2007, Akio and her husband invited us for a home stay.

While planning furlough for the following year, the Kudo sisters asked if their family could live in our home, which also served as church, during our year of absence! The parents and another sister were not Christians, but the Lord gave us peace about this arrangement. The Christian sisters and young people would keep the SS and Sunday morning services going. Pastors and missionaries would take turns preaching one Sunday a month. New young people were added to the church during that time. God's ways amazed us!

RICK

Meanwhile, Rick was enjoying his last year of high school in Tokyo. He did well on the wrestling team and was singing in the school choir. Rick had a major role in the school drama, ***A Man for All Seasons*** which I was able to attend. What a scare when the lights went out, and you could hear the man's head chopped off and roll off the platform! In spring Rick was MC at the junior/senior banquet. It was the year of decision. He had to decide where to attend college and he applied to Wheaton College near Chicago, Ill. We all waited apprehensively for the answer.

During Rick's junior year, his studies had slackened. Not only that, but while our church had evangelistic meetings, we got a telephone call from the principal, telling us that Rick was being sent home for a week because he and some friends had gone drinking. What a shock and embarrassment! The evangelist was staying in our home.

After our talk with Rick, he apologized to the church. He promised to study hard again. When he returned to CAJ, his marks improved immediately. What a relief when Wheaton College sent him an acceptance letter! June 18 we attended Rick's graduation at Christian Academy in Japan.

Years later Rick and his wife Marilyn went to Zaire, Africa, where they spent 22 years as missionaries. God's miracle!

THIRD FURLOUGH 1971-72

Rick graduated in June 1971 and spent one last summer at home. Life always seemed to get busier: packing, farewells, people calling all day, invitations for meals, and hundreds of things to attend to. We stored our belongings in the attic under the eaves, so the Kudo family could move in. The condition was that the eight mat room would always be available for church activities.

In the meantime, back in Abbotsford, Peter's parents had sold their farm and built a large home on Grant Street for their growing family. Our kids were sorry that we would not be living on the farm. We moved in temporarily with Ma and Pa Derksen, and also spent time with my parents. Mother Klassen was in the Menno Hospital in Abbotsford, and Dad lived alone in his home on Autumn Street. However, we were itinerating most weekends, and often on week nights. On one trip Lily asked, "Where are we going now in the car that we live in?"

On August 20, 1971, we said good-bye to our B.C. family, and headed east. No seatbelts yet, so our family of eight squeezed into the car for the long trip. We stayed with friends and family along the way. Lily was sick, but we kept on going. Vangy and Rick had both passed their drivers' exam, so there were four drivers.

It was great fun to spend a weekend with sister Martha and husband Ed in Regina. In Winnipeg Tante Anna and Tante Tina treated us like family. That became one of our favorite stopping places.

Finally, we were off to Ontario again. Here we visited sister Frieda in Kitchener, whose wedding we had missed, sister Hilda in Kitchener, Oma Rempel, my grandmother, who was 94 and in the old folks home in Vineland, my brother Walter and family in St. Catharines, our many uncles, aunts and cousins, and a host of friends.

It was lonely to have no parental home in Virgil since Mom and Dad had moved to BC. We took turns staying with my brother Walter and Grace, and with our dear friends, Jess and Hardy. Jess and I had been best friends since childhood when we walked to elementary school together. They always made us feel as if their home was our home.

Hilda had come to Virgil, too, and of course, we were excited to see our old homes. Early Sunday morning Hilda and I drove to our three former homes, first to Creek Road where Mom and Dad had lived most recently, then to Plum Street where we had all grown up, and last to the farm with the creek where I had lived until I got married. But instead of the creek, we saw a large body of water! The creek had been dammed. As we turned into the driveway, Hilda got so excited that she kept driving until the car stalled. Stuck deep in mud! Our kind neighbor pulled us out with his tractor. We barely made it to church on time!

SEMINARY AGAIN

Monday morning we headed west again. Destination? Elkhart, Indiana. Peter was finally going to finish seminary. On a previous furlough when we had spent one semester in Elkhart, I had vowed never to go back. We had lived off campus when the twins were only one year old, and I had felt very isolated.

We made one stop in Parkhill to visit Jack and Ann who had a ranch for delinquent boys in western Ontario. The kids enjoyed their first horseback rides! The next morning, we left for Elkhart, and moved into a lovely furnished apartment on campus. However, we had no bedding or dishes. Our dear friend, Ethel Kambs, who lived in Elkhart at the time, came to the rescue, and soon our new apartment was home to us. We felt so blessed when we found a piano for $60; Now Rose could continue piano lessons.

Peter had orientation the next day, and the following day I took Rosie to the sophomore division of high school in town. And who had us for faspa the first Sunday? Ethel! We were with Japan family again!

What a busy week getting everybody off to school! Early Monday, September 5, we drove Vangy to O'Hare Airport in Chicago and she flew back to Vancouver for her second year at UBC. Tuesday Billy and Wanda registered at Pierre Moran junior high school. Rosie attended Elkhart high school. One day she came home pale and tense. Violence had broken out in the school halls, and the police were called in to control the tensions between blacks and whites.

On Tuesday, September 14, we took Rick to Wheaton College in Chicago. At last all were settled in school again. We were close enough to Wheaton so Rick could come home occasionally for weekends.

That left Lily and me at home. Lily became my constant companion. On one shopping trip I got out of the car, opened the back door for her, and closed the door a bit too soon. She screamed! The lower part of her thumb was caught in the door. I had locked the doors already, so it took time to get them unlocked and free her hand. Can you imagine how I felt? Her thumb was very bruised, but thankfully no bones were broken.

I joined an inspiring women's Bible study fellowship. I had homework, too! Lily loved the Sunday School, as she called child care. We had wonderful fellowship with Krisetya's from Indonesia, and Tanase's from Japan. What a difference from the previous time at seminary. Of course, the children were older, and that helped. Lily was four, Billy and Wanda thirteen, and Rosie fifteen.

HEAD-ON COLLISION

On Sunday, September 26th, we were to present our mission work at the Silver Street Church in Goshen. We followed directions and thought we must be nearing the church. Suddenly over a small hill a shiny red car came driving straight at us in our lane! I shouted, "Peter!" He saw the car and debated whether to change lanes but made a split-second decision against it. By the time we crashed head on, our car was almost stopped.

Peter's sister Erna and husband Jake had loaned us their Chrysler for the year. I jumped out of the car and got our four children out. They could all walk, and so could we! Our car front was smashed!

I hurried over. Their windshield was broken, and the four siblings were cut and bleeding. I helped them to lie down in the grass. By this time traffic had come to a halt, and people surrounded us. A policeman who lived opposite the accident came out to help. The young lady driver and her three siblings had been driving to a church in the opposite direction. The car was brand new. They had all been occupied with a seat adjustment in the front and their car had gradually moved into our lane.

A couple going to Silver Street Church took the children and me to church, while Peter stayed to make arrangements for the car. The most serious injury was an eight-year-old with a broken jaw. I had a bleeding knee and a torn stocking. Billy was in shock. The church people were very helpful and took care of him in the nursery, while the rest of the family carried on with the program we had prepared. They had switched SS and worship times around, so it all worked out. That night I could not sleep. My heart kept singing "Thank you, Jesus. Thank you, Jesus!" He protected our family and even the others from serious injury.

When we weren't scheduled for meetings in other churches, we made Silver Street our church home for the year. It was fun to make sukiyaki, a Japanese meal, for 29 young people. Everybody liked sukiyaki!

In October we drove to Wayland, Iowa, for a missions meeting. On the way we stopped to pick up Rick in Wheaton, and met a young student, Marilyn Carter, who would become a very important person in our family, Rick's future wife! Of course, we didn't know that at the time! They came for a weekend in February. We were quite impressed with Rick's choice! Here is Rick's story of how they met:

HOW MARILYN AND I FIRST MET

It was part way through orientation week my first year at Wheaton College that I first met Marilyn. All first year students lived in the same dorm and one day as I was heading down the stairs from the main floor lounge to the basement with a friend from Japan, Dave, I met Marilyn and a friend of hers coming up the stairs. As soon as she saw me she asked if I was Steve Savage's brother. Steve was an older Wheaton student whom she knew, and evidently thought I looked like him. I thought she had said 'Steve Sandwich,' and thinking that was a rather strange name, I replied without a moment's hesitation and a straight face, "No, I'm Joe Hamburger." Marilyn believed me and for a couple of days she called me Hamburger and I called her Sandwich.

She found out that my real name was Rick Derksen and not Joe Hamburger, so when we met again at an all school picnic and I told her I was from Japan - which was in fact where I had lived most of my life until college - she didn't believe me. Now it just so happened that she had gotten to know a Japanese exchange student during high school, and one of the only Japanese words that she remembered was "Aishitemasu," which means, "I love you." By that time, I had a pretty serious crush on Marilyn - she had a beautiful smile and a friendly personality - and when she said "Aishitemasu" I turned to my friend and said, "I just met this girl and she tells me she loves me!" As you can imagine, Marilyn was a little embarrassed, but I didn't mind at all. One thing led to another and here we are after almost 35 years of marriage. We got married after finishing college in 1975 - still very much in love!

BLESSINGS

That was an unusual furlough year. There were various Christian movements. On the west coast it was the Jesus People. In Saskatchewan revival fires were burning. And in Canada and the US. the charismatic movement was gaining strength. We prayed that God would keep our hearts and minds open to whatever He wanted to teach us that year. We attended charismatic prayer meetings in Notre Dame University, and were richly blessed to see so many denominations, including Catholics, singing and praying together. If God had special blessings for His people, we wanted to be a part of it.

Our family was complete again for Christmas! Rick surprised us by hitchhiking home to Elkhart. Peter drove to O'Hare to pick up Vangy as she flew in from Vancouver. We often had company for meals, but we missed not having responsibilities in a church. No SS programs to practice. No Bible class parties! It certainly was different. The biggest shock came when we wanted to attend a Christmas Eve service but had to search through all the newspapers to finally find a church far out in the country that had a meeting! The same was true of Christmas morning. No church services anywhere! So it was family time, and then we drove to the County Old Folks Home with friends to sing.

We all missed Japan's New Year. No one was busy, whereas in Japan every home got a thorough cleaning before the New Year. In America most of the cleaning was done before Christmas, so no need to do it again.

One exciting experience in the New Year was meeting my childhood Sunday School teacher, Evangeline Mathies, formerly from Virgil, ON, now married and living in Elkhart. She had been such a great influence in my life, that we named our first child Evangeline! Perhaps because of her influence, I felt it very important to organize Sunday Schools as soon as possible in each new place where we worked in Japan.

Soon all except Lily and I were back in school. I felt lost. Then sister Hilda phoned to tell us of her engagement. The wedding was to be in March, and of course, we would all attend. Just two days later Dad phoned from B.C. that Mother was very sick. On January 10 he phoned again. Mother had gone to heaven. She had suffered much from Parkinson's disease for the past 20 years, and we were thankful that the Lord had taken her Home!

The next day Peter took me to South Bend. I flew to O'Hare, where Rick came to see me off for Vancouver. Vangy met me at the airport in Vancouver. All my siblings except Frieda, who was expecting her first child, came to Abbotsford for the funeral. We had wonderful family times in Dad's home.

Peter and the younger children were all at South Bend to welcome me home again. A Japanese student, who had been at our place when I left, was still there. Many friends in Elkhart had invited them for meals.

WEEKENDS

We were able to take in exciting events. Peter attended The General Conference of our churches in Fresno, CA. Rosie and I had the privilege of going to Probe '72. I felt quite insecure being a delegate, because I thought I would have nothing to contribute since many older and wiser leaders would be taking part. I quite surprised myself that … yes, I had opinions and experiences worth sharing, too!

When Peter returned from a COM study conference of staff, national leaders from overseas churches, and missionaries, he said, "It's great to be a part of such a world-wide fellowship and ministry!"

In March we spent a weekend in the Normal, Illinois Mennonite Church where we met Franzie and Dorothy, former short termers to Japan. During their time in Japan, Dorothy had given free piano lessons to the children in the mission school. The long Easter weekend we served in the Pretty Prairie Mennonite Church in Kansas, where Peter and Lois Voran, our coworkers from Japan, were pastoring during an extended leave.

Another weekend we served at a missions conference in Leamington, Ontario. Many of my high school friends from OBS lived in Leamington, so my former roommate, Helga, hosted a school reunion. Peter returned to Elkhart after the last meeting. Rick, Lily and I went to Kitchener and St. Catharines/Virgil, visiting Oma Rempel, and helping with preparations for Hilda's wedding.

There we met Hilda's fiance, Colin, for the first time. Peter, Rosie, Billy and Wanda came from Elkhart in time for the wedding. Hilda had asked me to sing a solo. I had only one practice with the church organist and was quite nervous. But God gave grace, and I sang ***O, Lord Most Holy*** with all my heart! Singing from a balcony without facing the audience eased my fluttering stomach. At the reception our family sang, with Wanda playing guitar. We didn't think about it again until we were back in Japan, and a letter came from Nancy, a close friend of Hilda's whom we had met at the wedding.

Nancy wrote, "Your family song touched me deeply. I want what you have!" In my enthusiasm, I just praised the Lord, and wrote Nancy a long letter on how to become a Christian. But I never heard from Nancy again, and begged the Lord to forgive me for my blunders.

It wasn't until a year later that I received a joyous letter from Nancy, telling me how she had seen a picture of Jesus in her church (Catholic,) which touched her deeply. She took out my letter and reread and finally, she wrote, "It all fell into place!" Nancy gave her heart to Jesus. Not long after, she died of cancer. This was not the first time the Lord turned my blunders into blessings! How I thanked God that Nancy was ready to enter into the presence of the Lord Jesus.

GOOD BYE SEMINARY

After the wedding it was back to our busy life at seminary. Peter had a call from Mom Derksen saying Dad was very sick but he needn't come. He went anyway. His Dad improved and Peter was back within the week.

We made an important visit to Rev. and Mrs. John Suderman, who had retired to Winona Lake after a life of pastoring churches. Our acquaintance with the Sudermans dated back to another furlough when we lived in B.C. On December 24, a snowy winter day, these dear folks had braved the storm and had come from WA, not just for a visit, but to take us shopping. They told us to put on our winter wear, because they were taking us to a family clothing store in downtown Abbotsford. Each member of our family of seven was to choose any item of clothing that they liked in the store, not what Dad or Mom wanted them to pick. What a shopping trip! And what a Christmas gift! I still remember my black skirt, which served me well for years.

Our year in Elkhart was coming to a close. I had been so involved in choir, auditing a course, hosting, and having family to our home, that there was no time to be lonely. Peter kept up with his seminary studies in spite of busy weekends in churches. I typed his many papers. Peter was finally graduating from seminary with a Master of Divinity degree. It had taken him seventeen years, including a year in NY before going to Japan. What an accomplishment. What joy. What relief!

When we finally arrived in BC, we were shocked that Dad Klassen had sold his house. We had hoped to live there for the summer until our return to Japan. Mom Derksen came to the rescue. She found a rental house on Townline Road and collected furniture from friends. Dad and Reiko from Japan lived with us that summer. We were tired and discouraged.

However, we still had a big family event to look forward to, Ma and

Pa Derksen's Golden Wedding anniversary! 50 years ago they were married in the Ukraine, and emigrated to Canada in 1925. Their family had grown to five children, spouses, and twelve grandchildren, plus foster children they had cared for during their years on the farm. On August the 19, 1972, family and friends gathered in their spacious yard on Grant Street in Clearbrook to celebrate. The program of poems and songs by grandchildren, family, and friends was disrupted by a rainstorm, so everybody squeezed into their home to continue rejoicing. Peter's message, "Great is Thy Faithfulness," was from Lamentations 3:22-24. We were thankful that we had been able to take part in this important celebration.

Every weekend that summer we had three or four meetings in BC churches. God did a miracle in my heart as I listened to Peter enthusiastically sharing about Japan. This had a healing effect on me, and by the time we had said most of our good-byes, I was eager to return to Japan.

This time we would be leaving Vangy and Rick. We had already moved Vangy to Jake and Lillian Elias in Vancouver, where she would board for her third year at UBC. Rick was returning to Wheaton College. The day before we were to leave, our family of seven went to our favourite meadow on a hill with a grand view of Mt. Baker. It was a beautiful calm evening. We sang, prayed, laughed and just relaxed. It had truly been "a great day!"

August 30, 1972, was a time to rise and shine again, as our BC families and friends came to Vancouver International Airport to see us off to Japan via San Francisco. We never thought of our mission to Japan as sacrifice, but it was very difficult to leave our children.

The plane we boarded in San Francisco flew along the west coast before circling toward Japan. When I knew we were flying along the BC coast where our two oldest, Vangy and Rick were still with their Opa and Oma, my heart could hold the pain no longer and I burst into tears. Good-bye. Good-bye. We're going home to Japan!

MEMORIES OUR CHILDREN HAVE OF HYUGA AND OITA

Memories of My Last Year in Hyuga – Rick

- We were living in Hyuga, but I was still going to Miyazaki Christian School (MCS) – a school for missionary kids – in Miyakonojo, by train every week. I would leave earlier than my siblings to go to my violin lesson in Miyazaki every Monday afternoon before continuing on to Miyakonojo for another week of school. I was in the eighth grade with Sharon Kruse, Doug Voran, Lawrence Boschman, and Tim Oxley and our class was by far the largest class in the one room school that had grades 1 through 8. Our teacher, Agnes Dueck – we called her "Miss Dueck" – was quite strict, but a very good teacher. Our dorm parents were Fritz and Ellen Sprunger and they were very nice, even though I'm sure that we drove them crazy at times. My memories of that year in Miyakonojo are taking turns with the other eighth grade guys to get a big container of milk from the milk factory early every morning by bike… often going beyond the boundaries of how far we were allowed to go from the school and dorm after the school day was over… playing "go narabe" with "Aunt Ellen" on occasional evenings in the dorm… playing kick-the-can… and convincing the conductors on the train going home to Hyuga on Friday afternoon to allow me to sit in first class even though I had only paid for second class.

- My memories of Hyuga are of going to ships in the harbor to see what country they came from – we had a sugar refinery and sometimes got ships from Cuba or the Soviet Union
- trying to board them and make friends with the crew, and sometimes get invited to eat with them on board and sometimes invite some of them home for dinner. Poor Mom… I never gave her any forewarning of the guests I was bringing home! Other memories include learning to drive a scooter and getting stopped by a cop and pretending I didn't understand Japanese so he would let me off the hook even though I didn't have a license, which he did… going with Dad to Bible classes in different villages when I was home from school
- places like Mimitsu and Kadogawa and sometimes into the moutains…
- yummy faspas on Sunday evenings at home…
- Oba-chan helping us with housework, and her two sons… Aratake Sensei who had such a great laugh…
- panshoku, bread lunch, at church some Sundays after the worship service…
- and of course the beautiful beach at Isegahama with a perfect combination of rocks and sand.

Oita Memories – Lily

- I don't know what to say, as I was only three and a half!
- Of course a big part of my life then was becoming friends with Jun Chan and Kumi Chan, and even the boys on the street, Satoshi Kun and Yoshinori Kun
- I don't think I actually remember anything. But, I know I enjoyed having stray dogs and cats as pets, having people like Fujibuchi San around who played with us kids.
- I think that's about it!

Oita Memories – Wanda

- first of all, the arrival of Lily - and we couldn't see her until we came home from school after we had to go to Vorans the first weekend
- going to OCS, Oita Christian School, by bicycle every day, even when it was freezing cold over the bridge
- school at our little OCS with Miss Claassen, and Aunt Ethel who was such a good and gentle music teacher
- working at Mister Donuts - oh joy!
- little summer holidays at the beach on the other side of the bay
- watching Shiro give birth to two puppies by our back porch - quite amazing
- watching Lil play with the neighbour kids
- the elderly grandparents next door who were so kind
- going to the outdoor pool in the summer after chores were done
- speaking of chores - weeding, window washing, laundry, dusting, etc.
- having the family of cats sleep on the upstairs deck outside our bedroom window

Oita Memories – Bill

- I don't remember the actual physical move from Hyuga to Oita. What I do remember is thinking that we hit the jackpot when the Southern Baptists let us move into their Western-style house with a huge lawn, in the middle of Oita City, for four months while we built our new church house. That is where we met Mrs. Koga, our new neighbour, and her twins who were the same age as Wanda and me. It was unusual for a Japanese family to have twins that were a boy and girl.

- One of the weekly highlights during the early part of life in Oita was coming home by train from Miyakonojo and being greeted by Dad at the station. There was always the anticipation on the ride home of seeing any new additions to our house in Nakatsuru. The new concrete gate posts come to mind as one of those additions. Arriving home from the station to the smell of Mom's waffles with vanilla pudding or our favourite gravy was pure ecstasy. Sometimes we brought guests with us, foreigners whom we had met on the train.

- Watching our yard take shape at the new house was fun. The hedge, which I eventually had the responsibility of trimming, seemed almost extravagant when we first had it planted. Our neighbour, Kawano San, was impressed with how I managed a perfectly straight top without using a string as a guide. Speaking of extravagant, we thought the Kawano's new house next door was very ritzy. I loved our magnolia tree in the front corner as well as the tsubaki, camellia bush. One thing I hated about the yard was weeding. I can still see those fern-like weeds that refused to come out by the roots

- My favourite past-time was playing a baseball game by myself by throwing the ball against the block wall on the side of our prefab garage. I tried to hit a small ledge at the bottom that would make the ball fly, and then I would play all the positions appropriate to where the ball went. I had two teams going, one of them always being Daisho, Oita Shogyo, making sure that my favourites won the game in the end. Baseball was a huge part of my psyche in Oita. Often I went over to the field across the road where Daisho's baseball team practiced. I either watched the outfielders from the fence by the road, or if I had time went to the dugout area where there was a string of onlookers cheering our local heroes on. During the prefectural tournaments that decided who went to Koshien, Dad and I went on occasion to the baseball stadium across town to watch Daisho play. And, of course, no matter who represented Oita, whether it was Daisho or Tsukumi or Hita Rinko, we watched (onTV) both the spring and summer tournaments from start to finish on TV.

- I don't remember which winter it was, but we had lots of snow one time. It even drifted into some spots in our yard, which for some reason made me proud to be Canadian. Typhoons were another highlight, especially when we had to shut the amado, wooden shutters, to protect our windows.
- I loved watching Oita grow as a city. The Nishitetsu Grand Hotel along the banks of the Oita River was so modern, as was the company that built it—Shin Nittetsu Steel Co. Their new factory, built on the former Oita Airport land, was the biggest and most modern steel factory in the world. Another world-famous structure was our new concert auditorium that was built inside the old castle walls. I forget what it was called.

Oita Memories – Rose

- Here are a few scattered memories of "home" in Oita.
- I can clearly see our two-story house on the corner with the hedge and small lawn surrounding it
- I remember coming home to snack in the kitchen Friday nights
- playing with Lily in her crib
- laundry done in the wringer washing machine
- dusting Dad's study with all those books
- his call Sunday mornings to "***rise and shine***", and then "*last call for breakfast* "
- wonderful faspas with tea, served on our best china lots and lots of ocha, tea, served to lots and lots of people
- the park two blocks over with the pink elephant
- the baseball team yelling at each other in the spring
- riding bike to the pool in the summertime
- sharing hot water bottles with Wanda in the winter
- biking along the river banks
- going for Sunday drives along the ocean
- trips to Monkey Mountain and the drive along the bay towards Beppu
- shopping downtown with Mom
- standing in line with Dad at the train station to get tickets to

go back to school after New Years for hours in the middle of the night

- working at Elle folding t-shirts all day long
- going to see ***Sound of Music***, our first movie
- saying goodbye to Vangy at the airport when she left Japan
- teaching English classes
- playing piano for church
- candlelight Christmas Eve services
- carolling in the neighborhood and coming back to the house for hot chocolate
- the spectacular sights of kimonos at New Year's
- buying sweet potatoes from the old man selling them with his cart
- listening to Rick's rock 'n roll from CAJ
- devotions at night
- looking at the moon from our bedroom balcony
- reading when I was supposed to be dusting
- watching TV in our living room/mom and dad's bedroom
- And of course all the church services, the Sunday schools
- the people who became our friends and family
- I could go on and on.
- But most and foremost, the tatami rooms
- the red and white checkered kitchen floor
- the back porch
- this is what I think of when I think of home where I lived and grew and felt secure and loved.

Oita Memories – Rick

- I remember moving into a large, western style house, belonging to the Baptist mission, when we first moved to Oita between my eighth and ninth grade
- buying a property to build a Japanese-style house which would also serve as the church
- cutting my finger while cutting grass with Dad at the new property and having to get stitches at the hospital (I still have the scar on my left index finger)
- staying up half the night or sometimes all night in the cold train station with Dad in order to get tickets for the sleeper

car to go to Tokyo for school with Vangy

- meeting Furushiro-kun, a high school student who lived nearby and became one of my best Japanese friends
- having fun singing and doing other things with Fujibuchi-kun and the other high school students who came to church
- meeting Sato Shigeyuki when I went to get my driver's license and inviting him home with me
- getting a baby sister, Lily, when I was in the ninth grade, very exciting
- getting baptized with Nakano Sensei between ninth and tenth grades at Oita Mennonite Christian Church
- working for Pepsi-Cola two summers in a row – one of those summers I had a bicycle accident on my way to work one morning when I changed lanes without looking and got hit by a car and ended up with bruises and scrapes, but no broken bones
- another memory of my time with Pepsi was the intense rivalry and competition with Coca-Cola in particular, but also Seven-Up – so intense that my driver would sometimes get into fights with the other drivers
- working for a bridge company my last summer in Oita and quitting two days before a tragic accident involving the partial collapse of the bridge resulted in the death of two of the men I had worked with
- cheering for whatever Oita team made it to the annual national high school baseball tournament
- getting suspended from school during the eleventh grade and having to come home and face my parents and younger siblings as well as the church – a trip that was extra painful because I was bumped off the plane from Tokyo to Oita in Shikoku and had to take an overnight ferry to Beppu in order to get home
- and recuperating from a motorcycle accident at Larry Ledden's home near Tokyo the weekend before getting suspended!
- going to Monkey Mountain and the aquarium between Oita and Beppu as well as the hot springs in Beppu with visitors
- going to the Bunka Kaikan and thinking it had to be one of the coolest-looking buildings in the world – it was a modern

concert hall built on the site of an old castle with the moat and walls intact

- going to the nearby airport from time to time to watch planes land and take off – the most exciting time was when President Mobutu of what was then Zaire flew into Oita because of a trade relationship with a local company that imported copper – little did I know at the time that I would end up in his country many years later with my wife Marilyn to work with the Mennonite church there and stay until after his downfall in 1997!
- It is time for bed and I need to send this off to Mom by e-mail, so my memories from Tokyo are going to have to wait for another time

Hyuga and Oita Memories – Vanj (Vangy)

- Before moving to Oita, we had one last year in Hyuga after my grade 8 year at MEI in Abbotsford. I had been dropped off at CAJ in Tokyo on our return to Japan for my grade 9 year. It was a new school and dorm experience for me, so I didn't feel like I had "come home" quite yet. Returning to Hyuga for my first school holiday was exciting and satisfied my yearning for home. "Home" meant being with my family, my obachan, my church and my loyal friends who had come to our house to welcome me back. Hisayo Takahashi remains my friend to this day.
- I loved rice fields, iron basin ofuros, puffed rice, and everything inaka, country style, and hoped that our family would be moving to Tashiro, a small village that we had visited as a family for meetings. When Dad and Mom informed me that we would be moving to Oita, a large city instead, I was very disappointed. It had been a decision made by the Japanese Mennonite pastors together with Dad and Mom.
- During my first year at CAJ, I was introduced to Christian beliefs that were not Mennonite. My theological discussions with Dad, each time I returned home for a school holiday, became very significant in forming my core Mennonite beliefs of becoming a sincere follower of Jesus and choosing a path of peace and non-resistance. On March 26, 1967 during Easter vacation, I was baptized at 14 in the Hyuga Men-

nonite Church by Dad and the Japanese pastor. I had received a Japanese Bible as a Christmas gift from the church already three years earlier, and on that day, I held it close.

- Rick joined me for my second year at CAJ. I was so very happy to have a brother with me! The move to our new Japanese house in Oita happened in the fall of '67 while we were at CAJ. Besides a beautiful house with tatami, straw mat floors, shoji, paper sliding doors, and a tokonoma, alcove in the living room, to enjoy, we had a brandnew baby sister to meet! We met Lily when she was just two weeks old. To hold her was amazing. We all loved her. Mom even sewed identical dresses for all four of us sisters more than once.

Vangy's Random Memories include

- teaching English to women and students during vacations at home
- family trips to the beach
- volunteering at a camp by the ocean for handicapped children and being assigned to a boy who couldn't easily walk
- Arubaito, part time job, in a coffee shop
- fireworks at the river
- bouncing small balloons filled with water off my hand
- receiving a beautifully sewn heart by Mom for Valentines while at CAJ
- looking forward to weekly letters from Mom and Dad
- all our favorite baking of Mom's arriving in special packages from home
- taking the "futsu" (lowest class train) and camping in Aoidake with old and new friends
- church meetings and English classes in our home
- many expected and unexpected visitors
- professional beggars
- getting paid to weed the yard on a hot summer day
- checkers with Dad
- watching Koshien baseball together on TV
- watching the Americans land on the moon
- listening to Japanese pop singers on Sunday evenings
- hearing the news about JFK's assassination, the Vietnam

war, etc.

- Mom canceling her classes whenever we came home for vacation
- voice lessons from Mom that made me feel so special
- singing in choirs at CAJ, with our family, in church, from house to house on Christmas Eve's
- many Christmas parcels from Canada, that were so exciting to open as a family, filled with halvah, cornflakes, chocolate covered cherries, and many treasured gifts for each one of us
- special birthday parties with friends and family
- Mom's delicious crazy chocolate cake
- sharing an upstairs tatami bedroom with my sisters when I was home
- braiding Rosie's hair
- telegrams from Canada
- many, many train rides on all kinds of trains for both day trips and overnight trips
- flying home standby
- the gift of a kimono for my high school grad from Mom and Dad
- saying a big and tearful good-bye to Lily, Wanda, Bill, Rose, Rick and Mom together with Japanese friends and leaving Oita Airport with Dad on our way to Tokyo before saying good-bye to him and to Japan and finally boarding a plane flying to Seattle with Karen Johnson
- arriving at Vancouver International Airport with Oma and other relatives there to greet me
- starting UBC in September 1970
- weekends with Oma and Opa Derksen and Klassen
- eagerly welcoming my family on furlough one year later
- taking my first mission board paid flight to Japan as an MK of GC Mennonite missionaries in the summer of 1973 and arriving back home in Oita!

Memories have just begun flooding in and I am so grateful for all the beautiful experiences that were made possible because you decided to love God and go to Japan. Thanks Mom and Dad!

Rick, Billie, Rosie, Vangy, and Wanda; happy for a baby sister, Lily

Babes in arms

Xavier in Oita, 1549

Peter's English class with dentists

Worship service; sitting on floor - every Bible open

Carolling

MCS - Our Mission school and dormitory

Fritz & Ellen Sprunger, dorm parents and children - mealtime

Oh, oh! Lily and Satoshi are in trouble

Amahl, by MCS students

MCS Christmas program

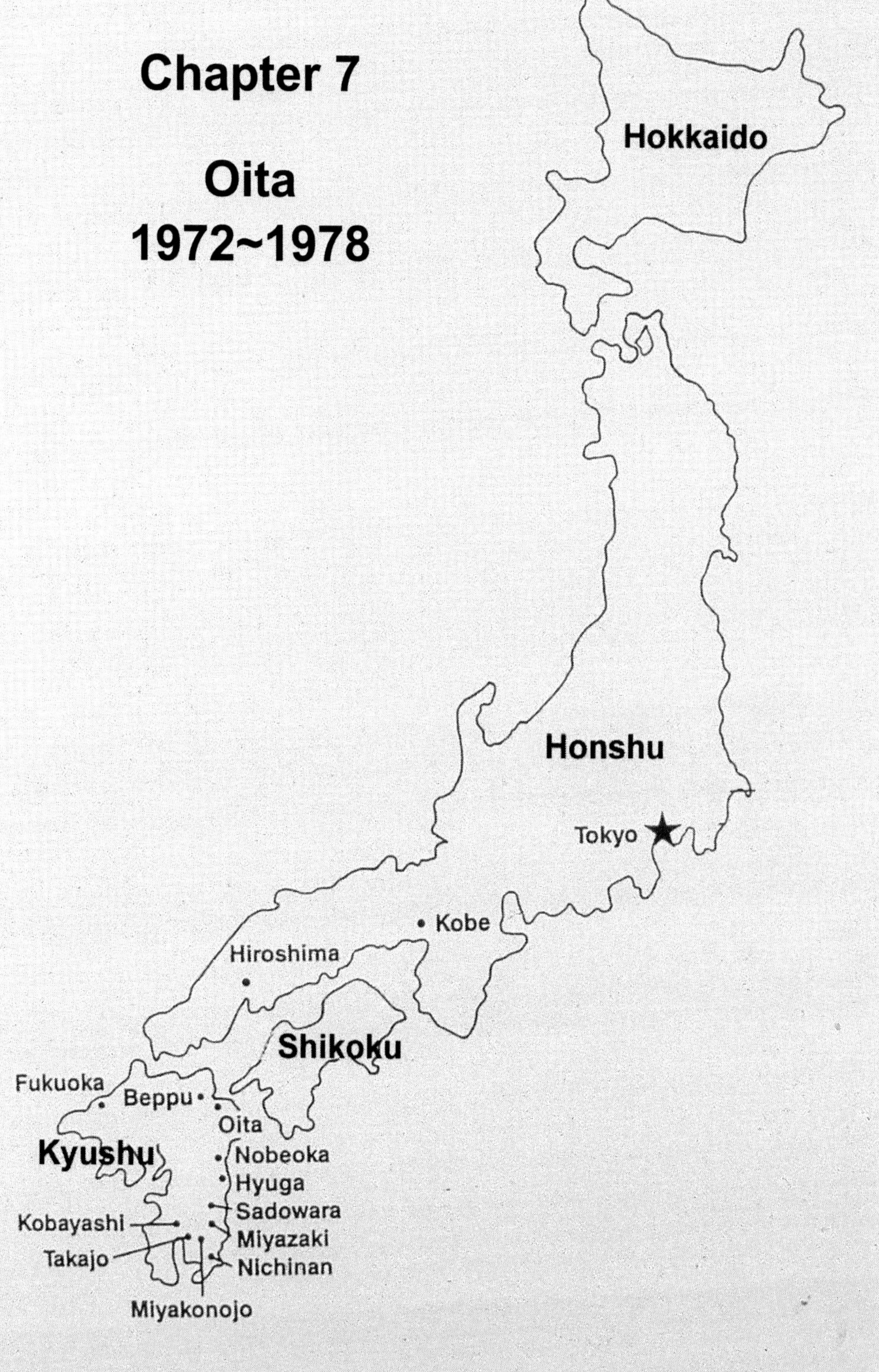
Chapter 7
Oita
1972~1978
Hokkaido
Honshu
Tokyo
Kobe
Hiroshima
Shikoku
Fukuoka
Beppu
Oita
Kyushu
Nobeoka
Hyuga
Sadowara
Kobayashi
Miyazaki
Takajo
Nichinan
Miyakonojo

HOME AGAIN

The sun was rising as we flew home to the Land of the Rising Sun for our fourth five-year term. Faithful Ferd met us at Haneda Airport at 6 AM. He took us to their tiny apartment in Tokyo. We were amazed that they found space to sleep! Thank God for mission family who took care of us along the way.

The next morning, we said good-bye to Rose, Bill and Wanda as they left for their boarding school, Christian Academy in Japan, in Tokyo. Our family of eight was suddenly reduced to three, Peter, Lily and me. We flew to Oita that day, Friday, September 1, 1972.

What a welcome at the Oita Airport! Three church young people took us home to a feast with 15 friends. The next day two came to help us settle. The same day Virginia Claassen, our former mission school teacher, arrived at our home in Oita from her furlough.

Sunday the SS kids sang ***Iesusama wa Ichiban****, Jesus is the greatest*, and welcomed us back. What a joy to see the church young people, some not even baptized yet, taking responsibility for the Sunday School. I had worked myself out of a job. One mission accomplished. Thank you, Lord!

The Kudo family had lived in our home during furlough. The house and yard were spic and span. The sisters, Misuzu, senior high and Hiromi, junior high, not only kept the church going, but new people were attending.

There was no time to readjust to the sixteen-hour time difference. Monday missionaries Fritz and Ellen Sprunger arrived by ferry with their parents for lunch. A few days later we helped Virginia move into an apartment two hours by car south of us. The church in Nobeoka had asked her to work with them. Virginia adjusted well to her role as missionary instead of teaching missionary children.

One day a beautiful photo of our six children arrived. That released a flood of tears! No time for self-pity. We needed to call on neighbors and friends to reconnect with our Japan family. Japanese usually don't show outward emotions. When Kurahashi San, a single woman who owned a tea shop in town, saw me, she ran into my arms. We were home!

On a hot and sticky September day, I did laundry, a major undertaking when you run it through the ringer spinner and hang it under the veranda roof to dry. We hauled our stuff out of the attic, welcomed church young people who dropped in, aired the bedding, and I biked to town for groceries. What a day! It took weeks to settle.

OUR CHILDREN

Meanwhile, Rick had returned for his second year at Wheaton College. Flooding had ruined the books that he had stored in a basement suite. His clothes were a mess and needed to be laundered or dry cleaned. No Mom or Dad around to help.

Rose, Bill and Wanda in boarding school in Tokyo, Rick in Wheaton, and Vangy at UBC in Vancouver all wrote letters faithfully. One week we received eight letters from the kids! Occasionally we had a big day – five letters from five kids!

Can you imagine the joy in our hearts when Wanda wrote: "... reading my Bible, talking to God, and singing for a long time." Rose wrote: "Mom, I like that verse, *'Look to Him and be radiant.'* Just yesterday I went past a beautiful blossoming cherry tree, and it made me smile and feel radiant. I thought that's how it is when we look up to Jesus, taking our minds off our problems. He makes us radiant and happy again."

Our mission board had a wonderful arrangement to help missionary families. They paid for one trip home for each college student whose parents were overseas missionaries. Vangy and Rickie came home to Japan in 1973 to complete our family of eight again. What a happy noisy household! Rick preached his first sermon one Sunday morning. In my diary I wrote, "Tremendous!" We enjoyed discussions and singing. Guitars, trumpet, violin and ukulele helped us *make a joyful noise unto the Lord.*

At the end of that summer, Vangy returned to UBC in Vancouver, and Rick to Wheaton College. Then Rosie, Bill and Wanda took off for Christian Academy in Tokyo. Rosie graduated the following spring and left for Canada. Even though she had Vangy to help her through the adjustment, she missed Japan.

Canada was not home. Japan was. When she and Vangy went for a walk in Grant Park next to Oma's, she cried out, "I hate Canada! I hate these trees!" However, soon she was writing positive letters, saying, "I'm not homesick yet." Then fearing she might have hurt our feelings, was quick to assure us, "But don't worry. I will be soon."

The day after her five siblings left for school, Lily entered the local kindergarten, and our home was empty. Empty! That was too sudden. I struggled with my role as mother. Why did I have to be deprived of my children for such long periods of time? It didn't help to think that Lily was also lonesome in kindergarten. It took time for this little foreigner to be accepted, especially since she was the only girl with fair hair and hazel eyes. We needed to draw strength from the Lord, knowing he had called us to serve him. How your prayers encouraged us.

There was no taking time off even with a bad cold. Guests kept coming, classes and meetings continued, shopping and cooking, cleaning and laundry were never ending, and eventually the colds healed!

Many Sundays the congregation, sometimes sixteen, stayed for lunch. Everybody pitched in with preparation and clean up. The meals were simple: pan-shoku, a bread meal. Two or three would head for the bakery and choose a variety of individual breads. Sometimes we slurped instant noodles, or enjoyed rice and curry prepared the day before.

Often the young people stayed until 7 PM. Two were excellent guitar players, and they loved to sing the new Gospel songs. Most of the kids had no Christian support at home, so they needed the extended church family.

HIGH SCHOOL EVANGELIST

The high school kids kept up enthusiasm for their Adam and Eve club. When a local high school was planning the annual cultural festival, they decided to take part. Yurika, a freshman who played guitar and sang well, bravely asked the teachers if she and her friends could sing Gospel folk. The immediate answer was "No. No religion allowed in school events." Yurika left crestfallen.

However, the idea persisted, and she thought, *If only*... A few days later, she determined to make another effort. Yurika had just dedicated her life to God at camp. God seemed to be speaking to her, *Now is your time. Why wait for the future*?

With a new spring in her step, she approached the teachers again. "Please let me sing for you. Won't you please listen," she begged? No harm in that. Yurika sang a favorite, a new Christian folk song.

The teachers liked what they heard. "Why, these songs are different than the usual Christian songs. They speak right to the needs of kids. We'll let you know." And with that she was dismissed.

The days dragged by. Less than a week to the festival. Saturday she was called to the office. (In Japan students attended school six days a week.) "You may have forty minutes for Gospel folk on the school grounds Thursday, and ten minutes for your performance at the grand program in the city auditorium Friday!"

"O, thank you! Thank you!" Yurika said. It took all her self-control to walk out of that office quietly and with dignity. Wow! Witnessing to over 1500 kids in their school!

The Adams and Eves were busy making fifty booklets of gospel folk songs, and later setting up sound equipment for the occasion. Yurika knew that her heart must be prepared, so she spent long hours every night reading her Bible and Rosalind Rinker's book, ***You Can Witness with Confidence.***

On the big day, Yurika struck some chords on her guitar, and began to sing. Soon a crowd gathered, and her church friends passed out song books, inviting them to sing along. When some began to leave, Yurika called out, "Don't leave! Please don't leave!" How could you forsake a pleading fellow student?

Next day Yurika was on the stage alone. Nearly 1,500 spot lights danced before her eyes. A welcome quiet pervaded the auditorium after the ear-splitting rock group performance. Her fingers rippled over the keys and Yurika burst into song -

I am singing a new song / that Jesus gave to me.
with my new heart /Jesus chained me
with my new mind / with the chain unbreakable.
for a new purpose / for he chained me
I am singing a new song / with the chain of love.

with the new experience / I cannot go back to my old ways...
with the new life / for He chained me with the chain of love.

Yurika sang on and closed her performance with a word of praise for her homeroom, bringing wild cheering from that section. "Sayonara, sayonara!" and the curtain fell. "And thank you Jesus," she whispered.

CHRISTMAS HIGHLIGHTS

Christmas parcels for overseas had to be sent in mid-November so that Vangy and Rick would get theirs on time. We eagerly waited for Christmas parcels from home, too. Peter's mother always sent gifts for each of us including my favorite, her fruitcake. After mother died, Tina Loewen, a dear friend from our home church, sent home-made fruitcake every Christmas. Tina shared her recipe which I used for four special occasions in Japan. But that story is for another day!

Best of all was sharing the Christmas message of the Savior with the largest crowds of the year. Christmas was the best time for evangelism. The rampant commercialism made people curious about Christmas. The angels brought *...good tidings of great joy...Unto you is born this day a Savior, which is Christ the Lord."* What glorious news to share with Japan.

That joy was multiplied seven times at Christmas,1973! Machiko's father and six young people, Shigeyuki, Osamu, Eishiro, Kayoko, and our twins, Bill and Wanda, were baptized. A rare occurrence with five men. What a day of rejoicing! Now our family had five members in the Oita church. Vangy had been baptized in Hyuga, Rick, Rose and now Bill and Wanda in Oita. Our cup of blessing was running over! Oita was a church made up of mostly young people. Energy plus!

One of our Christmas traditions was sending Christmas greetings to three hundred supporters in Canada and the US. Peter's sister Erna and husband Jake in Abbotsford copied our letters and mailed them. One year we sent out a greeting written by Lily, using the word CHRISTMAS for her poem.

C *– Christ was born!*
H *– Hallelujah!*
R *– Rejoice!*
I *– It's wonderful!*
S *–Sounds of bells ring!*
T *–Tell to everyone!*
M *–Message of salvation*
A *–All the world*
S *-Sing His praises!*

TRADITIONS

On New Year's Eve Japanese eat a hot noodle soup at midnight. No one goes to bed early, and our family was no exception. Bill would open the window at midnight and play his trumpet to the world! No one complained! One New Year's Day we were at the breakfast table when an international call came from Vangy and Rick who were spending Christmas with Oma and Opa Derksen in Abbotsford, BC. What a special beginning for the New Year! Although we couldn't see each other, we could talk together.

January 15 every city and town held big celebrations for young adults who turned twenty during the past year. Young ladies wore beautiful kimono, while most of the men wore western suits and ties. We drove around town enjoying the beauty and taking pictures of the rainbow colored ladies. At the ceremony the young adults were told of their new responsibilities and were challenged to be good examples. Sadly, many used their new privilege for drinking sprees.

KIMONO ACCORDING TO COLOSSIANS 3:14

The kimono is not simply slipped on like a dress. Dressing is a complicated, time-consuming affair. The kimono is a loose garment open all the way down the front. The obi is the band that ties it together at the waist. Seven different ties complete the obi.

In our English version of Colossians 3:14, we are simply told *And over all these virtues put on love, which binds them all together in perfect unity.* In the Japanese Bible we are told to put on the *obi* of love, *which ties everything together in perfect unity.* The kimono is useless without the obi. In the same way, we need God's obi of love to be useful in building the Kingdom of God in our world.

LILY, MADE IN JAPAN

Three little girls, including Lily, and two boys, all lived on the same dead-end street. When they were babies, we mothers often chatted outdoors, babes in arms. Jun Chan became Lily's best friend. The family was so accepting of Lily, that when we had to attend conferences, we sometimes left Lily with them. It was a happy arrangement.

Lily says, "My best memories of Oita are playing with Jun Chan and Kumi Chan. It was wonderful to grow up with them and play on the street with the other kids, too. I enjoyed the stray cats and dogs we had. Some died, and we buried them in our yard."

Our five older children had all attended our mission boarding school away from home. However, the school closed long before Lily was ready for school. We had always dreamt of trying the Japanese school system. This was our opportunity. Peter and I decided to send Lily, our youngest, to the local schools.

Lily and her four neighboring friends started kindergarten together. The three little girls Jun Chan, Kumi Chan and Yuri Chan, (Lily) marched down the street hand in hand in their blue smocks, blue tams perched saucily on their heads.

Soon it was obvious that I would be learning more than the kids. Almost every day Lily brought notes from the teacher. I could not read them, so I checked with my neighbors to see what the school wanted.

Instructions! How the children had to brush their teeth, how much allowance they could have; they tried to keep it balanced so the kids from rich homes would not be getting much more than the poorer ones. On a certain day mothers should all come to clean the classroom windows. Once a month parents were allowed to observe their children in the classroom. Teacher's not only taught the kids but the parents!

On kindergarten graduation day mothers all wore black kimono with the family insignia on the back. Fathers wore suits. Moms and Dads came armed with white handkerchiefs. I couldn't escape the emotional tugs surrounding me; the tears came. Yes, Lily graduated from kindergarten and kept right on going.

Our little neighborhood kids were all in the same first grade with over 400 other youngsters in their school of more than 1000 children. Each classroom averaged 40 or more and had only one teacher. Elementary children did not wear uniforms unless they were in a private school.

The change from kindergarten to elementary school was drastic. Now she was beset with name calling. Gaijin, Gaijin, foreigner! One day several boys chased her, knocked her book bag off her back, and ran away. She quickly collected her scattered books and ran home, falling into my arms sobbing and shaking.

Distraught and worried, I visited the principal the next day. He called a school assembly, addressing the problem. He said, "Lily was born right here in Oita, and is just as much a Japanese as you are. No one will call her 'gaijin' again." Problem solved.

Picnics! Everyone loves picnics, right? But nothing was just for fun. Every new school year began with a picnic. This was the best way to get to know your new classmates. Ah, yes, classmates were rotated, so in a class of 40, there might be two or three that you knew from your previous class.

Another big reason for picnics was to challenge physical health. Lily's doryoku pi-ku-ni-ku, or effort picnic, was a seven-kilometer walk taking four hours, two each way. Students had two hours for lunch and play. When Lily got home from those picnics, she dropped exhausted, too tired to move.

Lily made it her job to recruit classmates for Sunday School, and succeeded in bringing 26. A few mothers came to women's meetings in church. Having a child in the local Japanese school was great for outreach.

Schools play a big role in society. Each mother had to sign up for one of many clubs the school organized. This would ensure that everyone would have friends in the community. Since I enjoyed singing, I joined the Mama Chorus. I loved the many Japanese folk songs which I would not have learned otherwise. Best of all, I made many new friends.

The Japanese Mombusho, the education system, was in charge of schools. Music was a big part of the curriculum. All children had equal opportunities in music. In grade one every child learned to play the recorder, in grade two the pianica, a mini piano that you carried in your hands, and for sound you blew into a tube connected to the pianica, and in following years, they could choose a violin or other string or wind instrument. The school supplied the instruments free on loan. For school functions, they had an instant orchestra, with hundreds of grade one's playing recorders.

Sports were the life of every school. Students practised months for the annual fall undokai, sports festival. Moms rose early to prepare fancy lunches for the family. Fathers and kids hurried to the huge school playground early to claim a space for their picnic blanket.

The school divided students into four camps. Competition for first place was fierce! All kids wore colored headbands according to their camp: red, white, blue or green. Parents and grandparents joined the cheerleaders and by the end of the day all were hoarse.

Undokai was always on a Sunday unless it rained. Since Sunday was the church worship day, we went for the afternoon. If it rained, it was postponed to the next good weather day. That suited us fine.

A cousin, who had spent ten years in concentration camps in Siberia because of his Christian faith, had been released and was visiting churches in Japan. One cold winter day we passed the school where Lily and her classmates were having PE outside. He was shocked to see the hundreds of girls wearing short bloomers and short sleeves. "That is torture!" he said. It was our turn to be shocked because we knew that he had been severely tortured in Russian prisons.

CHURCH CAMPS

Our favorite summer activity was attending Camp Aoidake, our church conference camp in the mountains between Miyazaki and Miyakonojo cities. The churches planned camps for children, youth, and families. How refreshing to breathe the cool mountain air! Excitement filled the camp at arrival time, wondering which friends would come from the other churches.

In the afternoon kids hurried down the mountain for a cold swim in the river. By the time they hiked back up, they were hot and sweaty again. Everybody helped with dishes and clean-up. Evenings we sang and shared testimonies around the campfire. At camp we met God and grew in our faith. Many young people made decisions to follow Jesus. After the evening sharing, it was off to bed, but usually not to sleep! The men and boys stayed in cabins, and the women and girls and babies slept on the floor in a large tatami room. The cold-water showers cooled us quickly! Year after year a large old frog outside croaked us to sleep.

We hosted a camp in our home for kids that couldn't go to Aoidake. Eight boys stayed with us, and eleven girls stayed at Virginia's for night. We enjoyed Bible lessons, singing, playing and eating. What a thrill that parents who didn't even come to church trusted their kids with us.

MISSIONARY KIDS AND FRIENDS

Marilyn Carter, Rick's girlfriend, a Wheaton College student, was on a summer mission trip in Tokyo. She added a visit to our home. What a special young lady! While visiting, she kept her hands busy knitting. She never finished her project, but later I received a beautiful afghan and pillow she had knit for me. Marilyn loved the Lord, and we loved Marilyn. We toured Monkey Mountain, Marine Palace and showed off our city. When Marilyn left, the family piled into our car to see her off at the airport.

The growing church in Oita was a challenge but also a source of great joy. Most of the congregation was made up of eager young people. Many came to church through friendship with our kids during summer vacation.

Summer jobs kept the family busy. Rick was on a construction crew building a new bridge across the Oita River. He was earning money for a motorcycle. A few weeks after he quit, the bridge collapsed, killing two men he had been working with. What a shock!

In the meantime, Rick had bought a motorcycle, met his friend Gary, and they wound through Japan, including Fukushima, where the monster tsunami struck many years later. Rick tried to sell his motorcycle after the trip, but without success. Dad was left with that job long after Rick had returned for his third year at Wheaton.

SHIGEYUKI

When Rick went to get his motorcycle licence, he met Shigeyuki. who farmed with his parents an hour's drive into the mountains. Shigeyuki had spent a year in the US and was fairly good in English. Sometimes he came to visit. However, I thought he was just interested in practicing English. How often I make hasty judgments.

Shigeyuki began attending English Bible classes and worship services and became a friend to all. He made a decision to follow Christ and was baptized. He took his faith seriously. His sister-in-law was dying of cancer; he believed that God would heal her if he prayed in faith, even though she wasn't a Christian. The next time he came, he shared that she had improved enough to sit up in bed. The following week she was walking and was released from the hospital with a new lease on life. What an encouragement for this new Christian and for us!

He also persuaded his parents to read the Bible with him. They listened to Christian radio tapes. When his mother was sick, he prayed in faith, and the Lord gave healing. His father made a decision to believe in his son's God!

Soon Shigeyuki was teaching Sunday School. The added bonus was that in summer he took the SS children to camp in an abandoned house on his farm in the mountains. The steep climb down the path to the old house would have made a good slide on a rainy day. We slept on mats on the floor. I could hear the monstrous cockroaches running by my head! I'm sure those camps will never be forgotten by teachers or kids. What a treat when Shigeyuki piled all the kids on the back of his pickup for a swim in the river.

I helped where help was needed and landed in the kitchen. The farm kitchen had a dirt floor. Cooking pots rested on a stove that was fired with wood on floor level. The living area was a high step up from the kitchen. We sat at low tables on the floor to eat. After my first day I wondered if I would ever be able to straighten my back again. No wonder so many Japanese obaachans, grandmas, had bent backs.

Looking over the valleys and mountains beyond, the farm became a natural setting to teach the children about our Creator God and his Son Jesus Christ.

Campfires were special times for the 42 children that summer. Tender hearts were open. A fourth grader told her mother, "Okaasan, (mother) I became a Christian at the camp fireside." Mother and daughter were both in church the following Sunday.

At our next worship meeting, Shigeyuki read some of the notes the kids had written. "The hike was almost too difficult. Then I remembered how Jesus carried the heavy cross for me."

Another wrote, "I had wanted to become a Christian for a long time, so I was very happy that I could become one at camp." Sunday School mushroomed.

The churches in Japan had many single girls, but single men were scarce! Shigeyuki was single, but he was a farmer. Yoko from the Hyuga church was a music major in college. Yoko had come to high school English classes in our home when her father was mayor of Hyuga city. When she visited us in Oita, she caught Shigeyuki's eye. Oh, no! That might not work we thought. But he prayed and persisted. He won out! It was a happy ending, but we were sorry that we had to miss their wedding because we were on furlough!

Living in the country was a far cry from the city life that Yoko was used to. She was also the oyome, bride, daughter-in-law living with Shigeyuki's parents, which is normal in Japan. After both parents died of cancer, Shigeyuki decided to change his occupation in midlife. They sold the cattle and moved to the big city of Fukuoka where he took nurse's training in a Christian hospital/hospice. Yoko taught piano to support the family. Shigeyuki became a very devoted hospice nurse in Eiko, (Glory) Christian Hospital in Fukuoka.

YUKO

Vangy taught English classes. One of her students, Yuko, began attending church services. One Sunday church was exceptionally full. Our kids were attracting more young people. We always served Japanese tea and snacks after a service. Vangy was quite busy talking to Yuko, so I leaned over (we sat on cushions on the floor) to ask for help in the kitchen. Usually she would jump up and help without the nudge, but she said, "Mom, this is very important!"

Yuko had been attending the One World Unification religion but could not find rest for her restless spirit. She was searching for peace. This Sunday she found what she had been searching for and gave her heart to the Lord right there among all the noisy chatter surrounding them. Yuko and Vangy were both first year university students, so they had much in common. Now they were also sisters in the Lord.

Yuko's joy was overwhelming. She couldn't keep quiet about her new faith. She printed 100 invitations for a Bible study on campus. On a cold windy November morning she stood at the entrance of Oita University handing out invitations to students as they passed by. As the gusts of wind blew her long black hair across her face, she prayed,

"Lord, please send at least one student back to check it out." Her face lit up as one returned to ask what this was about. God had answered her sincere prayer.

Yuko started a Bible study on campus. As time went on, students from other churches came. They asked their pastors to help. Peter also took his turn. The university allowed them to meet in a classroom, and the group continued to grow.

The following spring Yuko was baptized, followed by others from the university group. We always encouraged students from other churches to be faithful to their own church.

Yuko came for special evening meetings in our church. One night when she returned home, her parents had locked her out. Many years later she discovered that her grandmother, who lived with them, had at one time been baptized in a Christian church.

Japan Kirisuto Gakkusei Kai organization in Osaka, Japan, similar to Canada's Intervarsity Christian Fellowship, asked Yuko to help with summer camps. KGK planned summer camps for the Oita students. The following year the camp was held at Oita's youth centre for four days, attended by 70 university students.

Among them were students who played guitar. They loved to sing the new gospel folk songs like ***Tomo Yo, Utau,*** Friends Let's Sing. An idea took shape. Why not have a Gospel rally at the university? Invitations went out to churches. A huge poster on campus announced the rally. High school kids weren't going to be left out. It's hard to capture the joy that this event brought to these new Christian students.

When KGK discovered what a stable Christian Yuko was, they asked her to start the first KGK on Kyushu Island, one of the four major islands in Japan, after her graduation. The headquarters would be in Fukuoka City on the northwest coast of Kyushu. Thus began a cycle of Christian witness in universities throughout Kyushu. Summer camps, meetings and churches got involved, all because of one student's decision to follow the Lord.

In 1977, Yuko graduated from Oita University with a degree in education. On March 27, the Oita Mennonite Christian Church had the joy of commissioning Yuko to full-time service with KGK. The congregation was moved as many joined to lay hands on Yuko. After the last Amen, tears flowed freely.

A university professor and lay pastor, Tojo Sensei, took notice of Yuko. Although her parents opposed her choice, Yuko and Takanobu had a beautiful Christian wedding. They moved to Tokyo where Tojo Sensei taught in a university and also pastored a church.

In 2013 Yuko and a friend came to Canada to thank the churches for sending missionaries to Japan. How special to have Yuko visit us in Abbotsford, BC after our retirement. Yuko brought a gift from her mother who had been opposed to Christianity. Yuko shared her testimony during the adult SS class and also the worship service, which happened to be youth Sunday. The church heard first-hand one of the results of their years of prayers and offerings for overseas missions! Perhaps some youth were challenged to follow the Lord wherever He might lead, as Yuko had.

INOUE FAMILY

The church was thrilled to have a new family in church. Our children taught their children English. Alas, two years later the father was transferred back to Tokyo. We kept in touch and discovered Yuka's many talents. She wrote children's books and played the harp. Her daughter became a famous harpist giving concerts throughout the world.

One year the daughter played harp in a concert in Vancouver. We were retired and living in Abbotsford, BC. What a thrill when the Inoue's came to visit and took us to their daughter's concert. Yuka had cancer and knew her time was limited. "I think I could be a Christian," she confided. They had to leave, but we trusted God to finish the work the Holy Spirit had begun in their lives.

HAPPY BIRTHDAY

Friends in Abbotsford, BC, had surprised me with a birthday party on furlough. Japan usually didn't celebrate adult birthdays. There would be no celebration this year, and I was feeling lonely and sorry for myself.

Then the doorbell rang, and there stood three beaming friends, Tomoko, our school teacher Virginia's neighbor, Izumi, and Yuka. All were seekers attending our small church. In unison they called out "Otanjobi omedeto gozaimasu," happy birthday in Japanese, and set down a beautifully wrapped gift. I was so overwhelmed that I just collapsed on the floor and cried.

Finally realizing that they were still in the genkan, entrance, I invited them in. In Japan you don't open gifts in front of the giver, but I asked them to make an exception. Carefully I unwrapped the gift and opened the box. Slowly I took out a large brown flower vase with a simple elegant design. A short teardrop was running from a narrow neck, and a longer teardrop slid across its bulging stomach with more teardrops on the other side. It must have come from a famous pottery shop. Now this vase has a special spot on the family antique organ in our retirement townhouse in Abbotsford.

FAMILY WEDDINGS 1975

Vangy and Rick were not idle in their relationships. Vangy met Ernie Thiessen at Intervarsity Christian Fellowship meetings in UBC. A weekend IVCF retreat became quite special, until both attended Urbana in the US. There Vangy thought God was calling her to be a single missionary to Japan. When she told Oma Derksen in BC. Oma asked her, "Do you know what you're doing?"

When Vangy wrote us about her calling, Dad asked her the same question! "Do you know what you're doing?" On second thought, they began dating again. Then Ernie wrote a letter asking for our permission to marry Vangy. How could we refuse such a gentle polite young man, even though we had never met him?

Rick and Marilyn were also talking about marriage. In a visit to Marilyn's home, they had a good conservation with her parents about their hopes and dreams.

Our Japanese friends were quite concerned that we would allow our daughter to marry a man we had never met. They thought it was irresponsible of us. They also wished me to receive a good oyome san, daughter-in-law. In Japan it was still common for parents to arrange the marriage or to ask friends to find suitable partners for their children. Our Father in heaven did the arranging for us. What a great job!

Both couples were very considerate and planned their weddings a week apart to make it easier for us to attend. But when we sat down and took a look at our finances, we decided only one could go. How could we make such a difficult decision? We prayed. Before they knew of our problem, a sister and her husband came to the rescue. They offered to pay fare for one, but only if both were going. Thank you, Lord, and thank you Hilda and Colin!

When we finally had it all figured out, there was enough to take nine-year-old Lily, too. Oh, joy! Rose was attending UBC that year, so that left out Bill and Wanda, seventeen. Not only did they have summer jobs at Mister Donuts, but they agreed to be in charge of the church during our absence.

Wedding dates loomed. Vangy and Ernie set their wedding for August 2, 1975, and Rick and Marilyn for August 9, 1975. Sounded good, but there was a slight hitch. The weddings were a continent apart, the first in Abbotsford, BC, Vangy and Ernie's hometown, and the second in Elmira, New York, Marilyn's home town. Of course, both couples wanted Dad to marry them. Our plans suddenly changed when Vangy asked me to sew her wedding dress! Wait! I had enough trouble getting used to my new Brother sewing machine. Could I handle a different one? It also meant that I needed at least a month for such a big job. She was our daughter, and the first one getting married. How could I refuse?

WEDDINGS

I left a month early, and Wanda became head cook at home in Japan. When Peter and I were young, men didn't get involved in the kitchen. Peter's family didn't even allow the men of the family into the kitchen!

Soon I flew into the arms of our children in Canada. Vangy had graduated from UBC a year earlier, was teaching in Vancouver, and had an apartment. It was summer vacation, and Rick, who had just graduated from Wheaton College, had a summer job in Vancouver. Rose was also living with Vangy, so here I was in Canada with three of our children. How blessed I was!

My big concern was the sewing machine. Would I be able to use a sewing machine I didn't know? What an answer to prayer when I saw that Vangy had borrowed a Brother, exactly like mine! Our first task was to buy a pattern and material. When I saw the pattern Vangy chose, I worried again. The little pleats across the bodice looked so complicated. Next we shopped for material, and I wondered. But she was the bride and my oldest daughter, so I agreed to her choices. Wonder of wonders, it all happened. Beautifully!

Peter and Lily arrived on July 28. A minor problem arose. No men had beards in our family, at least, not until then. Lily had quite an aversion to beards and ostracized Ernie and Rick who had both started growing beards!

What excitement in the Derksen home. The wedding took place on August 2 in the Ebenezer Mennonite Church in Abbotsford, where Uncle Jake was pastor. In those days, everybody, including the bride and groom, sat for the long service. A general invitation had gone to our home church and many friends. The church was full. The Lord blessed us through Peter's message, the vows, and the songs of Vangy's friends. She had requested that I sing a solo, and I chose ***O, Lord, Most Holy***, which I had sung at my sister's wedding. Church ladies helped with food for the reception in the church basement. God had taken care of all the details. Beautiful!

On Monday, August the 4, Peter, Rick, Rose, Lily and I left in Rick's van for the long cross- country trip to Elmira, New York for Rick and Marilyn's wedding. Four drivers took turns driving and sleeping on the mattress in the back. We dropped Rick off at O'Hare International Airport, so he could fly to Elmira to give him and Marilyn time together before the wedding. The rest of us arrived just in time for the barbeque with family and friends in the Carter's garden the day before the wedding.

Rick and Marilyn made a last-minute decision to have Lily for a flower girl. A shopping trip brought no results, except that I bought a yard of pretty pink to add a wide frill to her lovely white dress. I was frantically sewing until midnight.

The outdoor wedding was August 9, at 8 AM at the Hilltop Restaurant on Jerusalem Hill overlooking Elmira. Wrapped in early morning fog, several of us searched the fields for Queen Ann's lace and other wild flowers for the tables. The mist gradually gave way to sparkling sunshine. White chairs on the lawn were soon filled with 130 wedding guests. As Marilyn's friends played guitar and flute, Peter and I walked the green cushioned aisle with Richard. We turned to welcome Lily scattering flower petals for the bride, and then a beaming Marilyn with parents, Mary and Dave Carter.

Brunch was served at beautiful tables in the restaurant garden. During the meal, Mary Carter shared the funny story about Rick and Marilyn's first meeting. Nature added its praise with interludes of singing birds surrounding us. All too soon the weddings ended, and so did our short summer furlough.

Bill and Wanda had kept the home fires burning, literally. Wanda told me years later that she had accidentally spilled scalding water on her hand, which was very painful. She hid it well. I hadn't even taught the kids the basics of baking soda on burns. She never went to the doctor, and Dad never found out. During our absence they made many new friends and developed a close relationship with the church people.

And Lily? When she returned to school in Japan with homework piled up, she rebelled. "I'm going to quit school and get married," she said. One month in Canada had loosed her English-speaking tongue considerably, and she no longer spoke only Japanese to us. Now we were all bilingual!

BUSY YEAR

Busy became a meaningless word. Visitors added spice to life. Family was always special. My sister Hilda, husband Colin, and their toddler Susan got an enthusiastic welcome from our family of six. Rose was home from Goshen College. This was Bill and Wanda's last summer before college. A guest family from the US, popping with questions that kept our minds and hearts going, were warmly received by our family.

Then Stephen and Barick from India came. In the morning I asked Stephen if he had a good night. With a broad smile he said, "Oh, yes. I have the peace of Christ in my mind and the joy of Christ in my heart!" That kept me going for days.

English classes continued. I served ocha, tea, to every guest and every class. We learned to appreciate this typical Japanese custom, no matter how often I had to heat water. Actually, in summer it was fine to serve cold tea.

One day Hilda said, "Mary, this is like Grand Central Station. How can you stand it?"

Japan was constantly making changes, and Kyushu railways entered a new era. Amid sad farewells and bouquets, Oita Eki, the station, paid its last tribute to an old friend, the *Takachiho*, name of the train that plied between southern Japan and the big metropolises of Osaka and Tokyo. Probably no other country could make me feel actually sad to see the end of the slow dirty old train that still belched black soot! The *Tokaido* line opened its tracks between Hakata and Tokyo. Now we could get to Tokyo from Oita in seven hours and forty minutes. People slept in the station all night at Hakata station just to be the first to get on the new Hikari, Light, train! Japan kept on fascinating us.

HIGHLIGHT

In August 1976, we celebrated our twenty-fifth wedding anniversary. Thirty-six, including our family of six, enjoyed a wonderful time of singing, sharing, and enjoying a meal with the church. We were sorry that Vangy and Ernie, and Rick and Marilyn couldn't be home that summer. Phone calls were reserved for emergencies, so no overseas calls, but we spent a relaxing day listening to the tapes they had sent. Rose, Wanda, Bill and Lily made a special meal served in style as they waited on us. We were as proud as they were of their beautiful and delicious accomplishments.

Shigeyuki's family invited our family to the farm for a night. It was probably the only time they ever hosted a foreign family! We made a side trip to the Oita Safari to check out the wild animals living in our community. My terror of wild animals surfaced briefly. I did wonder what would happen in case of an earthquake!

The summer ended abruptly when we took Rose, Bill and Wanda to the airport to return to Canada and the US. Rose returned to Goshen College, and joined Goshen's overseas program where they took students by bus to Florida, from where they flew to Costa Rica for a three-month homestay. Our family was scattered in five countries: Vangy and Ernie in Canada, Rick and Marilyn in Belgium studying French for a year before going to Zaire as long-term missionaries, Rose in Costa Rica, Bill and Wanda in Wheaton, IL, and Lily keeping us happy in Japan.

Vangy and Ernie presented us with our first grandchild, Jayden, on September 22, 1976. We were happy, but I wasn't so sure that I was ready to be labelled Oma, grandmother. That changed when we met Jayden and spent as much time as possible with our new family member. Oh joy, what a blessing!

FILM MEETINGS

Japan is a movie going nation, and Christian films were a wonderful way to attract people. We started churches in our homes, but for special meetings we rented facilities. Junji Sasaki was first attracted to Christianity as a high school student when he watched ***The Ten Commandments*** in a theatre. He was so impressed, that he watched the same movie several times. Not knowing anything about Christianity, he decided he was going to be an evangelist. One day he dragged five friends to visit the foreigners in his city. Usually when high school students came to our door they asked, *Please teach us English*. Junji asked, "Please teach us about the love of God."

Junji became a devoted Christian. He brought a happy atmosphere into the church. Junji felt God's call to attend a Bible college in Tokyo. His parents paid us a visit and bowing to the floor (we always sat on the floor), implored us with tears to stop their son. What chance did he have in life as a pastor? We told them it was not up to us to make that decision. "If God calls him, God will take care of him," we said. Junji went to Bible College.

The Oita church nurtured many young people. Four young men became pastors, and two young ladies became pastors' wives. Of course, not all at the same time. What joy and challenge for the church.

After a movie in church, a high school senior shyly handed us a letter written in English. "A few days I don't feel lonesome," he wrote. "Rather my heart is calm. The sky and mountains that are seen through the windows of the school bring me some meaning that I have never found. As I said, I had not been able to believe in God and his miracles. To tell the truth, even now I don't know how faith to God and the miracles harmonize with various things, such as scientific knowledge. But I want to believe it! And you said with confidence, 'God is! What the Bible says is true.' Those sounds went to my heart. I will try to gain faith more and more. Please help me to do so."

Another student wrote: "Thank you so much for letting me see such a wonderful film. To tell the truth, before I met you I was indifferent towards Christianity. However, after hearing from you, I came to believe, although still vaguely. Through the film the other day I understood how much Jesus suffered in bearing our sins and dying for us. I am grateful to God and also want to thank you for leading me to the joy of faith."

I believe one of the best ways to reach out in evangelism is friendship. No, our neighbors didn't all become Christians, but living in the neighborhood changed the atmosphere of indifference to acceptance and friendship. Many came to special meetings. God's seed was planted, and He will bring it to fruition.

Ladies were eager to learn western cooking, so I started a monthly class. After a devotional, we cooked and baked, and enjoyed the fruit of our labors. Baking was not a Japanese tradition. Dessert for them was usually fruit or steamed cakes. Most families did not have ovens. However, due to western influence, small ones were available. The ladies were quite surprised to see our western oven. We also cooked borscht, pluma mousse, made salads, and katleten, hamburgers, that they had eaten at our table. Finally, I ran out of ideas and said, "O.K. Now it's your turn. I want to learn Japanese cooking, too!" Then they took turns making their favorite Japanese foods.

OHTA

The church had a big group of high school, college and university students. A few faithful adults helped to stabilize the church. Periodically I would make the rounds of our neighborhood to pass out tracts and get acquainted. Children were coming to SS, and I wanted to meet their parents.

The Ohta family lived one street over. Their son and daughter attended SS. One day the father, a medical doctor, suddenly became sick and died. I visited Ohta San, expressing my sympathy. She was in shock. A few days later I went again and read some comforting words from the Bible. Ohta San followed my invitation to church. The ladies in church became her friends, and she kept coming.

However, one Sunday she said, "I cannot become a Christian. That would take a miracle, because I can't forgive my mother-in-law for the terrible way she treated me when I married her son and lived in her home. Now she is a complete invalid, and I have to take care of her." Since her deceased husband was the chonan, oldest son, she was also responsible for worshipping fourteen generations of ancestors.

Ohta San liked her church friends and kept coming. One Sunday during testimony time she said, "The miracle has happened! I can forgive my mother-in-law!" She was ready to follow Christ and was soon baptized. In her new enthusiasm, she bought two hundred Gospels to give friends and clients. End of nice story? Not quite.

When the church began to talk about inviting a Japanese pastor, she quit. In her mind, financial burdens stretched unending. I took the weekly church bulletins to her and kept up friendship but was ready to give up. Suddenly she reappeared in church and said, "The Lord has been speaking to me, and now I am ready to even give up my daily cup of coffee to help the church!" A good lesson – never give up!

TOSHIKO

Toshiko began attending church while still in high school. She was interested in English, so she came to English Bible class faithfully. Then she started attending worship services. However, she did not want to make a quick decision to become a Christian. After high school graduation, she took nurse's training. It took six years of searching before she finally decided Christ was for her.

Toshiko was not satisfied with being an ordinary nurse. Her tender heart was touched by the great needs in the world, especially in Africa. She found a government program where she could serve in Malawi, Africa.

When Toshiko returned from Malawi, she explained her Christian faith to her mother. They began to study The Apostle's Creed, checking the Bible for references. God as Creator captured interest as they read the creation story from Genesis. Through a thorough study of the Creed, God opened her mother's heart, and she became a Christian. Fully convinced that our Creator God was truly God, she said, "I don't need my gods anymore!"

Meanwhile, Toshiko kept on studying midwifery. As an expert in maternal and child health welfare, she was selected for a Japanese government overseas program in Sri Lanka. After Sri Lanka, Toshiko studied in the US at Tulane University's graduate school, where she got a master's degree in Public Health and Tropical Medicine. She went to Ghana in Africa for four years. Toshiko fulfilled her childhood dreams of helping people in underdeveloped countries. Now Toshiko has returned to her home city of Oita and is a strong supporter in the Oita Mennonite Christian Church.

OUTREACH

The ***Adam and Eve*** club attracted more students. Yuko's university class also brought new students to church. Four young people were teaching SS. The Christians were witnessing to their families.

One Easter the SS teachers took to the streets with the children. A parade! The idea kept mushrooming, and the kids got excited and began making placards. On a Sunday afternoon they marched in the neighbor-hood, some playing recorders, followed by 30 lively kids and teachers. We paraded around a park, singing favorite S.S. songs. The Pied Piper of Hamelin would have been proud of this following. By the time we got back to church, 80 youngsters squeezed into the rooms without walls to watch a Christian kids' movie, followed by a special treat. What a boost for the Sunday School.

Another Easter Sunday, Sunday School teachers and children walked to a park by the beach for breakfast, and then performed Christ's resurrection story. The children loved it. Those who heard the Easter story for the first time asked, "Did Jesus really come alive?"

The church tried to keep contact with each Christian and seeker. Occasionally someone who had made a sincere effort, or even decision to follow Christ, quit. A few said, "Leave me alone!" Even a Sunday School teacher reneged. What a blow! That did not stop the church from praying for them. Zephaniah 3: 17-l9 gave us courage to keep on; *Though the fig tree does not bud and there are no grapes on the vines, though the olive crop fails and the fields produce no food, though there are no sheep in the pen and no cattle in the stalls, yet I will rejoice in the Lord, I will be joyful in God my Savior. The sovereign Lord is my strength; he makes my feet like the feet of a deer, he enables me to go on the heights.*

Walls and doors came down during evangelistic meetings, and the rooms were packed with people night after night. 80 people signed cards indicating interest, and 33 made decisions for Christ. A new Christian stared in disbelief as his mother, sister and her husband, and cousin responded. Impossible. His brother-in-law was a communist! His mother burned her fire god the next day. One youth said, "I believed in miracles before, but now I really believe in them!"

Japan Steel, the world's second largest steel company, built a mammoth plant in Oita city. This brought new families to the area. Michiko (pseudonym), wife of an executive, started attending English Bible class.

She was a Christian and brought a dozen friends to the evangelistic meetings. Some made decisions for Christ. We know from experience that initial decisions do not always lead to a lasting commitment. Jesus indicated this in his parable of the sower and the seed.

Company families lived in a new housing area of Oita. There was no church nearby, so Michiko invited us to have meetings in her home. Neighbors and friends came. We looked forward to this happy monthly outreach.

Big companies in Japan transfer many of their workers every few years. A number of those, attending the outreach in Michiko's home, moved to Tokyo. We connected with them again after our retirement when we made two visits to Japan. Each time these women and their husbands hosted us in their company's exclusive restaurant and kept us in their homes for night. We continue our contacts with them through Email.

After evangelistic meetings when our doors and walls were in place again, Lily said, "Why can't we leave the rooms like that all the time?"

A PASTOR

Church members began taking on more responsibility. After years of prayer and financial giving, the Oita Mennonite Christian Church purchased the mission building. It was time to pass the baton to a Japanese pastor. Another furlough loomed on the horizon. However, the church couldn't wait years for a pastor, they needed one now.

In Japan it is a great blessing when a man with a family feels called to the ministry. It also means a tremendous sacrifice – their job, moving to a big city with family for Bible College, and cutting family ties. Non-Christian parents are not in favor when their sons give up jobs for very unpredictable, to them, meaningless work that is not recognized in normal society. There were never enough graduates in the Bible colleges of Japan to fill the need for pastors.

Shozo and Emi Sato packed up their two children and moved to Tokyo where Shozo enrolled in Bible College. Emi was able to work in the school to help with support. The Shozo couple had given up a prosperous agricultural business to follow God's call to the ministry. He studied four years in a Bible college, and three years in seminary. Now Shozo was graduating, the only student from one of our churches, so the invitation went to him. The church didn't just get a pastor. They got a pastor with a wife and five children!

Now we had to hustle. We wouldn't be leaving for furlough until summer, but Shozo was graduating in spring of 1977. The family would be moving into what had been our mission home for many years. Now it belonged to the church. Renting for a few months was almost impossible, but God saw our need. We found a house in the community. Church friends helped us move. We stored our stuff under the eaves of the church and packed only bare necessities for furlough. The church was excited about their new pastor family, and we were happy for the nudge to get our house in order. What a joy to see the church with their own meeting place and a pastor family.

In preparation for furlough, we made five big posters of pictures depicting the history of the Oita church. 1. Beginnings, 2. Children's ministry, 3. Meetings, 4. Special occasions (weddings, baptism, church dedication, etc.) 5. A poster filled with pictures of members, seekers, families, and neighbors, with a challenge in the centre: "Are you praying?" We used these for displays at churches, conferences, and schools. When Oita celebrated their fortieth anniversary, we gave these historic posters to the Oita church.

FURLOUGH 1977 - '78

When we left for Japan in 1954, we took for granted that even if our parents died, we would not be attending their funerals. Peter's Dad, also Peter Derksen, was a quiet person about his faith. However, on furloughs he followed his son to every meeting in the area, always sitting in a back bench. His comments were short but encouraging. "You always speak and share with enthusiasm," he said. After a stroke, he struggled with poor health for many years and died June 6, 1976. He was 84.

Peter's brother Henry phoned. The family insisted that Peter return for the funeral. The prodding finally took effect when Pastor Shozo, who had just come to Oita, told Peter he had to go, or the pastor could not have a relationship with him anymore. That's how important it is in Japan to attend a parent's funeral!

Peter arrived in time to preach at his father's funeral. Mother was happy to have him home. Rick and Marilyn were there, too. They had finished a year at seminary in Elkhart, Indiana. Peter was able to spend a few hours with them before they left on the journey that would take them to Belgium for a year of intensive French language study before beginning their long-term ministry in Zaire, Africa.

In the September, 1976 missionary newsletter, Gecomen, Alice Ruth Ramseyer wrote: *This summer's final high point was seeing Rick and Marilyn off at the airport when they left for Belgium before going on to Zaire. Emotional, because it seemed a symbol of God's continuing call to men and women to serve Him. I couldn't help but remember the farewells in Seattle (1954), with Rick crawling around on the deck – couldn't even walk yet. Now to see him and Marilyn leaving as missionaries themselves can only be called a thrilling experience. Mary and Peter, you have a lot to be grateful for.* Yes!

A difficult decision faced us. Where should we live during this furlough? We would be travelling to many of our supporting churches across Canada and the US throughout the year. Vangy and Ernie lived in BC; Ma Derksen was living alone in her big house. We decided to begin our furlough living with Ma in Abbotsford.

News came in May, 1977, that Peter's Mother was gravely ill. His family asked him to come home immediately. Shozo, the new pastor, added to the push. Thankfully, Peter was able to spend a few days with Mother before she passed into the presence of her Lord on May 14, 1977. Peter spoke at her funeral in West Abbotsford, our home church.

Lily and I were left alone to finish packing to leave Oita. It was lonely without Peter, but Lily and I got a bonus. We were able to attend the baptism of Machiko, her mother, and a high school student. At the close of the service, Machiko's simple prayer of thanks touched us all.

In Japan, Lily had just started grade four. We were concerned about how she would fit into her grade a year later. No problem. Her teacher armed her with a pile of books to keep up her Japanese subjects. Fortunately, Peter was quite fluent in Japanese, and he spent an hour studying Japanese with Lily on days when he was home.

WEDDING BELLS

Rosie's turn. Rose met John Snyder at Goshen College where both were students. She was halfway through her nursing program when they decided to get married. Where could they possibly have a wedding? Why not at our seminary in Elkhart? Our Japan missionaries on furlough, Ramseyers and Virginia and other friends were ready to help.

On August 13, 1977, the happy couple was married in the beautiful seminary chapel in Elkhart, IN. Peter spoke and officiated. Wanda, Bill and Lily, Vangy, Ernie and Jayden were there. Grandparents and relatives from Ontario were able to come. Rick and Marilyn, studying French in Belgium, were missing.

When the reception line finally ended, the wedding party moved downstairs for the meal. We met people coming up and told them it was time to start. However, when we entered the dining hall, half of the people were already finished eating and were leaving. What a funny surprise! Weddings in the US must be different, we thought. I told our remaining three kids to be sure to have their weddings in home territory next time.

Living in the parental home without parents was lonely. Week-ends we shared about our life in Japan with many congregations in BC. Bill and Wanda joined us for the summer months. Bill preached mini sermons, Wanda gave a testimony, and we sang as a family. Wanda accompanied us with her guitar. Folks always enjoyed our song ***Jesus Loves Them All*** where Lily sang a little solo part. As we sang, "*Too small*?" she would answer, "*No*."

We attended conferences in Toronto and Bluffton. Exhilarating as it was, nights were short. The theme in Bluffton at the General Conference was *Focus on the Family*. Late night visiting with friends took its toll. Bill said, "It almost put our family out of focus." At the end of summer, Bill returned to Wheaton, and Wanda transferred to UBC in Vancouver.

Wanda responded to an ad for tour guides. What a surprise for Japanese tourists. What sort of magic was this, a blonde young lady who spoke such perfect Japanese? She was the private guide for the Hokkaido governor's wife, who called her, "Itsu no ma ni ka umareta Kanada no musume! (From where did this Canadian daughter suddenly appear?)" Wanda toured Canada and the US with many Japanese tourists.

In a note to Gecomen, our Japan mission paper, I wrote, "Lots of folks must be praying for the kids. They are all happy."

A FAMILY OF STUDENTS

Lily enjoyed grade four in Abbotsford. Her English was a bit stilted, but she had learned such good study habits in Japanese school, that she kept up. What a surprise to learn that she was far beyond her peers in math and science.

We arranged for missionary housing in Wheaton after the New Year so that Bill could live at home. A Christian organization rented housing, furnished with dishes, furniture, and linens, to missionaries on furlough. What a big help.

I took the opportunity to audit some writing courses at Wheaton College. It was no secret, but we just never talked about it. Until then. Bill said, "Mom, you mean you never graduated from college?"

My response shocked him. "I never graduated from anything. Actually, I graduated from a two-year business course in high school, but never finished high school, either." I always told folks that I received my MD, Mary Derksen, when I married Peter Derksen! My dream of studying journalism (which only came after writing hundreds of prayer letters to our supporters), was partly realized. At the age of 49, I joined Bill as a college student.

Lily entered grade four in a local Wheaton school. We didn't think of it in time, or she could have been in grade five. After one long week-end of meetings, Lily said, "Why don't we just go back to Japan where we belong?" Then the afterthought, "O, well, I guess that's what it means to be an M.K!" (missionary kid)

We heard that the Oita Mennonite Church had decided to send monthly support for Rick and Marilyn's ministry in Zaire. We had started the Oita Church, and Rick was one of the first to be baptized there. Now the church was helping with their support. We felt rich indeed. Full circle!

On furlough, no matter how often I listened to Peter telling how we share the Gospel in Japan, I never tired of it. After our last meeting, a young couple said, "We've never been so excited about missions in our life!" Neither had we! We were eager to return to our beloved Japanese people to tell them more about our wonderful Lord and Savior, Jesus Christ.

Our 25th wedding anniversary

Baptism
Back: Bill, Shigeyuki, Peter, Fujibuchi
Front: Kurimoto, Wanda, Kai, Furushiro

Lily, in the Grade 1 band

Gospel - folk

Children's Sunday School Christmas choir

Best friends, Jun, Lily & Kumi off to Kindergarten

Sasakis cut wedding cake

Vangy, Rosie, Wanda, & Lily

Lily in grade one

Ethel

Sunday School parade

Camping at the river

Church youth on 'Coming-of-Age' day

Yuko passing out invitations at university

Yurika, high school evangelist

Baton touch - Peter and new pastor, Sasaki

Oita's 30th anniversary, 1997

Oita's 40th anniversary, in new sanctuary

Peter serving as judge

Peter's parents, Oma & Opa Derksen's 50th wedding anniversary

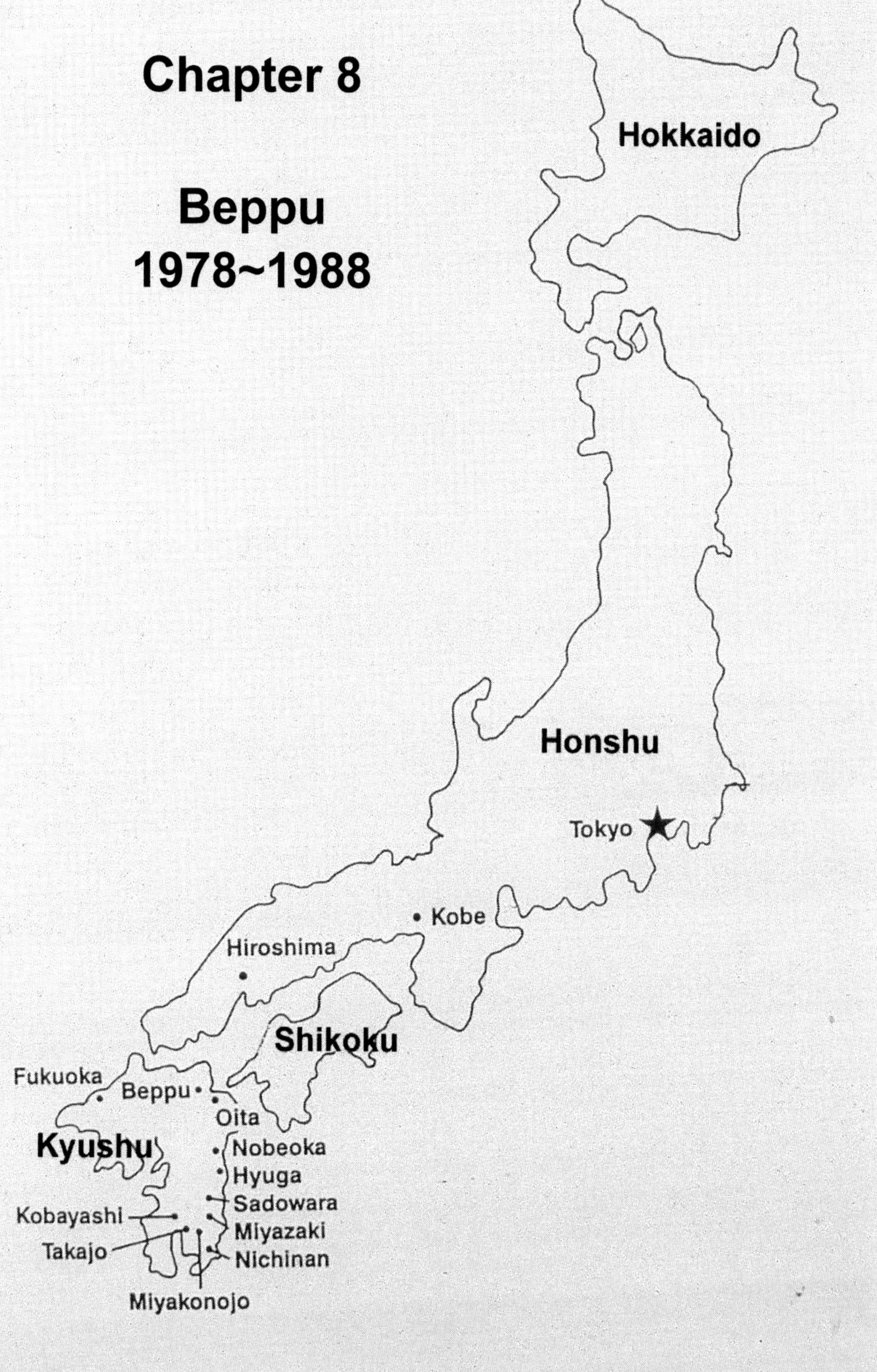
Chapter 8
Beppu
1978~1988
Hokkaido
Honshu
Tokyo
Kobe
Hiroshima
Shikoku
Fukuoka
Beppu
Oita
Kyushu
Nobeoka
Hyuga
Sadowara
Kobayashi
Miyazaki
Takajo
Nichinan
Miyakonojo

TOURIST CITY

When the Japanese church conference suggested that Peter and I start a new church in Beppu, we balked. Beppu? That tourist city? Other cities were difficult, but local pastors called Beppu the *Sodom and Gomorrah* of Japan. However, we accepted their decision as God's challenge to a new ministry.

Beppu is built on the hillside of the Tsurumi mountain range stretching up from Beppu Bay, a scenic drive half an hour north of Oita. As we drive along Beppu Bay, layers of mountain ranges gradually disappear in the distant haze to our left. Ahead, hundreds of hot spring columns climb Ogi (Fan) Mountain. Miriads of lights turn Beppu into a sparkling mountainside at night. Beppu, set on a hill, cannot be hid. Mt. Tsurumi, the highest peak of the range, is a dead volcano looking down protectively on the city. Sometimes I wondered if this mountain could come back to life.

The natural hot springs make it a famous year-round resort, adding millions of tourists to the population of 140,000. A thousand large and small hotels offer hot spring baths with a night's stay. Hot spring public bath houses are cheap and plentiful, so it is not unusual to see a family walking along the sidewalk in the evening, carrying towels and their own little wash pans to their daily bath. The eight major viewing hot springs have one common word in their names, Jigoku, or Hell, with a Blue Sea Hell, Red Blood Pond Hell, the Waterspout Hell which erupts with a roar every half hour, and other dreadful sounding names.

Homes fortunate enough to own a hot spring have free cooking and heating. A friend who was cooking eggs for tourists with their private hot spring tap, told me how the ground behind their house began to shake one day, and a geyser of steam spewing flames shot into the sky with a boom that could be heard a kilometer away. As it roared to life, city officials, police, and newspapermen hurried to the scene. What a rush to cap that noisy monster. And what a vivid reminder that Beppu sits on fire!

Pastor Sato of the Oita church and Peter scoured the streets of Beppu for a rental house in the summer of 1979. The area of Minami Ishigaki north of the city centre had no church, but real- estate agents told us no house was available. They finally found an empty house tucked into a short dead-end street. It was not for rent. We prayed for that house, persuaded the owner that we would keep it in good shape, and he gave in. We put up a sign advertising Christian meetings.

MOVING ONCE MORE (EEK)

We were cleaning the house to move in and Peter was vacuuming the kitchen. As he opened a low cupboard door, huge cockroaches came skittering out. Lily and I began screaming and jumping around to avoid stepping on these yucky creatures. He kept the vacuum going until they were all sucked in. After he switched off the vacuum, a line of very dusty coachroaches slowly emerged, bereft of their energy for the time being! In the evening without screens in the windows, we discovered that they could fly right into our home. I never did make friends with these hard shiny giant insects as big as ripe prunes.

Lily, nine, Peter and I moved in. From our kitchen window we loved watching the ferries coming and going into Beppu Bay far below. We could reach out and touch our neighbor's roof. We had never lived so close to people.

One night after we were asleep, Peter suddenly screamed! "Something bit me!" I switched on the light, and saw a giant centipede scurrying under the piano. The bite on his chest caused intolerable pain. We grabbed our insect killer and sprayed till it succumbed. Friends told us that a child could die from such a bite.

A huge storage shed took up half of the yard. A few blooming shrubs cheered the drabness. There was barely room for the car to squeeze in. The first time I tried, I needed twenty-five times of backing and moving forward, inch by inch! Eventually I learned to do it in three.

Shopping meant zooming downhill by bike and pushing it back up. One day Lily discovered that her brakes were not working. Not daring to speed across all the streets on the way down, she deliberately crashed her bike into the wall of a temple, bruising herself quite badly.

It didn't take long to discover that Beppu, though affectionately called

The Smile of Japan, had a whole world of darkness and evil. Much of life was bent on sensual pleasures, represented by the thousands of bars, cabarets, and houses of prostitution. Beppu was home to one of Japan's crime syndicates. Biking down the street one day, I suddenly found myself between two columns of men dressed in uniform on either side of the road. A crime syndicate was guarding their territory during the funeral of one of its members in a funeral home nearby.

A NEW APPROACH

How does one begin to "*Rise and Shine*" amidst the darkness? It was only because we came in the name of Jesus Christ that we had courage to begin a witness in this city. With help from the Oita church, we distributed gospel literature to four thousand homes and nine hundred high school students.

Noguchi San, an older Christian from another church, and a Gideon, visited us soon after we moved in. He brought two gifts, a loaf of bread, symbolizing our unity in Christ, the Bread of Life, and a box of grapes, symbolizing Christ's blood shed for our sins. Noguchi San came with a proposition. Would Peter distribute New Testaments to the hotels of Beppu with him? We prayed together, and then planned.

Suginoi Palace, Beppu's largest hotel that could house one thousand guests a day, was world famous. If Suginoi Palace accepted New Testaments for each room, other hotels would follow. Suginoi responded with YES! A few of the smaller hotels refused, but Peter and Noguchi San kept on with the task. Beppu was in need of the *Light of the World*. What better way than to distribute the Scriptures that could filter into the whole country, or even the world?

Our home was situated in a quiet but heavily populated residential area that had no church. This was a time to wait on the Lord. Sometimes we try so hard. Sometimes our faith shrinks, and we become impatient with the Lord. Other times we don't know what to do, and just cry out to the Lord. The song *Sometimes I'm up, sometimes I'm down, sometimes I'm almost to the ground* expressed our feelings. Only because of Jesus could we sing, ***Glory, hallelujah***!

BEPPU BEGINNINGS

The first Sunday meetings were on September 20, with 15 children for Sunday School, and 14 adults for the worship service. The small room was comfortably full. Attendance fluctuated, with the lowest, three. But there was always someone! By Christmas, we had moved to the larger room upstairs.

Isaiah 61 says, *The Spirit of the Lord is on me, because the Lord has anointed me to preach good news to the poor…bind up the broken-hearted, to proclaim freedom for the captives and release for the prisoners…to comfort all that mourn, and provide for those who grieve…a crown of beauty instead of ashes…gladness instead of mourning, praise instead of a spirit of despair…for the display of his splendor…and everlasting joy will be theirs.* The Lord sent us to the needy city of Beppu.

We lived and worked in the name of Christ who does the impossible. Thirty people responded to the literature distribution, some coming to English Bible classes, and others to church services. One man showed up at the end of a service. He had been searching for a church with a cross on it for over an hour.

Toshiko, the nurse from the Oita church, was working in a hospital in Beppu. She brought a fellow nurse, Kimiyo, a troubled young married woman. Kimiyo had gone to a Buddhist priest to ask how she could get rid of the burden of sin in her heart. He said, "I can't help you with that. Why don't you go to a Christian church?" She came.

Other hurting people came. An elderly Christian widow brought a friend and her daughter. Both were among the first to make decisions for the Lord. Both learned to forgive wayward husbands as Christ's love enveloped them. Some had already sought relief through suicide and failed. One young mother came a few times after receiving a Christmas tract. Later she tried to kill her child and commit suicide. The small church was visibly shaken and prayed fervently for this little family. All three survived, including the child the mother was carrying at the time.

We discovered that in many cases the seed of God's Word had been planted long before a person's contact with a church. Some adults who found their way to church had attended Sunday School somewhere in their childhood. Some had their first introduction to Christianity through a tract, others through radio ministry, and others through church attendance years ago. One woman in a bar had shown a tract to a customer.

"If I ever get in trouble," she said, "I'll know where to find help."

GROWING CHURCH

When growing churches had to support a pastor and fund a building at the same time, it was a struggle. We decided to try a new strategy and provide a church building first. We found a suitable lot several blocks down the hill from our rented home. Thanks to an enthusiastic Sunday School child who brought her New Year's money, the church started a building fund. Soon they had $5,000. A modest beginning, but it was a start.

We know the spiritual body of the church is more important than the building, and as meetings continued, a young man asked for baptism. How exciting when he married a Christian from the Oita church.

Our first formal business meeting took place with all twelve baptized members and two seekers. Sound boring? It wasn't. With a spirit of unity and eagerness, Christians volunteered for positions, which made it one of the most exciting business meetings we had ever experienced. When Nagano San said, "I think we need a foreign missions committee, too," all agreed. He willingly took charge together with Kozaki San. Then Hatata San, a folk-singer university co-ed said, "We should have a music committee, too." Three music lovers quickly filled the role.

When Nagano San won a free trip to Taiwan at an All-Japan Youth Missions Festival, he declined tourism in favor of meeting with Taiwanese pastors in the Mennonite churches.

Sato San, our nurse, phoned one day to share. "I'm just so happy that the Lord is blessing my witness. Please pray for me so that I won't get proud." I told her about my struggle with pride, and she was relieved to find a fellow sinner!

Have you ever been surprised by a robber at night? That happened to me when Peter had gone to Miyazaki for a few days. We slept upstairs, so I was up in a flash when I heard the safety chain rattle at the door downstairs. When I looked down in the dim light, I could see a hand reaching in trying to unhook the chain. I hollered "Kora!" grabbed a slipper and threw it down, hoping to scare him long enough so that I could call the police.

Then a familiar voice called out, "What are you trying to do to me?"

Peter had driven home instead of staying another night. I flew down the stairs and collapsed into his arms relieved! It was 3 AM.

Our short alley had great community spirit. Neighborhood kids came to play with Lily as soon as we moved in. The first day of school in September, ten kids from kindergarten through sixth grade from our dead-end street were at the door. “Yuri Chan, let’s go to school!” they called in unison. She went with misgivings but came home all excited. “I love it!” she said. What more could we ask?

Lily’s new friends loved Sunday School. By the first Christmas, three young Christians were helping. Eventually there were seven Sunday School teachers, with children from nursery through junior high. Not only was this reaching children, but mothers became Christians as a direct result. Attendance averaged 25, with peak seasons bringing over 40 kids.

Our house was too small for the Sunday School Christmas program. We found a local hall for rent two blocks away. What a parade. Children walking down the street carrying Christmas gifts for the kids, outfits for the Christmas pageant, snacks to serve after the program, and a small Christmas tree. A number of parents and grandparents came, and we had a wonderful Christmas celebration, the first ever for most of these people.

Parents of a sixth grade girl who refused to attend school were at their wit’s end, and so were the teachers. The principal sent the father to the church. “Maybe they can help you,” he said. Receiving recognition from a school was a major victory. Later a junior high school endorsed a film our church was showing, encouraging its students to attend.

One day three elementary aged boys stood at the door. “Please teach us about God,” they said. I invited them in and we got acquainted. I got out a kamishibai, paper drama, and told them about how the living God created the world. They were very attentive, but they never came back. God is working at that link.

LILY GRADUATES

Lily loved animals, and one day a dog followed her home. No one came to claim her. Lily begged to keep her and promised to take care of her. Reluctantly we allowed her to keep the dog, and we had a pet. A pet needs a name. Since this one had followed her home, she decided that "Tag" was a good name. Unfortunately, Tag was a she, and soon a litter of puppies followed!

Lily did well in her studies and enjoyed school in spite of many hours of homework. When she was in grade 6, the class planted a time capsule at the school entrance, to be opened in 25 years. Unfortunately, she had to miss that future event.

The highlight of my Japanese education had arrived: Lily's grade six graduation! We had been in Japan 25 years, and felt like Japanese, even though we could never look like them. The gym was not big enough, so only one parent was allowed to attend. Peter sneaked in and stood at the back for a while. Most mothers wore black kimonos with the family crests on the back. Some wore black dresses, and so did I. Finally, I was in harmony with the country that I had come to love.

The huge rising sun flag draped across the gymnasium stage reminded me of my foreign status. However, I was surrounded by friends, and so was Lily. I squeezed my eyes to keep back the flood of tears that threatened to erupt as I listened to Lily and her 240 classmates sing and recite their six years of experiences.

After long weary speeches, the students marched to the podium one by one to receive their diplomas. When Lily started her way up the steps, something inside me began bursting. We had struggled together. We made it! Lily spoke Japanese like any other Japanese child. She had learned good study habits. She had many friends. I also had many friends, classmates' mothers, and neighbors. My heart was overflowing in gratitude to God.

My heart almost burst with pride when Lily marched to the front, bowed politely, and stretched out both hands to receive her diploma. Banzai! Yeah! I felt as if I was graduating, too. I wasn't the only one with wet eyes. When the graduates marched out to *Auld Lang Syne*, a wave of white hankies seemed to float over the auditorium! My tears rolled.

NEW CHURCH HOME

What a big year! The new church building was finished in March, and we moved in. Neighbors stared in astonishment when they saw us rolling our washing machine down the hill. We had brought it from America after our last furlough. With a spinner attached, it was big and pear shaped. It took both of us to roll it to our new home, but that was easier than loading and unloading it on a truck which we didn't have. It took a bit longer than our usual five minute walk to our new location down the hill.

On one of our evening walks, Peter and I saw a bookcase on the sidewalk in the midst of debris. "Just what we need," I said to Peter, "a bookcase!"

"Are you sure it's okay?" he asked?

"Oh, yes," I persuaded him. "Otherwise it wouldn't be sitting out here." We carried it to our new home. The new church had a wide entrance where shoes are taken off, a pastor's study, a sunny meeting room that could seat 50, a tiny kitchen for serving ocha, tea, and a tiny washroom.

Our upstairs apartment had a small living room, kitchen, two small bedrooms, and an ofuro. It was the first time this builder had ever put an ofuro into a second floor. Our washing machine was outside behind the new building. On laundry days we ran a hose through the tiny church kitchen window to the machine! It worked. I hung my laundry upstairs under the patio roof.

Peter's question about the bookcase was disturbing. Finally, I stopped at the little shop where we had picked it up. When I mentioned the bookcase, the lady said, "We wondered what had happened to the bookcase. We were renovating, so put it out there for the time being." I wanted to bring it back, but she refused. I baked a cake and took my "sin offering" to her. We became friends.

Palm Sunday the neighborhood was challenged to *Rise and Shine* as the parade of Sunday School children waving palm branches and singing loud ***Hosanna,*** skipping down the hill for their first Sunday in the new church.

That afternoon over 70 friends, neighbors, seekers, and Christians from far and near joined us for a thanksgiving dedication service. After the meeting chairs were stacked and everyone sat on the floor in groups for tea and fellowship. Serving tea on the floor is no small feat. I left that for the locals.

ONES AND TWOS

New people kept coming. A mother came to the door with her two children. A close family member had just committed suicide. Her request? "Please teach my children about the love of God." They came to Sunday School regularly. The daughter loved church. It was thanks to her gift that initiated the building fund.

Another mother brought her two girls to Sunday School. The mother, a music teacher, needed to upgrade her electone, similar to an electric organ, so she donated hers to the church. The girls loved Sunday School and soon the mother started coming to services. She agreed to play for worship services so the church not only acquired an organ but an organist as well. She brought her sister and her mother to church. Her husband came to her baptism, his first time ever in a church.

An elderly Christian widow moved to Beppu and found our church. The mother of a teacher who had been baptized in the Hyuga church twenty years ago lived in Beppu. She brought two friends. And so the church grows as one brings one who brings another.

Often, we heard excuses, "My parents are too old," or "They are strong Buddhists." The widow of a Buddhist priest was guest speaker at a church retreat. Her husband was 82 when they became Christians. She cried when she told us how her husband travelled up and down Japan for ten years sharing his faith in the living God.

A younger man had to work Sundays, so he arranged for a late evening Bible study in his home. He told Peter, "Reading the Bible is so enjoyable."

A young Christian transferred to Beppu and was soon involved. He was a big help in stabilizing the church group and he married one of the Christian girls in the church.

Seiji became a Christian at Cambridge University in England and found our church when he returned home. He was so concerned about the need for Bibles in China, that he made several trips to smuggle Bibles into China.

Seiji and Tomoko, new Christians, wanted their formal engagement in the church. When the parents talked of wedding plans, this young couple said, "We want the wedding and reception in the church. The church will take care of everything!" What a big order! How could we take care of the one hundred guests they were inviting? We needed a few miracles! A tent to the rescue, which opened right against the four window doors of the church. Christians and regulars eagerly helped prepare food for the reception. The sun and God's love shone on this beautiful wedding.

Tomoko had a healthy eight-year-old niece who suddenly became very sick. Tomoko asked us to pray and visit Hisae Chan in the hospital. A few days later, Hisae Chan died from the virus attack. The grieving parents were so touched by the caring church that they asked for a Christian funeral. Since we had no graveyard, they brought their daughter's urn with her ashes to the church. When they drove past the church, the father put his hands together and bowed. Hisae's mother kept coming to church and became a Christian. One by one the family came to faith in Christ. Years later one of Hisae's brothers became a Christian pastor.

Cremation was law. The small country of Japan did not have room for burials. Now the church realized that we needed a burial plot in a cemetery. All were enthused, and soon we had the needed $5,300 to buy a small lot with a cement hut that could hold over one hundred urns. The church had a meaningful celebration of dedication, and Hisae Chan was laid to rest in the new graveyard. The widow also transferred her husband's ashes to our new plot. This was one of a few plots that had a symbol of the Christian cross in the cemetery. The Christians were relieved to have a burial place of their own.

Kimiyo, the nurse, attended regularly, and read her Bible at home. She made her decision and asked for baptism. A few weeks before the birth of their first baby, she was baptized. Big family problems arose but each one brought her closer to God.

The daughter was in child care. Her mother brought her to church faithfully and taught her about Jesus at home. When the little girl was four, she was on a walk with her preschool class. The teacher took the children to a temple. However, the little one refused to enter the gate. When the teacher asked her why, she replied, "I don't want to go in there. Jesus is my God. I pray to Him."

When giving her testimony with a quivering voice on baptism Sunday, one young lady said, "My parents were very opposed to my church attendance, but since my mother has seen how early I rise on Sundays to get laundry and cleaning done so I can get to church on time, she has stopped scolding."

Another broke into tears when she shared, "Life was so dark and empty. All I could think of was death. But now Christ has filled my life with joy and peace!"

A young lady had come to church regularly for years and wanted to be baptized. My husband always asked young people to consult their parents. Hers parents refused permission. She was an only child and would be responsible for worshipping fourteen generations of ancestors. She chose to wait. We waited too. God's link was in process.

My sister Hilda and family visited us during the time of a very difficult problem involving mobsters. One evening while I was typing a letter on our electric typewriter in our second-floor apartment, my sister came in pale and shaking. "Mary," she exclaimed, "I thought it was a machine gun, and someone was shooting at us!"

BONDING

The church became a caring community. When someone had to move, some Christians took a day off from their job to help. If someone was sick, they took meals to the family. When a family was in financial distress, the church collected $10,000. in two days to help them through the crisis. With happy tears, one young mother brought her bank savings to help. Within a month the money was all paid back.

Christians were eager to liquidate the building debt, and five years later they were able to pay for the church building. What an accomplishment!

Discouraging times came, too. One couple told us they were quitting. They had been baptized, married, and dedicated their baby in church. Suddenly her mother died. "Why didn't God answer my prayers for my mother to become a Christian before she died?" she asked.

"What about my father who died before hearing about Christ? And what about all my ancestors?" the husband asked. Questions pleading answers. We were crushed, and also fearful of the impact this might have on others. However, God was keeping watch over his flock.

Christmas blessings abounded. Ninety attended the S.S. program. It was so great not to have to cart a hundred and one things to a rented hall. When the curtain was opened in the darkened room, revealing 45 starry-eyed angels in white capes and red ribbons holding candles, a gasp rose from the parents. Even the monotones took on angelic sounds! The four teachers had done an excellent job of practising their plays with the children. Hearing the Christmas story from the mouths of children was always a highlight.

The Sunday School teachers wrote their own drama once. ***The Light of the World,*** portraying Jesus' birth, and then people through the centuries who received this Light, and how they in turn shared their Light. They took us right through time; the Apostle Paul, Luther, Helen Keller, Florence Nightingale, Handel, and a famous Japanese writer, Miura Ayako. What a dramatic education!

Christmas Eve candlelight service was a highlight. After the meeting was finished, our enthusiastic young people went carolling, and returned to church for tea. Suddenly the doorbell rang, and in walked a family with three young children. They were so impressed with the carollers, that they got dressed and brought chocolates for the singers to celebrate Christmas some more.

Christians had distributed 5000 Christmas tracts in the neighborhood and to three high schools. Several responded. A mother brought her two children Christmas Eve.

MORE RESPONSES

Baptism during the Christmas worship Sunday filled our little church with joy. Nakajima San, a young mother who had been attending the women's Bible class for over a year, gave a radiant testimony before her baptism. Mayumi San, who had moved from another city, transferred her membership.

Christmas was a time of giving. When Christians heard of the famine in Africa, the church topped their goal and collected 600,000 yen. Forty percent was designated to MCC for the famine.

When we heard about my cousin Rudolph Klassen spending six years in prisons in Russia for preaching the gospel, we started a campaign for his release. Amnesty International sent us a form, and we collected over three hundred signatures in our church and community. We rejoiced to hear that he had been released shortly after Gorbachev took the helm in Russia.

If all those who had made decisions for Christ in Japan were still in church, the churches would be full. Some had made decisions on the spur of the moment. Sometimes after many years they would come back and renew their faith. Others lost out for lack of a church in the community where they had moved, or because of opposition in the home.

A senior couple who became Christians when they were young, found no church in Manchuria where they had been transferred. After WWII, they returned to Japan, and moved to Beppu. Walking by our church one day, the husband dropped in to talk. We were all thrilled to have these seniors.

The grandfather of a neighbor in our secluded little street died. After cremation, the family gathered around the ashes with chopsticks to choose bones to transfer them into the urn. They were surprised to see two bones in the shape of the cross. Was grandfather a Christian?

A crowd of sixty attended the Mother's Day meeting. The S.S. kids loved singing for their mothers. Then each child presented their mother with a potted plant.

Three young neighbor boys came to SS regularly. We were sad when they moved to Kurashiki, famous for its historic ancient village. Peter and I contacted them when we made a stop in Kurashiki and were surprised that the husband took a day off work to show us around. The best part was singing all the songs the boys had learned in SS while driving around in their car.

A young couple plagued with physical problems often talked about suicide. Yet each time they said, "There must be a better way." When they heard a Christian radio broadcast, their hearts opened to Christ. The radio program sent us their names, since they lived in Beppu. We looked them up, and found them just around the corner, and helped with babysitting and taking her to doctor appointments. They came regularly. Gradually her health improved, too. They had found that ***better way*** when they opened their hearts to Christ.

We benefitted from the work of others, too. Kei San first heard the gospel via radio. He wrote to the program sponsor asking them to introduce him to a church in Beppu. He became a faithful Christian, often bringing family and friends. The church could always count on Kei San. One of his gifts was finding jobs for the jobless among us.

Mayumi San was a gift to the church. She loved the kids, was a musician, and was good in English. She translated the musical, ***Mary Had a Little Lamb*** which I had brought from Canada. A sixth grade girl was an excellent pianist, and the children eagerly practiced for Christmas. But I had a problem trying to conduct the jazzy, syncopated music. I practiced in front of a mirror until I caught on! The recurring theme: ***GLORY TO GOD – PEACE ON EARTH,*** engraved itself so deeply into my heart that I was singing it waking or sleeping.

Eri (pseudonym) our night guest, was sleeping off her drunken stupor upstairs on the morning of the SS program. ***Peace on Earth!*** Her husband and boys were waiting for her at home. Would they ever have a normal wife and mother again? My tears spilled over. Only the Lord could restore peace to this family. Eri San was sent to the only hospital in Japan solely for alcoholics. We lost contact, but the Lord didn't.

When Mayumi San graduated from seminary in the spring of 1986, the Fukuoka Mennonite Church called her to be their pastor. The Beppu church held a commissioning and farewell service for her, as they sent out their first full time worker.

Minako, (pseudonym) walked by one day and stopped to read the sign in front of the church. *Come to me, all you who are weary and burdened, and I will give you rest* (Matthew 11: 28). Could she possibly ever find rest again? She had married her high school sweetheart, but the family didn't like the son's choice, and they were divorced. Minako was devastated. Now she came every day to unburden her woes. She became a Christian, and soon her new Bible was underlined throughout.

On baptism day, Minako's 93-year-old grandfather attended. He asked to speak and thanked the church for all the help and love they had shown his granddaughter.

One day Minako came, shaken. "I tried to end my life today, but couldn't do it," she told us sadly. The Christians gathered that evening to pray with her. The depression lingered, and the family put her into a hospital. Whenever we visited, she ran into our arms for comfort. She loved the song, ***Because He Lives***, which we often sang together on the phone. Minako took comfort believing that someday the Lord would heal her.

BILL COMES HOME

Our children were free to make their own decisions. Peter and I prayed much, and secretly hoped one of them would return to Japan. When other young couples came, I wished it could have been Rick and Marilyn, who had felt called to serve the Lord in Zaire, Africa. I asked the Lord, "Why so far away?" However, we loved the newcomers, and embraced them as our own!

Bill had spent a year in Japan after graduating from college, and lived with Junji and Yoshihara, young Christian guys from the Oita church. It was a good year for Bill, immersing himself in the culture and language in the land of his birth. After he left, he wrote, "I left Japan and the best year of my life!"

Years later, in 1984 Junji Sasaki, the new pastor of the Oita Mennonite church, invited Bill to begin a ministry in the southern area of Oita. This ministry became the Minami (south) Oita Mennonite Church. What a joy to welcome Bill home, this time as a fellow missionary to Japan! He was happy to have his friend James for a short term, and with the support of the mother church, started meetings in their rented quarters. A small enthusiastic group emerged. Lily was thrilled to have a brother nearby.

WEDDING CAKES

Pastor Sato left Oita to begin a new church in his home community. Junji Sasaki had graduated from Bible College and became Oita's new pastor. Sasaki was engaged to Mami, a lovely Christian from another church. With wedding preparations looming in 1982, he suddenly said, "Maria Sensei, you are going to bake our wedding cake!"

"No way! I've never baked a wedding cake in my life, and I'm not going to start now," I said. End of conversation.

A month later, he approached me again. "Maria Sensei, you are going to bake our wedding cake!" I was shocked at his persistence and didn't want to appear rude. "I'll pray about it," I promised. I was quite sure I wouldn't do it. I added a few impossible conditions to my prayer. "God, if you want me to do this, I need your help. I have no idea how to bake a wedding cake." In Japan wedding cakes were like ordinary cakes, soft and delicious. Our wedding cakes in Canada were even more delicious, fruit cakes. That's what it had to be.

I picked up the first recipe book that caught my eye and opened it at random. I couldn't believe my eyes. There was the recipe for wedding fruit cake! I dallied. "God, this isn't enough. I have to know how to decorate the cake." I opened another recipe book, and what did I see? A recipe for decorating a wedding cake that I had copied from a missionary friend! "O.K. God. I give in!"

The job was even bigger than I had anticipated. Making the three layers was no problem. But where would I find columns to separate the layers? Ah! Empty film canisters. I iced them, and presto, problem solved. Decorating was a tedious job, but the cake was beautiful! Finished. Thank you, Lord.

Not finished! Another couple wanted a wedding cake, too. How could I refuse? I was in business. Two couples in the Beppu church joined the cake requests.

I was in the middle of baking the third, when my oven quit. Peter was becoming quite adept at taking appliances apart and fixing them. He painstakingly began taking one small part out at a time, while my cake sat in the oven waiting. Good thing it was a fruit cake! We finished baking in the wee hours of the morning!

By the time I was doing the fourth one, I felt quite confident. Soon the cake was sitting ready on my sewing machine upstairs in our apartment. The wedding party was practicing downstairs in the church room for the big day. Suddenly the building began to shake and sway! I am terrified of earthquakes and normally would have looked for a safe spot. But my cake! I ran upstairs to make sure my cake was o.k. It wasn't. My little columns couldn't support the weight, and one side slid right down on top of the other. Forgetting about the earthquake I searched for something to put the cake back in place. No one except my husband knew what had happened. It looked fine!

EVANGELISM

As if weddings weren't enough excitement, the church planned evangelistic meetings with Koji Honda Sensei, the Billy Graham of Japan. Peter and a Christian from the church went to the city office to rent the beautiful New Life Plaza that could seat three hundred people. The answer was, "No. No religious meetings." Not taking "no" for an answer, Peter's final appeal was "The constitution guarantees freedom of religion and of expression. If necessary, I'll appeal to the governor of Oita Prefecture!" A few days later a phone call granted permission not only to rent the 300-seat hall, but also to print invitations.

Miracles happen. Honda Sensei's office told us that he does not go to one church's invitation, but only when area churches cooperate. A spirit of prayer pervaded our little church and spread in the city. Several other churches committed to work with us for this evangelistic endeavour. The Nazarene and Immanuel churches made this their evangelism meetings for the year. All three nights the hall was packed. "Tears filled my eyes," I wrote later, "as I watched people walking to the front to make decisions for Christ."

A seeker in our church had a dangerous confrontation with her father. Both were at the meetings, and both made decisions for Christ. Later Peter visited the father when he had cancer. The father asked, "Will God accept someone like me?"

The Ouchi couple both had their doctorates and were very interested in English literature. Since the Bible was the most popular book in the world and in Japan, they started attending Bill's English Bible class in Minami Oita. They were not interested in becoming Christians. Bill had introduced them to us, and we became friends.

We invited them to these special meetings, and they came. The room was filled to capacity. After the service I was in the crowded lobby with the Ouchi's. Suddenly we came face to face with Honda Sensei, so I introduced them. Honda Sensei raised his hands, laid them on the heads of this couple and prayed for them, out loud! I was touched, but I wasn't the only one.

The next Sunday the Ouchi's were in the church service for the first time. "Something happened when Honda Sensei prayed for us," they told Bill. Both accepted Christ, and their world changed. The husband was scheduled for research in Marburg, Germany. Now the small church in Minami Oita sent this new family out as their missionaries. Another of God's surprises!

Face beaming, a young lady who had been coming to church recently, told of the joy in her heart that Christ had forgiven her sins. Her friend said, "I've never believed in instant conversion. I went forward with my friend to encourage her. I saw the change before my eyes. At that moment Christ seemed to be speaking right to me, and I was no longer in front for my friend. I was there to allow Christ to do a new thing in my heart," she cried.

FAMILY REUNION 1980

Our family had not been together since the kids went off to university one by one. Now we had multiplied to fourteen, including three grandchildren. It took a lot of planning, but finally, all were able to come for one month to our new home in Beppu. What an exciting day when Peter, Lily, twelve, and I drove to the airport to meet the first ones, Rick and Marilyn, who had just completed their first term of service in Zaire (Congo), Africa. Wanda came from B.C. where she was attending UBC, and Bill from Wheaton, where he had just graduated from Wheaton College. Rose and John Snyder arrived from Lansing, MI, and last, Vangy and Ernie Thiessen from BC with Jayden four, Carissa two, and Micah six months. Our family of fourteen was complete!

We laughed, cried, sang, shared, ate, and played under the same roof all of July. Drying diapers, towels, and clothes for fourteen people in the rainy season was no joke. However, showers of blessings kept us cool. Ernie, an agricultural engineer, put a drainage system into the back yard. The kids visited many of our churches, like going home to places where they grew up. They also visited Hiroshima where the first atom bomb was dropped, ending WWII.

The Oita church had special ties with Rick and Marilyn. Rick was baptized there in 1968. Two years ago the church had decided to send a small monthly support for their work in Africa. This was a first in the history of General Conference Mennonite Church where a church begun by missionaries now in turn began supporting an overseas missionary from their midst.

The three little ones added spice, sticky fingers, and fun to our full days. Devotions were times of sharing and praising the Lord with the help of piano, guitar, and violin. We took turns leading devotions which added variety and uniqueness to these special times.

Lily had been looking forward to this reunion, but also had misgivings. She was not on vacation until July 19. That day she came home and announced, "The teacher said we had to study at least four hours every day during the holidays!" She managed to study most days, even on our three day family trip to Miyazaki Ken to visit our former homes.

The kids had taken off from their jobs to come to Japan. Not so Dad and Mom. When you live in the church, people come at opportune and inopportune times. During this time we had guests from India, Taiwan, America and Japan. They just became part of the extended family. Friends were taking my suggestion of "Come and join the family" seriously.

Like most families, we experienced hurts, misunderstanding, confrontations, and relationship problems. Those were difficult times, but they made us stronger as we realized the joy of forgiving and being forgiven. We were stronger to face the loneliness and trials in the various cultures where we were living and working. After the children were gone, I felt responsible and apologized to the kids. Rick wrote back, "Don't worry, Mom. Most families wouldn't even try what our family did."

Now we were scattered far and wide in five countries, Zaire, Nepal, Taiwan, Japan and the US. Who knew how long it would be before another family gathering?

And the family became *fruitful and increased in numbers.* Rick and Marilyn were in Zaire when their first baby, Karina Kasai arrived. How many of us would think of walking to the hospital when labor begins, and a few hours after the baby is born walking home together in the moonlight as a family of three? Marilyn is a midwife and had delivered many babies in her few short years in Africa. During labor she said to Rick, "Build my coffin!"

LIFE MOVES ON

Christians distributed five hundred Christian newspapers a month as well as thousands of invitations to services and monthly film meetings in the neighborhood. Two years later we had our first response to this ministry. Two people phoned to thank for the paper and ask about the coming film meeting.

An excellent way to bring new people to church was through Christian movies. We used this in every place where we worked. Before the first movie in Beppu, we told the Sunday School children they could only come if they brought an adult. Eighteen came, and only one had no adult. We were packed out in our small home.

Shiokari Pass*,* a popular new Christian movie, was recommended to each school by the Beppu board of education. The board also put up thirty posters in the schools advertising this movie. Perhaps a season of unrest and violence in schools and homes was the reason. Ayako Miura, the author, was a best-selling writer and a highly respected Christian in Japan. Many people have searched the Christian faith through her books. Over 300 came to the rented hall for this movie. It was a time of seed-sowing.

JESUS OF NAZARETH COMES TO BEPPU

After we moved into the new building, the small church of 20 took a giant leap. We rented a 2,000 seat hall in the centre of the city to show the film, ***Jesus of Nazareth****.* This time it was not free. Everybody was busy selling tickets. One of the seekers sold one hundred tickets. We wavered between faith and unbelief. Would people really come? We prayed and worked. Worked and prayed.

On opening night the young people were at the doors early setting up a table with pamphlets. People kept coming, and soon hundreds filled the hall. No, not hundreds, a thousand two hundred! The impossible had happened. Our hearts thrilled as we sat with the crowd watching the life of Jesus unfold. *Behold the Lamb of God who taketh away the sins of the world,* and of Beppu, I thought.

One young man asked, "Did Jesus really die for me?" A business man cried as he watched the story of Jesus. We felt that Christmas had arrived!

Other churches got involved. The pastors asked, "How did you get so many people out?"

We had discovered long ago that big meetings didn't make much of a dent in attendance, but it was an excellent way to get Christians enthused in sharing the gospel. God has promised *so shall my word be that goes forth from my mouth; it shall not return empty.*

The little church loved the involvement, and the following year decided to use the film ***JESUS.*** Would God do the miracle again? The Christians put up three hundred posters and distributed five thousand invitations. The goal was to sell l,500 tickets. People were slow in responding.

By Nov. 6, we had sold only 289 tickets. The movie was on November 13.

A local paper carried a feature article with the headlines, ***Continuing to Proclaim the Love of Christ!*** A TV reporter came for an interview and advertised the movie on prime time.

An old man asked if this was the same film as last year. "No? Then I want a ticket."

An elderly lady came to buy several for herself and her friends. "Jesus is so wonderful. I want all my friends to know about Him, too!" she said.

November 13 dawned bright, cold and windy. The wind ripped off the posters. But it didn't matter. Ticket count was 1,025 sold. The Christians were filled with excitement. And the people came. At first by ones and twos, then families, mothers with babies strapped to their backs, little old bent people, students in their smart uniforms, nuns, priests, pastors with groups, and a group from the orphanage. The crowd kept surging in. A multitude, Overwhelming! The total count was 1,300, not counting children under six who were free. In spite of the low cost of tickets, all the bills were paid. The church decided to give the *twelve baskets of crumbs* to the city welfare office. They were impressed and promised to cooperate next time.

Although we could not count visible results, these mass meetings were fulfilling important tasks. They were creating a unity among the pastors. As Christians saw how the Lord answered prayer, they were becoming bolder in sharing their faith. We were spreading God's Word far and wide. Yes, Jesus came!

Seiji, Peter and I attended a church growth seminar in Fukuoka. The highlight of that meeting was the evening concert by a famous Korean singer. Hardly an eye remained dry when this Korean lady, dressed in a long white gown, and looking very much like we imagine an angel, fell to the stage on her knees crying. She begged the Japanese audience "Please forgive me! I have hated you in my heart all these years." I felt surely someone would run up from the audience and beg her, "No, we need to ask you to forgive us." No one moved. However, they had come.

CONTINUED SCHOOLING

After Lily's graduation from elementary school, there was no question in her mind or ours. She would go to Japanese junior high school. The first big change was that all students wore uniforms. The girls looked so grown up in their navy pleated skirts topped with wide sailor collars on the navy blouses. A maroon tie completed their outfits. The skirts were measured from the floor up for uniformity. At the opening ceremony the mothers said, "Don't they look pika pika?" (sparkling)

The kids were all scared stiff of junior high school. They had heard enough stories to keep them on edge. One day it happened. All the girls in Lily's class were five minutes late getting dressed for PE. Punishment was swift. They had to sit outside on the ground and listen to a scolding. Then each girl got a hard rap on the head. Ouch!

Junior high in Japan was like opening a Pandora box and finding one surprise after another inside. The first surprise came at the opening ceremony when the principal threatened, "Unless you rank in the top 50 of your grade, you won't pass into high school!" That meant 50 out of 413. The pressure was on!

Lily had long auburn hair and wore a ponytail to school. Hopping mad after school one day, she told us that the teacher had asked her to wear a black rubber band for her ponytail so the girls would all look the same. I laughed and sent her to school with a black band. A few days later the teacher called her in again. "Just wear your brown band. Black stands out too much on you." And that was the end of the story.

Now weeks were punctuated with tests and exams. Standings were on the bulletin boards for all to see. After the first test, Lily ranked 249. Not exactly high school quality. She hated and loved school in spurts. When a close friend came second in the school, Lily was inspired. By the second year she had worked herself into the top 50. Ready for high school!

Lily brought new friends to church, many on the fringe of society. We were amazed and learned to love each one. Lily began sharing her dreams for the future. She wanted to be a missionary! To us, she was one already.

When she entered the third year of junior high, weekly tests and exams escalated. The constant pressure was too much. Lily was ready for change. She wanted to attend the same school where her five older siblings had graduated in Tokyo, Christian Academy in Japan.

In September 1982, it was time for Lily to leave for CAJ. Lily and I travelled to Tokyo together. I helped her get settled in her first dorm experience. How had we managed to send our other children away at such a young age? Fourteen was even too young. And we were lonely.

Lily enjoyed her four years at CAJ. She was a member of the school volleyball team. Volleyball almost became her life. However, she began having trouble with her shoulder snapping out of place, and each time it became more painful. Finally, the doctor recommended surgery. Lily feared that she might never be able to play volleyball again. I went to Tokyo to be with her for the operation. The operation was a success, and we thanked God for healing. Lily claimed Jeremiah 29:11. *For I know the plans I have for you, declares the Lord, plans to prosper you and not to harm you, plans to give you hope and a future.* Eventually she was able to play again. Oh, joy! We also discovered that since her shoulder problems happened at school functions, CAJ's school insurance paid the bill.

When we took Lily back to the airport to return to Tokyo after a vacation, the road and airport were lined with police and security people. The Crown Prince and Princess of Japan had just attended Oita's International wheelchair marathon. We joked that Lily should have dressed up to travel with the royals. Well, the joke turned out to be true, as Lily was on the same plane as they were! We were in the lobby of the airport when the royal couple walked through. Princess Michiko glanced our way, looked surprised, and then gave me a bright smile, perhaps because we were the only foreigners there. Later Lily told us how the plane made a special tour over the city of Beppu. It had been a rainy day, but suddenly the sun burst through the clouds, illuminating Beppu and the surrounding mountains into a glorious scene. May God's Son and His church shine through the darkness, transforming Japan into His Light.

VARIETY

Mennonite tour groups came to visit. When the Kehler group came, Peter rented a minibus and took then to Mount Aso, the world's largest active volcano. On the way we stopped at a restaurant. Since there were no other lunch guests, we sang our table grace. When we were finished, the servers asked us to sing some more. We raised the roof singing ***Praise God...***, the # 606 version!

Our Japan mission commissioned George Janzen and Peter to sell the Kobe house. The value had increased tenfold. Peter came home with the proceeds in his pocket. He had never carried so much cash!

Decisions, decisions! We were praying with Lily about her college education. She wanted to attend Wheaton College, but the school had discontinued aid for foreigners. Yes, Canadians were foreigners. We marvelled how God undertook. The day she left Japan, a Christian in our church handed her an envelope. Inside she found nineteen crisp 10,000 yen bills. The church people told us, "Lily is part of our church family, and we want to help!" God's amazing provision happened again and again for each of our college and university kids. Lily went to Wheaton.

WANDA AND BRUNO'S WEDDING

Wanda and Bruno met at UBC in Vancouver. Timing was perfect for Wanda and Bruno's wedding. COM, our mission board, had a new policy, and we could choose to take a summer furlough in 1982. We were happy. No uprooting our life in Japan for a furlough year.

We had met Bruno on a short furlough. The Bergen family lived on the other side of the block where we were staying, in Opa and Oma Derksen's home in Abbotsford. What a pleasant and handsome young man! This was the first time we had met one of our daughter's boyfriends before the wedding. We were impressed, and I added Bruno to my prayer list.

Bruno was teaching, and Wanda had just graduated from UBC. The wedding was at Peace Mennonite Church in Richmond, BC where they were members. Wanda was teaching SS for teens, and the mothers decided to prepare all the food for the wedding. What a show of appreciation for her youth work.

had gone early again, this time to visit our scattered family: my family in Ontario who would not be able to attend Wanda's wedding, and Rose and John and Benjamin in Lansing, MI. Next stop: New Haven, where I had the privilege of attending Rick and Marilyn's graduation ceremony at Yale University. The highlight was taking part in an early morning communion service in Yale's chapel. I had been discouraged in our work, but in the communion service I met the Lord and could say, “Yes, Lord, I’ll willingly return to Japan to share your love.”

Peter and Lily flew from Japan in time for the wedding. Vangy and Ernie and Jayden arrived from New York State where Ernie was studying at Cornell University. Six of us went out early the day before the wedding to pick wild flowers. Half were wilted before I started making bouquets, but there were still enough!

Wanda was a beautiful bride, and Bruno was easy to love. God had made another excellent choice! They made their first home in Vancouver. Wanda would never have to spend another Christmas alone as she had done a previous year, which we only found out years later.

Peter, Lily and I took advantage of Visit USA tickets after the wedding, which made flying a fraction of regular costs. Our flights took us to Detroit, New York, Denver, Winnipeg, Chicago, and Vancouver. We were in New York to see Rick and Marilyn off to Zaire. In New York we also looked up the Baptist Church in the Bronx where we had lived for a year before leaving for Japan. We were sad to see it closed off with barbed wire. Since we would be leaving from San Francisco, we even got in a trip to Disneyland. Lily was thrilled!

After a visit with our ninety-three-year-old Uncle Gerhard in Virgil, Ontario, Lily said, “Mom and Dad, that’s how you have to be when you’re old!” He was still playing guitar and knew all the songs from the church hymnal by heart.

During our final week in BC, we paid a visit to our doctor who said, “Exert yourselves less and trust the Lord more.” Once more we flew home to Japan.

HOME

Back in Beppu, it was rewarding to see how the Christians had taken responsibility and grown through our absence. Thirteen Christians shared their testimonies during our first Sunday worship service back. Sad news touched us immediately. The husband of a church member was killed in a trucking accident. She returned to Beppu with her baby son but lived in fear that her husband’s family would take her son from her. Life gradually returned to normal, and she was able to raise her son without family interference.

Vangy and Ernie and the three kids stopped for two weeks on the way to their second term in Nepal. Peter seemed to get more exercise in two weeks than he usually got in two years. "Opa, can you come for a bike ride with us?" We packed several years' worth of picnics, outings, and late night talks into our time together.

Wanda and Bruno had applied to our mission board, and went to Taiwan for a two-year mission term, teaching English and leading youth and Bible studies. During their time in Taiwan, Wanda had an appendectomy. On their way to Canada after two years in Taiwan, they stopped for a wonderful visit with us in Japan, Wanda's birth country.

When they arrived home, they called us by phone. Our mission board, COM, had asked them to take the position of personnel secretary. They moved to Newton, Kansas, where their two girls, Tesia and Brina, were born.

We were on furlough the year Tesia was born and planned our visit to Newton so that we would be there for her birth. But that little one had a plan of her own, and we had to travel to our next commitment without seeing her. We did get to see her on our next visit and had lots of fun with our two beautiful granddaughters in Newton.

NEPAL 1980

Vangy and Ernie with Jayden, Carissa, and Micah, were serving with MCC in Nepal in the remote village of Andhi Khola. Peter kept referring to our new prophet, Micah, when Vangy and Ernie phoned about Micah's birth.

Nepal seemed like "the uttermost part of the earth" to us. We read everything we could about that country.

When they first arrived in Nepal, Vangy wrote: "We've reached the promised land!" Communicating via snail mail took weeks. Once when we hadn't received letters for over a month, my heart was burdened. News reached us long after the happening. One day when the parents were away, the woman caring for the children rescued Micah from his high chair minutes before their burning kitchen exploded! Now I knew why I had been praying especially for our family in Nepal.

Peter and I shared a dream. We wanted to visit each one of our children in their overseas homes. Then we made plans. Nepal was first on the list. Our dates were set. However, a big problem with one of our church families almost stopped us. I finally persuaded Peter that the problem would not disappear quickly, and God could take care of it without him during our trip. We compromised, so he would stay only one week and return home, and I would stay the planned two weeks.

In the wee hours of the morning, May 10, 1983, we left Fukuoka airport for Nepal, with a quick stop in Taiwan and an overnight stop in Hong Kong. That was before Wanda and Bruno's two years in Taiwan. Hugh Sprunger met us in Hong Kong and took us to their apartment and church. Security was tight. First we went through a big iron gate with their key, followed by another iron gate. Japan had big apartment complexes, too, but nothing like what we saw in Hong Kong. This complex was U-shaped. Windows on first floor where their church was located were secured with multiple bars. Looking up, we saw laundry hanging on each balcony. That was the main view most of these apartments facing each other had. How could so many people possibly live next to each other, on top of each other, and below each other?

Reiko and Brian were our hosts for the night. Reiko was from Oita, one of Vangy's best friends. After graduation Reiko had become a stewardess and married a British pilot. They made their home in Hong Kong. What a lot of catching up we had to do. Early the next morning Reiko took us to the airport for our flight to Nepal.

We made one more stop in Dhaka, Bangladesh, but no one was allowed out of the plane. A guard stood at the bottom of the stairs. I bravely stepped down and begged the guard to let me just put my foot on the ground, so I could say I had been in Bangladesh. Permission granted!

We saw Vangy and Ernie, Jayden, Carissa and Micah at the windows of the airport in Kathmandu, Nepal. My eyes filled with tears. What a joyous reunion! Taxis took us to the Sallyann guest house of United Mission to Nepal, under which all missions were cooperating.

The next day we were all at the airport again, planning to fly to the second largest city of Nepal, Pokhara. Ernie and Jayden left by motorcycle. A Japanese tour group was also at the airport. Then all flights to Pokhara were cancelled because a storm was brewing. We were stuck.

Peter and I listened to the Japanese group leader announcing their plans to rent a bus to Pokhara. I told Peter, "We have to try and get on that bus!" I edged over to some of the tourists. They were surprised to meet these foreigners who spoke Japanese, and we quickly made friends. We asked them to please make room for this family on their bus. They spoke to their leader. That instigated lots of discussion. Their insurance only covered the tour group. We assured them that we would not hold them accountable for anything. We waited nervously until they finally agreed to take the six of us. What a relief! Our trip would be free! The bus was leaky and cold, but no one complained. Bus drivers seemed to be chasing each other around the hair-pin curves. Seven and a half hours later we arrived in Pokhara.

Ernie and Jayden were waiting for us in the mission guest house. We were up again for the 6 a.m. bus to Galyang, the closest village to their home. The roof of the bus was loaded with boxes and suitcases. The inside was full, including a goat and a few chickens. Our young driver was in charge. We thought he was going pretty fast around those mountainous curves.

On an unusually straight stretch, we saw men on the road far ahead of us. They were standing legs spread across the road. Were those guns? Our driver slowed, but just before we got to the men, he gunned the machine, and the men jumped out of our way. The driver kept on speeding till the men were out of sight. Whew!

Our kids told us that not long ago men had stopped a bus, and told the young foreign passenger to hand over his passport. He refused so they shot him. We will never know what our driver saved us from, but we were very thankful.

At the rest stop, we watched fascinated, as donkey caravans, chickens, dogs, cows and people all vied for space, creating a scene beyond anything a movie might portray!

In Galyang, a small village with several open front stores, we left the bus. We hired porters to carry our suitcases and started the half hour walk along the mountain path that led to the kids' home in the centre of the village, surrounded by Nepali neighbors. The people in the numerous small villages high in the mountains were close to starvation. They carried water on their heads, walking twenty minutes to the nearest spring.

There was little rain, and it was back-breaking to till their small garden plots, where corn plants grew sporadically. The mission was making a dam in this area, which would generate electricity for the mountain homes when the project was finished. Then they would have water. The kids had a metal barrel and used water sparingly. Any water for drinking had to be boiled. There was no electricity.

The following morning, Vangy asked their helper Junkiri to get some food from the market where they could buy bread and a few groceries in Galyang. The only vegetable Junkiri found was a nice sized cucumber, which she sliced and put on the table for lunch. The three children crowded around the cucumber and counted the slices to see how many each one would get. We were eight people!

There was no church on Sunday. However, Saturday evening several Christians from the area gathered for fellowship. We couldn't understand, but our hearts understood. We sat outside in a circle. Christianity was illegal, and baptisms were carried out in secret. A Christian might be jailed for a year if baptized. Christians suffered persecution. However, the few Christians longed for fellowship, and took the chance to be in a Christian meeting. We were deeply moved and felt the Lord's spirit in our midst.

Peter left in one week, and I stayed one more. Vangy took me to Kathmandu, with a one night stop in Pokhara. Along the way the awesome Himalayan white peaks pierced the clouds and blue sky. At night I got up twice, climbed to the roof of the guesthouse, and marveled at the Annapurna range in the silvery moonlight.

Even in the big city of Kathmandu, one had to wonder why they allowed the cows such freedom. Cows were considered holy, and store owners were constantly on the lookout, chasing them away. The smells were overwhelming at times. Cow dung was a precious commodity which they dried for fuel. What happens when you get splashed with cow -dung walking down the street? Laugh it off! Chickens and dogs also had free run. The narrow eyes on top of Nepal's monuments) followed us wherever we went.

On the way home, I spent a day with Reiko in Hong Kong sightseeing and shopping. I shared Nepal stories about our visit with Vangy and family. There was no end to the stories, and on the ferry we laughed until our sides ached.

Perhaps it was the shock of re-entry that caused our stomach problems. I lost ten pounds in one night. We were so thankful that neither of us became sick during our Nepal visit.

OUR TULIP GARDEN

Every fall I planted tulips in the tiny triangle garden beside the parking lot. Planting the ugly bulbs was a venture in faith. Digging the soil was back breaking, but eventually all the bulbs were in the ground, neatly covered. Soon the first snowflakes softly added their covering of blessing.

After Sunday School one cold day, I glanced out of the window, quickly opened it and shouted, "Stopu! Stopu!" The kids were jumping around on the bleak tulip garden. I was sure there would be no tulips that spring. But lo and behold! In spite of the trampling, they rose from the dead with blooming beauty. I counted them every year, sometimes as many as seventy.

The tulips reminded me of the church. It hardly seemed possible that some of the "bulbs" God chose could contain such beauty, but God knew the potential of each one. Seekers struggled to put down roots amid the storms of life. As these hurting people found love, forgiveness, and a new reason for living, they showed signs of new life. God's garden began to bloom!

We had prayed that the Lord would send us needy people, and that we would be able to reach the "underside" of Beppu. They came. We realized anew that we were only one link used by God. Some had attended Sunday School during their childhood. Others came through Christian radio broadcasts or Christian literature. Some came through a Christian family member or friend. It was exciting to see God's new church plant come to bloom. In normal society, probably most of them would not have chosen the friends they found in church. Yet here they were, a happy growing church family.

The church began to pray for a pastor. A young student whom our fellow missionary Anna Dyck had led to the Lord, was graduating from Bible college. Yes, he was willing, but he was single. According to Japanese custom, he was introduced to a Christian girl from the northern island of Hokkaido. What a blessing to have the new pastor's wedding in the Beppu church.

Our time in Beppu was coming to a close. We had experienced the birth, development and growth of the Beppu church during these nine years of ministry. Tears flowed as we said farewell and commended them to God's grace and to the pastoral care of the "just married," Kesatsugi and Megumi Kuroki. Another chapter of our life in Japan had come to a close.

Memories of Beppu by Lily

- Sakaigawa Shogakko (elementary school) and our first neighborhood, full of fun times, with many friends! I even got to participate in undokai (sports event), which was such a treat! Also, I remember even beating all the boys in my grade when we had a jumping rope competition.
- Chubu Chugakko (junior high) and our second home were a bit more challenging!?! It was quite the learning experience; from all the people with mental health issues who came to the door of the church whom Dad counselled quite regularly, to being in junior high, and feeling like nobody understood me except for my dog.
- Obachan (friendly lady), next door neighbor taught me how to play volleyball, the beginning of my love of volleyball for life!
- Of course, there were the hot springs and amusement parks and the city beach,
- and then there was leaving the "Japanese world" and going to CAJ (high school in Tokyo).
- It was really sad to say good-bye to all my Japanese friends, knowing that my world would be different from now on. But I was also relieved to no longer be under the pressure of school exams, like we had in junior high when we were ranked every time, and relieved that I didn't have to take the high school entrance exams. I also knew that it was the right time to change – or else it would be difficult for me to fit into the western world.

Lily attended CAJ for four years and graduated. We were all excited when she was accepted at Wheaton College, in Wheaton, IL. The officials even found a scholarship for a Canadian student that had been waiting years for someone to claim it; unexpected help for Lily.

FURLOUGH 1987

We were taking a one-year furlough again. Leaving Bill in Japan, we arrived in Vancouver to happy reunions with Lily; Rick and Marilyn and their children Karina and Jeremiah on a summer furlough from Zaire; Rose and John, Ben, Luke and a new granddaughter Athalia in Lansing, Michigan; and with Bruno and Wanda in their new home in Newton, Kansas. Vangy and Ernie and three were in Nepal, so we would not see them this time.

Criss-crossing North America by car and plane, we visited churches in B.C., Saskatchewan, Manitoba, Ontario, Kansas, Illinois, Wisconsin and Michigan. Isaiah 40:3 challenges us to *"prepare the way for the Lord."* Imagine our surprise as we entered Douglas Mennonite Church in Winnipeg and found it bustling with preparations; two children's choirs and a ladies' choir practicing for their missions evening. That church celebrated missions! In another church you could feel the anticipation that three months of prayer and preparation had inspired. In still another, families came six nights in succession, some with five young children.

However, in other churches missions seemed to be delegated to the elderly. Children and youth were busy elsewhere.

EUROPE ASSIGNMENT 1988

"Konnichiwa! Yoku irásshaimashita!" A Japanese welcome in Germany? Our friends, the Ouchi's, on loan from Japan to Marburg University for two years of research, greeted us in Frankfurt airport on January 23, 1988. They whisked us off to a beautiful YMCA center overlooking the Rhine River for a week-end retreat with a Japanese church in Bonn.

Then the Ouchis gave us their car for our five weeks in Europe. Driving the autoban in Germany, where people were flying past us at 140 km or more per hour, was scary. Someone warned us, "If you drive faster than 140 km per hour, your guardian angel leaves you!" We felt pushed to keep to the speed limit of 120 km, with drivers zooming by.

The Canadian mission board had asked us to share world missions with the Umsiedler (resettled people) in Germany who had fled Russia. We took the opportunity to see a bit of Europe before the assignment.

When Olga, a missionary friend in Switzerland took us to a small village with a church that had been built in the 5th century, I caught Peter's enthusiasm for church history. In Worms, Germany, we stood in the massive Cathedral where the words of Martin Luther seemed to echo and re-echo, "*Here I stand. I can do no other, so help me God. Amen.*"

We lingered at the Limmat River in Zurich, Switzerland, where Felix Manz, one of the first Anabaptists, was drowned for his faith. In Witmarsum, Holland we stood at Menno Simons memorial and thanked God for faithful leaders who PREPARED the WAY for future generations to live and worship in freedom. Each historical place that we visited increased our emotions as we pondered how these Christians, centuries ago, had prepared the way for our faith in God.

Next destination? Haarlem, Holland to visit Corrie Ten Boom's *Hiding Place*. The Ten Boom family took God's Word seriously. "*...for whoever touches you touches the apple of his eye.*" Many Jews found refuge and were saved through this family's sacrifice. Corrie's father and sister died because they were discovered, and Corrie was imprisoned in Auschwitz, but the seven Jews they were hiding at that time all escaped.

Looking over the Berlin wall, we were reminded of a divided city, a divided country, and a divided world. Our hearts ached.

"UMSIEDLER" (Displaced Persons)

With joyful anticipation, but also misgivings, we made our way to Neuwied, where Hans von Niessen, who had set up our schedule, welcomed us warmly. These dear displaced people had suffered such hard trials and terrible persecutions. How could we, Canadian/Japanese, ever be a blessing to them?

Churches were packed whether it was Sunday or week night meetings. In Unemassen the people had just arrived two weeks ago, but they had already formed a choir for the evening. After the service the conductor said, "We knew that we were to 'go *and make disciples of all nations,' (Matthew 28:19)* but we didn't know it was possible."

The long road of oppression and suffering had produced deeply rooted, childlike faith in God and in His Word, uncluttered by intellectual questions and doubts. They made a clear distinction between the kingdom of God and the kingdom of the world.

Our experiences with the "Umsiedler" were such a blessing, and very humbling. At the end of a service, one young man said, "We'll see you again – in Japan!"

ZAIRE!

Although we often wished that we could visit each of our children in their country of service, never in our wildest dreams had we imagined visiting our kids in Africa. The opportune time came at the end of our furlough. What a joy to play with Karina and Jeremiah for the first time. What a blessing to meet Rick and Marilyn, and to be a part of their life for one month.

Two of the most striking impressions were: the dire poverty, and the radiant faith of the Christians. Other impressions: hundreds of children squashed on log benches for a three hour service;

- clapping and dancing people each taking their offering to the alter;
- a short visit into a women's all-night prayer and praise meeting;
- Christian songs echoing across a lake where women were washing dishes and clothes;
- the market with its mounds of meat, sugar, vegetables, fruit, and clothes;
- women with heavy loads on their heads (and in their hearts);
- eating monkey meat, and fried caterpillars, (not me, but Peter tried).

One last note; we never saw one wild animal during our month in Africa!

We left Africa with a new appreciation for mission work. How different from Japan. Whether it was a big church made of stone or wood, or a bamboo grass church, all were full. Perhaps when people are poor their longing for God is greater.

We had made reservations at a motel in New Jersey before we left for Zaire. However, when we called for courtesy car service, they were all out. Waiting was not an option, so we took a bus in that direction, but we had to get off at the end of the line, still too far to walk. I wanted to get a taxi, but Peter insisted we could walk. So we started walking. Peter rolled the big two suitcases, and I had a smaller one on a hand cart, my purse, and odds and ends. We went down a ramp, and found ourselves on a freeway. No sidewalks. Dangerous! We saw the area of our motel and kept going till we got to the next off ramp. Both were exhausted, and I was mad at Peter! Finally he called the motel again and asked for courtesy service. This time they came immediately and smiled. We had almost made it. Their motel was just around the corner.

Were I to write more, our Nepal, Europe and Africa experiences would fill another book. We flew from New York back to Japan, happy to be home again.

One of my most profound experiences during our month-long visit to our children in Zaire in 1988 happened in the village of Kananga, where our children used to work. We all heard the singing when we got back to our room for the night, but Peter was ill, and no one else wanted to go with me. Thus I ventured into the dark alone. We had walked through the village during the day, so I thought I could find my way alone. I left them at 11 pm, but awoke every hour hearing their singing, until 7 am! This prose (on the following page) was my experience that night. Not until later did it dawn on me that there could have been wild animals or snakes around!

SONGS in the NIGHT!

Hark!
Who sings on this moonless night in Zaire?
JESUS, JESUS!
comes the faint chant
hurry, hurry
find the singers before they fade away
a tiny flashlight guides the stranger's stumbling feet
nearer, nearer
the songs grow stronger
the voices clearer
eager
joyous
beckoning
drawing her like a magnet
to the church in the village center
a door gives way to the searching stranger
kerosene lamps bathe silhouettes in warm light
dancing feet
clapping hands
praising voices
praying voices of village women
all through the night they celebrate
as morning light dispels the darkness
they return home
refreshed
Renewed
ready
for a new day!
these who carry heavy burdens
on their heads
and in their hearts
have found release
and have shown this stranger
a path through the darkness
with their SONGS in the NIGHT!

Church in Beppu, centre, bottom

Preparing posters for evangelism

Peter & Mary - new Vistas

Lily and Shinobu, ready for Jr. High

Fellowship

Peter leading worship service

Sunday School class in kitchen

Christmas Angels

Last resting place

Let's go to school, Lily

Grandkids keep Opa in shape during their visit

Derksen family reunion in Beppu, 1980
Standing: Wanda, Bill, Marilyn, Rick
Front: John & Rose, Peter, Lily, Mary, Ernie & Vangy
Grandkids: Micah, Carissa, & Jayden

Is my name there

Lily's high school graduation

Please teach us about God

Congregation in Kananga following service. Mary in front, center, and Peter in back, right. Rick and children in front, right

Marilyn buying eggs in the market

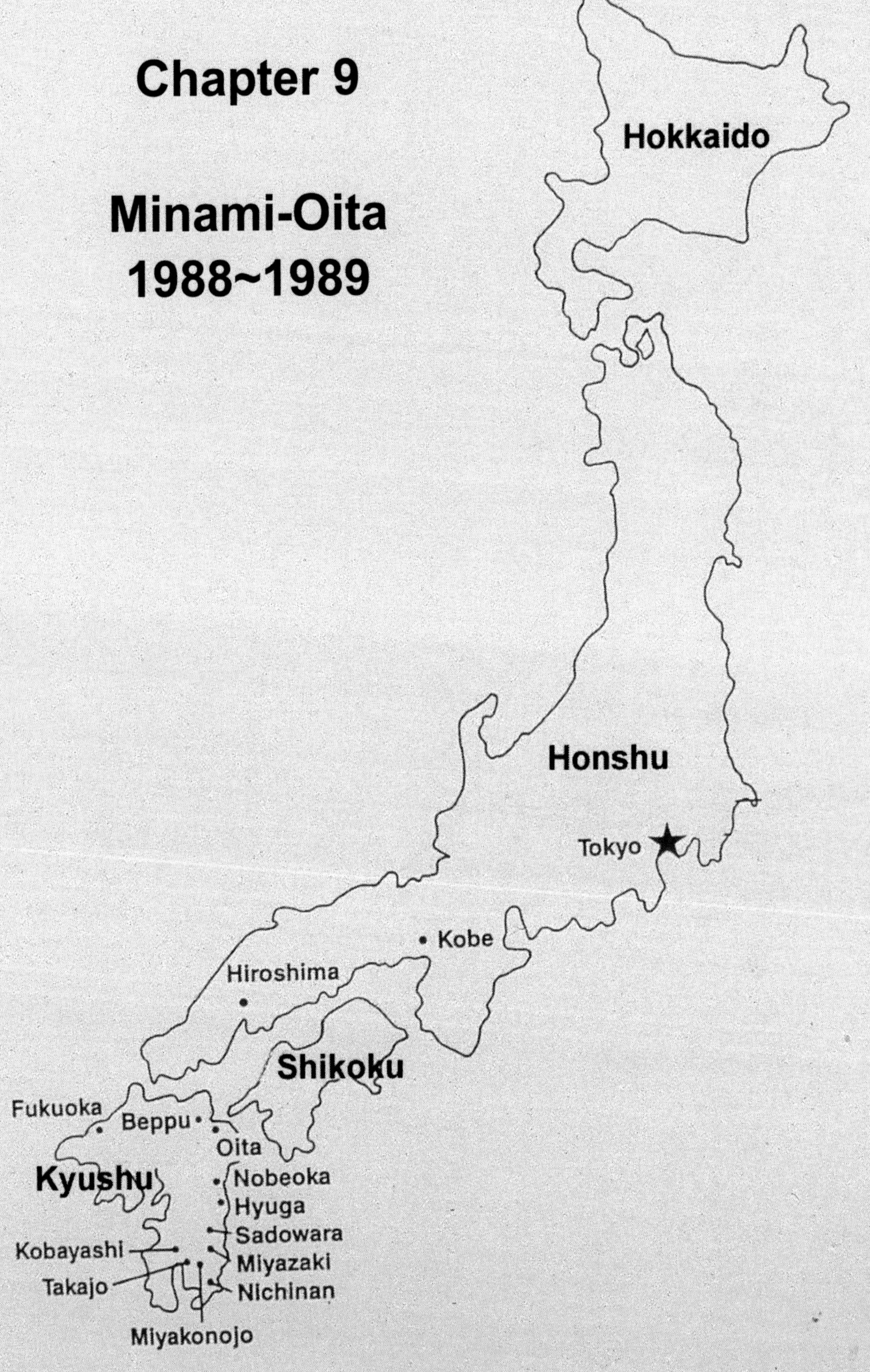
Chapter 9
Minami-Oita
1988~1989
Hokkaido
Honshu
Tokyo
Kobe
Hiroshima
Shikoku
Fukuoka
Beppu
Oita
Kyushu
Nobeoka
Hyuga
Sadowara
Kobayashi
Miyazaki
Takajo
Nichinan
Miyakonojo

A MOVING EXPERIENCE

The church conference had invited us to return to Japan after furlough to begin a new church in the city of Fukuoka. However, it was time for Bill's first furlough, so they asked if we could step in for him at the Oita Minami Mennonite Church. We agreed.

Bill's rented home in Minami Oita was also the church meeting place. The small group of ten Christians and seekers welcomed us warmly. Even though we would be in a different part of the city, we were happy to be back in Oita. The owner had sent out notices a few times that Bill would have to leave, but always changed, allowing Bill and the church to carry on. Now another notice came. No one seemed to take it seriously, except the owner. This time it was for real.

On our walks, Peter and I started looking for a house to rent. People were eager to rent to these foreigners. But it was a shock that no one wanted to rent when we mentioned church meetings. We found a lovely empty house within walking distance of our present rental owner. He had been transferred to Tokyo. "No way! No church in my house," he told us.

We kept on searching, and also contacted a real estate agent, but nothing turned up. We began to pray in earnest for the house we had found and phoned him again. He refused.

Our deadline was approaching, and the church was getting anxious. Some of the Christian ladies came to help pack dishes and household items. Our deadline was April 29. Neighbors kept asking if we had a place to move yet. Some were quite concerned. Others laughed.

We phoned the owner of that house again. He asked, "What are you planning to do, renovate my house?"

"Oh, no," we answered. "We only want to put a sign up outside." No response. We ordered a truck for April the 29 and waited.

The next morning a neighbor asked, "When are you moving?"

"Tomorrow," I answered.

That afternoon Peter and I walked to the house once more, and prayed in the garden, claiming the place for the church. In the evening we waited with baited breath. Surely God would answer our earnest prayers. There was no thought of going to bed. Then the phone rang. It was the owner. "You may move in," he said. It was 10:30 PM In my diary I wrote: *Our Red Sea Miracle day!*

Lily had come home for a six-month interlude of her studies at Wheaton College. It was good to have her share this experience. Now we shouted, "Yatta! Thank you Lord!" Lily and I jumped around the room in excitement.

THE NEW CHURCH

The next day it was time to *Rise and Shine* long before the truck arrived. It was Saturday, and ten friends came to help. The mother of an English Bible student brought a big lunch. Another mother brought food. Others stopped by. We were twenty-three for lunch. There was enough for all!

We moved on schedule! Neighbors were relieved and amazed! So were we. The Lord had done the impossible again! Sunday morning, April 30, the Sunday School children came to the empty house, and they walked to our new church home with the teacher. Peter's message that first Sunday was from Matthew 7: 7-12. "Seek. Knock. Ask." What perfect timing. Our new home and church did not even look as if we had just moved in the day before. Our high school students brought lunch for everybody.

Lily met Kazue (pseudonym) at the private tutoring school where both were teaching English. Kazue started coming to church services. There was something here that caught her attention. She had been attending meetings of a popular sect and was determined to win Lily over. Sometimes the Lord turns our world upside down. Kazue's whole family came to her baptism! The parents were relieved for the change in their daughter's religion. Another daughter had recently failed a suicide attempt.

Kodama (pseudonym) and his girlfriend came to church for help. She was losing out in her Christian life, and was expecting a baby. Imagine her shock when the police arrested him for drug involvement. Kodama was sentenced to ten months in prison. Now she cried to the Lord for his salvation. She gave birth to a baby girl, Hikari Chan, meaning light, for the Lord had once more become her *light and salvation*.

When Kodama was released from prison, he came to church for daily Bible studies. What a day of rejoicing when he accepted Christ and was baptized! Now they wanted a Christian wedding. It was a joyous day when her parents gave approval. Where sin abounds, grace abounds more.

A sad sequel to the story. The family had gone to the beach, where Kodama rented a boat to take Hikari Chan for a ride. Alas, the boat capsized, and father and daughter drowned. The funeral was sad, but also vibrant with hope, knowing Kodama had started a new life with the Lord. His wife gave a moving testimony at the funeral.

During the Christmas season we received hundreds of beautiful cards from friends. People who came to our house loved to check out the cards pinned on long red ribbons hanging from the ceiling. Fiends in Canada often asked, "Will your children all be home for Christmas?" We chuckled. We were happy for the family reunion we were able to have in Beppu when Lily was the only one left in Japan.

MY CHRISTMAS GUESTS

Every year I prayed that God would send me a special Christmas guest, like in the story of *Martin the Shoemaker*. I always wondered how God would surprise me.

The Sunday before Christmas, the teachers brought a black tree cut out of sturdy cardboard. Sunday School children and teachers were soon busy making macaroni ornaments. Sparkling dark eyes concentrated on their task, and paste was oozing between little fingers. Then a big boy, Hiroshi and his mother came in. Hiroshi watched a bit, and then went off to the kitchen. He opened the fridge door. His mother had a hard time getting him back to the meeting room.

When the children were finished with the ornaments, a teacher sprayed them with silver. After they pasted them on the black tree, behold, a miracle! A beautiful Christmas tree! It was fastened to the wall of the meeting room.

Christmas worship service followed. We sat on the floor, Japanese fashion, with our legs tucked under us. Hiroshi and his mother stayed. The room was comfortably full. He clapped his hands when we sang, ***Joy to the World*** and other carols. But the sermon held no attraction for Hiroshi. He began to talk out loud to his mother, repeating, "Suki. suki!" (I like you. I like you,) stroking his mother's cheeks. If she didn't respond, he kept on talking. I was feeling rather annoyed at the constant distraction. I knew how much time and prayer Peter put into his sermon preparations. This was our Christmas service. How could anyone concentrate with Hiroshi's ongoing chatter? Finally, the mother made a move to leave, and secretly I wished they would.

In the middle of his sermon Peter reassured them that it was okay. to stay. He continued with his message, "A church without love is not a church...."

The day was cold and cloudy, matching my mood. Suddenly the sun shone through and lit up the silver ornaments on the black Christmas tree. My heart almost stopped. And then Peter's words echoed in my heart: "A church without love is not a church!"

My heart was as black as the tree had been. "Oh, God," I sobbed quietly, "forgive me!" How could I become so calloused? This mother had brought her challenged son, probably hoping to find some encouragement and rest in church, and I had wished her away. I wiped my eyes. I was in need of God's forgiveness. My heart needed a deep cleansing before it could shine again.

I looked at the tree again and knew that God had answered my prayer. He had sent Hiroshi and his mother in answer to my prayer for special Christmas guests. And to think that I almost missed them!

COLLEGE STUDENTS

Birgit, a German exchange student, started attending English Bible classes. Occasionally we had fun speaking German. She started coming to church meetings and became a Christian. Birgit was *Mary* in the church Christmas pageant, and Mitsuya was *Joseph.* The church had made the decisions about the actors. Peter and I had no idea of the relationship that was developing. I suggested they were a bit too close together in the drama! We were probably the last ones to know they were in love.

Mitsuya and Birgit went to his hometown far in the mountains west of Tokyo, where they contacted the local pastor. Both were baptized there before they moved to Germany. There they married, found a church fellowship, and settled. They had four children, and soon the family was giving concerts in their neighborhood and in their city.

When they returned to Japan for family visits, they visited us. When Peter was sick, they called us in Canada from Germany and asked if they could come to see him. Peter's visiting times were very limited, but we were able to spend an hour and a half together. Financially, this was a very expensive short visit for them. How we thanked God for this Christian couple in Germany who had their roots in a small English Bible class in Japan.

OPPORTUNITIES

Every church must battle with relationship problems at times, and so it was with our churches in Japan. Sometimes Christians quit because of it, and sometimes they came back. Some we lost. However, they are not lost to God. *For the eyes of the Lord range throughout the earth…* Yes, I know there is more to the verse, but I do believe the Lord seeks the lost, even those who have forgotten him.

During Bill's furlough, he brought a tour of young people from our Canadian and American churches to Japan. The small church was a bit overwhelmed with eighteen foreigners at their Wednesday meeting. But our hearts warmed as they spent a lively evening sharing and praising the Lord together! This reminded us of the many friends in North America supporting missions around the world. Thank you all!

FAMILY TIES

Our kids kept us informed of life in the country where they worked. We were shocked when Rick wrote of his encounter with two bandits as he and Zairian friends were on their way to a distant village with two motorcycles. The bandits brandished a gun and demanded keys for the motorcycle. Rick refused and rushed into the woods to join his friends. Before the bandits drove away with one motorcycle, they shot holes into the tires of the other. The three were stranded on a lonely stretch. Their only solution was to walk to the next village pushing Rick's motorcycle.

From Nepal Vangy wrote: "This is the land where you can staple your blouse together when a hook comes off, where you can wipe your sticky hands on your clothes, wear the same things for a week, look into your kids hair and pick out the lice, hammer a nail in wherever you want to, get your exercise without trying, live without junk food, see lots of drama without going to the movies, be awakened without an alarm, and see beauty all around!"

Our family mushroomed to eight again when Vangy, Ernie, Jayden, Carissa and Micah visited us in May, 1989. They were on their way home from Nepal after their second term of MCC service. Lily was still home, too, so we were one big happy family most of the time. Readjusting from their village in the mountains of Nepal to city life in Japan had its frustrations. A friend gave us one child's bike, and we found two more in the local dump, where you can take any undesirable item to a collection point once a month. Biking was probably our favorite sport on that visit. Vangy, Lily and I had fun shopping. We all walked our streets and hiked to the river nearby. Nights were too short for sharing all that the Lord had done for us in Nepal and Japan. The month passed quickly.

Our sixteen months with the Oita Minami church were coming to a close. We were happy to have Bill back, and were looking forward to new beginnings in Fukuoka, the largest city on the island of Kyushu. Our hearts throbbed at the thought. What did the Lord have in store for us? Had we known, would we have started another ministry?

Bill and Pastor Sasaki; opening of Minami (south) Oita Church

Sunday School with the black Christmas tree

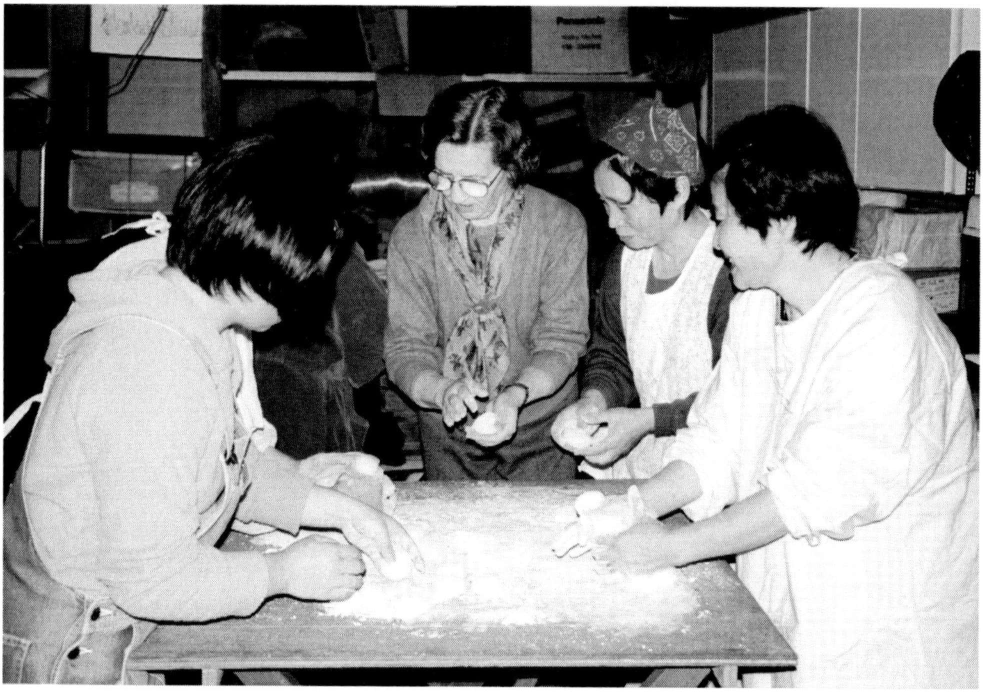

Making mochi - rice cakes for New Year celebration

Mennonite Women's Retreat

Mary shops
by bike

Junkiri's knitting class, Nepal

With grandkids, Carissa, Jayden, and Micah in Nepal

Junkiri, Mary, and Vangy in Nepal

Opa with grandkids in Nepal

COM—JAPAN 40th ANNIVERSARY 1951—1991
Missionary Fellowship October 23,1991

Japan Missionary family, 1991

Bill with Hashimoto family

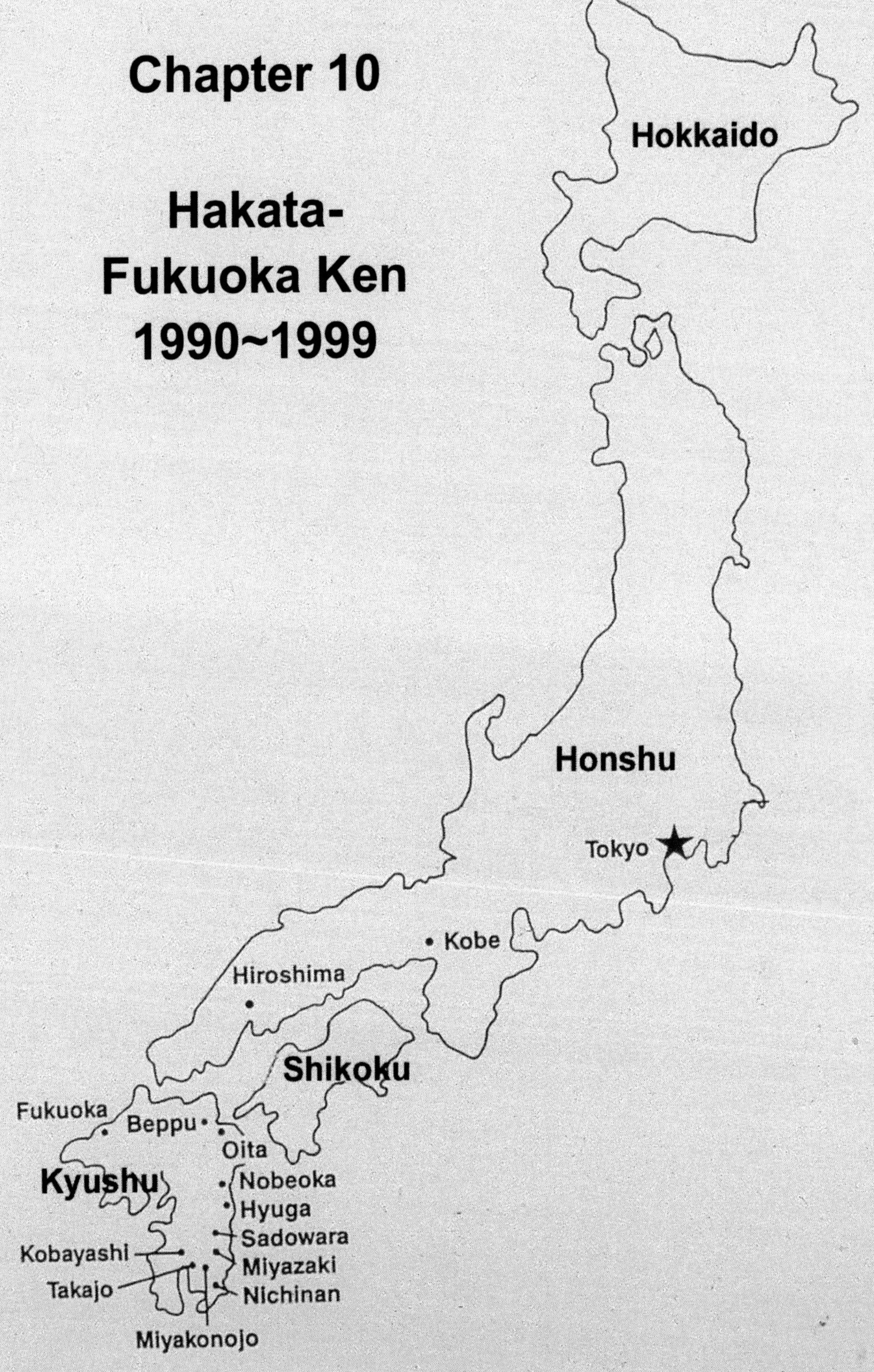
Chapter 10
Hakata-
Fukuoka Ken
1990~1999
Hokkaido
Honshu
Tokyo
Kobe
Hiroshima
Shikoku
Fukuoka
Beppu
Oita
Kyushu
Nobeoka
Hyuga
Sadowara
Kobayashi
Miyazaki
Takajo
Nichinan
Miyakonojo

LAST BEGINNING

Peter and I were sixty-two and counting. We had lived in Kobe, Nichinan, Hyuga, Oita, Beppu, and Minami Oita. In each town or city where we had worked, we had children, beginning with toddlers, and last but not least, our youngest daughter Lily, who was born when we started a new church in the city of Oita. We were on our own. No counting on kids to make us more user friendly. Except for Peter's occasional chest pains, we were healthy and eager to start again.

Now our six children were grown and gone, married with families of their own and scattered in as many places, except Bill and Lily. Vangy, Ernie and three were home in Abbotsford, BC again after six years in Nepal and four years at Cornell University. Rick and Marilyn and three were in Zaire, now Congo, Africa, where rebellion and instability were causing havoc. They were evacuated for a while. Rose, John and three lived in Lansing, Michigan; Wanda, Bruno and two girls in Abbotsford, BC; Bill in Minami Oita, Japan; and Lily in San Francisco, working under Mennonite Volunteer Service.

Fukuoka was the largest city on Kyushu Island, with a population of 1,200,000. Our conference already had one small congregation in the west end of the city, started by George and Martha Janzen, who had retired. Mayumi Sensei, sent out from the Beppu church, was pastor. The conference suggested we start another church in Fukuoka so that the small congregation would have a sister church nearby for fellowship and encouragement. We were happy to be able to work close to Mayumi, now called Sensei (teacher).

We moved to Hakata, which is the central region of the city, in January 1990. Train lines branch out in different directions from Hakata Station. We found an apartment a five-minute walk from Zashonokuma Station, half an hour from Hakata station.

This was the first time we would be living in an apartment. "Excellent 36," had six floors. Ours was apartment 602. One of our daughters jokingly called us her "excellent parents!" There were 36 apartments, but the number four was missing on each floor. “Shi,” the word for four, and also for death, was absent. Japan avoids that number whenever possible. For example, if you give someone a gift, you never give four apples, or four of anything. Our south windows looked down on our neighborhood of Mugino, meaning “wheat field.” A few homes had small gardens, but apartment buildings dominated the scene as far as the eye could see. On the north side we watched planes come in or take off at Fukuoka International Airport.

Our grandson Luke, fourteen at the time, was chosen to represent his school in Lansing, MI for a trip to Japan. After a one-week Japanese home stay, he visited us. Luke had done simulation training as an airplane pilot on the computer and was quite confident that in case of an emergency he could have landed the jumbo plane he flew on. Opa and Luke loved to stand under the flight path of airplanes taking off or landing at Fukuoka International Airport. After Luke was gone, a plane crashed on takeoff right where they had stood. “Don’t ever stand there with our grandkids or anyone else again,” I cautioned Peter. Not that he needed it.

Our immediate area had a short, covered shopping street with a variety of small stores. A department store nearby was called Nandemoya, meaning “anything and everything.” I did all our shopping by bike, and only used the car if I needed nandemoya when it was raining. To keep in shape, I walked the five flights of stairs once a day. Peter and I took walks most evenings, getting acquainted with our new neighborhood. I had also made a habit of planting a tree in each place where we lived. However, in this cement jungle there was not enough space for a tree to take root, so I failed.

Every city in Japan had designated days and places where you can dump your unwanted household items. On collection day, fridges, furniture, and a variety of anything and everything piled up. The saying was that you could furnish your home if you were on the ball. Once I found a small tape recorder. As I shook it to get rid of the rattle, a beautiful diamond ring fell out. Jeff, a nephew who used to work at a jewelry shop said, “This is the best imitation diamond I have ever seen!” Another day I found a large perfect Corning ware casserole dish. Someone dumped a like new Samsonite suitcase. No room in tiny apartments for such non-essentials after the trip is over. And then there was the heart-rending futon, sleeping mat, still in its new plastic wrap, a wedding gone sour so quickly?

Every apartment building had a niche for garbage twice a week and unwanted items once a month. I took the beautiful dishes and cookware I found to a thrift shop. Thrift shops were just making inroads in the market place. Was it easier to start over in a new place than to pack household belongings?

HOSPICE VOLUNTEER

The only people whom we knew in this megacity were the Shigeyuki's, the former farmer who changed his life occupation to become a hospice nurse, his wife Yoko, and their three children. They were members of a church where the pastor, Shimoinaba Sensei, was also a medical doctor. Dr. Shimoinaba was instrumental in opening Eiko Byoin hospital and hospice in Fukuoka, the second hospice in Japan. Shigeyuki worked at Eiko Byoin.

Shigeyuki's family came for a visit, and they soon discovered how lost we were without our children. We were lonely. Living in an apartment for the first time in Japan was a new experience. Shigeyuki suggested, "Why don't you volunteer at Eiko Byoin?"

"Me? A foreigner?" I asked? He thought I should try. Since we didn't have a schedule yet, I tried it. I liked it! The patients were very accepting of this foreigner, so the feeling was mutual. I chose Thursday as my volunteer day, and met volunteers from other churches, too. We served green tea to every patient on the third floor. I began to take along my zither, and we sang for patients. Thursday became my favorite day of the week.

Patients were coming to Eiko Hospice from every part of the country. Dr. Shimoinaba was a man of compassion and vision. Japan's medical professionals do not tell people if they are terminally ill. However, Dr. Shimoinaba's philosophy was that patients had the right to know. He explained the way of salvation to every patient, and many accepted Christ as Savior. He baptized new Christians on the hospital beds if they requested it. Some families chose to have wedding celebrations in the room of a dying family member. Since Dr. Shimoinaba was also a pastor, he performed the ceremonies.

The chapel had daily worship services for staff and patients who were able to attend. Once a year the hospital held a memorial service for families who had lost someone to cancer that year. At one memorial service he called on me for an impromptu speech. I was stunned, but with a quick prayer, went to the pulpit, and recalled many of the patients, giving them names. One was a "Hallelujah!" lady, always rejoicing in Jesus. Another was "I'm sorry," because she was always apologizing for all the trouble she was causing. Another was the "sock knitter," who spent hours knitting socks from her bed. I suggested we might see some socks falling from heaven.

In Japan I used the name Maria. Otherwise I would have been called "May-arri." As the crowd was leaving at one of these memorials, a lady greeted me warmly, "You are Maria, and your Mother's name was Agatha." Surprised, I asked how she knew. She reminded me of how we had sung for her sister, who had become a Christian in the hospice.

I had challenged her, "If you get to heaven before I do, please give my love to my Mother."

"Please tell me your Mother's name then, so I can find her," she said.

"Agatha," I told her.

Almost a year later, this sister had remembered.

Another day two volunteers and I were just leaving the room where we had sung for a cancer patient. A nurse in the hallway asked, "Would you please sing for the man across the hall?" We loved such requests. The family was gathered in that room. We sang a few fun songs with motions that had everybody laughing, and ended up with a favorite in Japan, ***What a Friend We Have in Jesus.***

As we were leaving later, we met family members outside. They told us, "Kuroki (pseudonym) died twenty minutes after you left." What a shock! How could I have been so insensitive, singing and laughing when the man was dying? I almost lost my courage to keep on volunteering.

Two weeks later the head nurse called me into her office, and I wondered if this was my termination. Instead, she handed me an envelope and said, "Kuroki 's wife left this envelope for you. She was very grateful." The note said, "While you were singing for my husband, it seemed as if you were ushering him right into heaven. On our way home in the train, my daughter and I saw a rainbow. Thank you so much." The envelope contained a 10,000 yen note, equivalent of $100. The family was Buddhist. They also had excellent care from Dr. Shimoninaba. Perhaps God did a miracle in their hearts while we sang. What an awesome God to turn my blunder into a blessing!

Ezekiel 1:28 reminds us: *Like the appearance of a rainbow in the clouds on a rainy day, so was the radiance around him. This was the appearance of the glory of the Lord.* We bow in worship.

NEW BEGINNING

How do you start a church when you live in an apartment? Most people in our apartment left for work early in the morning and returned after dark, so it was difficult to make connections, except for those who had young children.

Peter and I passed out thousands of invitations for Sunday worship services in our neighborhood. An elderly Christian couple from Miyazaki had moved into a care home in Fukuoka. They were happy for a church nearby.

Tomoko, Virginia's former neighbor, regularly attended church services in Oita. Losing someone who was so close to making a decision to follow Jesus was difficult. What a sad day when her family moved to Fukuoka. Now we were happy to have contact again. She lived in another city near Fukuoka. It would take her more than an hour to come to church services in Hakata.

Peter had been invited to a pastors' seminar at the Fukuoka Baptist Seminary. He found his way there by local train, which included a transfer along the way. When he came out of the meeting, he had no idea how he got there, so he asked a student for directions. The student, Satoru Hara said, "I'm going home in the same direction. We can travel together."

For the first Sunday worship service in our apartment three people came, The elderly Mitsushita San, Tomoko San, formerly from Oita, and Satoru San, the student. That was a good beginning, because all three came regularly.

NEW CONNECTIONS

A family operated a private tutoring school across the street. The teacher was interested in these foreigners and started coming. He even cancelled Sunday morning classes so that he could attend. Soon he was bringing his wife and children.

On a summer evening walk, a group of high school students surrounded us trying out their English. After a long visit, they suddenly asked, "Will you please be chaperons for our camp?" What? We were meeting them for the first time, and they came up with a wild request like that? They were not allowed to camp on their own, and no teacher was willing to give up a vacation for the kids they taught every day. The kids were not allowed to camp without an adult chaperon. Several students followed us home. They begged us to camp with them.

Camping was not exactly our cup of tea, but we finally agreed on the condition that they would behave! They promised! And they behaved. We slept on mats in tents. The kids took care of meals, and we enjoyed getting to know these teenagers. When we sang, ***Jesus Loves Me*** in English, Hiroaki sang along lustily. He had been to Sunday School when he was young, and after camp, started attending church services. Others came for a while. God's seed was planted.

We knew that we could not establish a church in an apartment, so we looked for a meeting place to rent. A three-minute walk around the corner from our apartment, we found Culture School Mugino. The owners taught calligraphy in a building on their property, which they also rented to other groups. They were happy to have a church meet Sunday mornings. What an answer to prayer! The wife came occasionally, and their son became a regular in Peter's English Bible class in our apartment Thursday evenings.

RENTING

We were happy to move into the rented room for church. Every Sunday Peter and I loaded the elevator with our keyboard, Bibles, hymn books, tea and snacks to serve after the meeting. On first floor we loaded it all into our car, and then drove to our new spacious room. This became our church meeting place for the remainder of our years in Japan.

Every Sunday after the service, all were invited to our home for lunch. Some had come a long way, and this was their only opportunity to get acquainted. Everybody pitched in to help serve and later clean up. When the numbers reached twelve, I quit. There was only room for twelve at our table, and I was beginning to feel my age, too.

After several months, a wedding company donated an electric organ, which the Mitsuyasus graciously allowed us to store in their room. A piano teacher, started coming. Soon she was accompanying singing for worship service. Ideal.

In 1990 our mission board sent Greta, a short termer from Niagara to help with English classes. Soon Greta was bringing new friends to church. What a joy to work with Greta! This was her third visit to Japan. Japan had grown on her, and Greta came to Japan once more to volunteer in the city of Kobe.

Greta was a welcome addition to the English Bible class, an international group including Japanese, Korean, Chinese and Canadians. We started class with singing. The students loved the English choruses. Noriaki occasionally brought his drum for added accompaniment.

A WEDDING WISH

Naoko (pseudonym), one of our English Bible class students, asked me to play ***The Hallelujah Chorus*** at her wedding. Since I played the choruses for our Bible study, she thought I could play anything. "No way!" I told her, sorry that I could not fulfil her wish. She finally persuaded me to play the hymns for the wedding service. I practiced day and night!

In Japan money is the customary gift for a wedding. You judge how much to take by the hotel where the wedding will take place. In any hotel, the minimum gift was approximately one hundred dollars in Canadian money. This wedding was in a hotel where you would be expected to bring about five hundred Canadian dollars. We were thankful that wedding invitations were few and far between. We could not afford it. Weddings in church were much cheaper.

Many hotels in Japan make a big business of western weddings and have a chapel for such occasions. For a chapel wedding the bride usually wore a western white gown and veil. I went early to practice on the electric organ. I was thankful that I managed the hymns without mistakes.

After the service, guests were ushered into a large reception room while the wedding couple left to change clothes. Peter and I were among the hundred or more guests, getting acquainted with those at our table.

Suddenly the door burst open. The bride, in a long red gown, and the groom, in a flashy western suit, arrived amidst a thunderous symphony rendition of ***Hallelujah*** on the speaker system. Peter and I looked at each other in utter astonishment! Naoko made her wish happen.

CHALLENGES and CELEBRATIONS

Japan was changing. Financial stability in most families may have been the cause of less interest in spiritual things. Never had it taken so long for a church to grow. Could our age be another cause? Or having no children? We were discouraged and asked our supporters to pray that we would not lose heart. Letters and prayers of family, friends and churches kept us going. Hebrews 11:1 held a special challenge for us: *Now faith is being sure of what we hope for and certain of what we do not see.*

We did not see a church steeple or even a cross in this densely populated area, our "grain field." But by faith we envisioned a community of believers emerging, quickened by the Spirit of God, serving and witnessing in the name of Christ.

Satoru left for a year to study English in the U.S. When he returned to Japan, he was ready to commit his life to Christ. In March 1991, Hara Satoru, the student who has shown Peter the way home, was the first baptism candidate for the Hakata Mennonite Christian Church.

In 1991 we celebrated not only the first baptism in our new ministry, but our mission was celebrating forty years in Japan. Our mission had grown to 18 small congregations, 14 with Japanese pastors. However, we were just making a small dent in the population of 122,000,000. Japan's Christian population remained less than one percent.

Special events brought new people to church. The Ayatsuka Family Band, a blind couple and their two blind sons, sang and shared their testimonies to a full room one Sunday morning. When they sang, *The Light of the World is Jesus,* all were deeply touched. *...Once I was blind, but now I can see."*At that point I was blinded by tears. In his testimony the father thanked God for his blindness, because it was through his blindness that he met Christ.

We invited the family to our home for a borscht soup lunch. A few weeks later a parcel came from the Ayatsuka family. Inside we found two big serving dishes and a creamer, an exact match to the dishes we had used for lunch with them. How did they figure that one out? We discovered that the younger son had a bit of eyesight if he held something close to his face. He must have done that on the sly! It was an extravagant gift, considering the time and energy it must have cost them to find these dishes.

CHRIST CALLS

Christ called Mitsushita San, our oldest member, to his heavenly home. Mochimatsu, the new young Christian in the Oita Minami Church, and his young daughter died in a boating accident. His wife testified to God's grace in their family life, and now in her loneliness. "Heaven is very near," she cried.

Christ was also calling new people to his church. Yoshiko and daughter Misuzu, twelve, welcomed Jesus Christ into their hearts. Without any prompting from us, Yoshiko asked her husband if she could get rid of the gold trimmed altar in their home where they worshipped a child who had died. He gave permission. Soon Yoshiko and her daughter were baptized.

Yoshiko's mother came for a visit from Osaka. Her daughter and granddaughter were excited about their new faith. They had the joy of leading the mother/grandmother, Takeshita San, to the Lord. What a joyous Christmas when Grandma Takeshita was baptized.

When Yoshiko was well, she was bubbling with life and joy. When depression came, things changed. During our New Year's Day service, Yoshiko's husband prayed to Jesus for the first time in his life, asking for healing for his wife. The following day when he went to the hospital to visit, she greeted him with a smile. Her depression had lifted on New Year's Day!

A miracle seemed to happen after we left Japan. She didn't have depression for many years. Her husband once said, "When my wife stops getting sick, I will become a Christian." We are still waiting for that decision.

In 2002 after retirement, we returned to Japan, and drove with Yoshiko and Misuzu to Osaka to visit Grandma Takeshita in her care home, a joyous reunion. When we said good-bye, Peter pointed up, and she responded, "We'll meet again!"

Eighty-year old Komaba San and his wife started coming after he had attended a Christian funeral. This made a deep impression on him, and the pastor of that church sent a card to our church telling us about his interest in Christianity. Peter and another Christian from our church went to visit the Komaba's, and they started coming. During a thanksgiving service he said, "I am so thankful to God from whom all things come…" He added thanks for his parents, for his faithful wife, and quoted from Colossians 1:16 by memory, "I am thankful to Jesus Christ." Six months ago this man knew almost nothing about our Creator God and Savior. Now he was always the first to recite the Bible memory verse for the week.

Mobility is a big problem for the church in Japan. Big companies transfer their workers every few years. Students come and go. Those living in the metropolises are on the receiving end more often, since that is where the better universities and big companies are. One year nine people who had been coming regularly moved away. Others came less often, and decisions were lacking.

Keiko (pseudonym) had been studying with a cult group for three years but found no peace in her heart. She lived quite a distance away but started coming occasionally. However, fear of in-law objection kept her from making a decision.

Anai San, a business woman, owned the local stationery shop. She came for grief support when her husband died. Here she found peace for her troubled heart.

A FIRST CHRISTMAS

Satoru was leading a Christmas celebration with our English Bible class. He asked each person, "When is the first time you heard about the meaning of Christmas?"

A new university student responded, "Now!"

Thinking she had misunderstood, he repeated his question. Her answer was the same. "This is the first time I have ever heard that Christmas is a celebration of the birth of Jesus Christ."

Churches in Fukuoka celebrated Christmas like other cities, only on a bigger scale. One thousand people gathered for the "Shimin Christmas," city people's Christmas, held in the city hall. Yuri Mori, a Christian TV singer soon had the stage full of children, getting them involved in the Christmas story.

In 1995 a devastating earthquake in Japan killed 5,500 people. Yuri told us what a difficult year this had been for their family. Her father, who lives in Osaka, went to the neighboring city of Kobe to find out if his only son was okay. All transportation was disrupted, so he walked for hours. Finally, he found the collapsed dormitory where his son had lived. Her father dug him out of the debris with his hands. Then he carried his lifeless son home.

Yuri compared the love of her father for his only son, to the love God showed each one of us when He sent Jesus to find us. In closing, she turned her back on the audience to face the big cross on stage and sang a song about the cross of Jesus.

We had our own little happening at the close of the meeting. A lady behind us got up courage to tap me on the shoulder. "Excuse me, but aren't you the Derksens?" she asked.

"Why yes, but how do you know us?" Fifteen years ago she had attended an evangelistic service at the Oita Mennonite church where Peter was the speaker. That night she made a decision for Christ. Later they moved to Fukuoka, where she was baptized in a Baptist church. What a special encouragement and gift from the Lord.

The Sunday School kids and teachers in our church had taped the Christmas story. They hid behind a huge cardboard box, holding up the appropriate cardboard people, Joseph, Mary, the angel, shepherds and wise men. The children didn't have to spend hours memorizing parts. Mari Yoshida, our guest singer, was so impressed that she asked to borrow the "people" for her church Christmas.

Christmas Eve brought 48 to the candlelight service. Eight of these, including my eighty-eight-year-old artist friend, were in church for the first time.

GORBACHEV

An event in 1995 tied me to my past. I was born in Ukraine, Russia in 1928. Severe persecution against Christianity and all religions broke out. My father was a preacher, and he knew his name was on the black list. One night after dark he jumped on his horse to visit a friend in another village who had been encouraging people to immigrate to Canada. Suddenly a loud knock froze their conversation! Police barged in and arrested his friend. Father rushed home and said, "We're leaving!" I had a new baby brother, and mother was not well. But we packed the wagon and left at night from another town to avoid suspicion.

We took a train to Moscow and waited with 15,000 others in refugee camps for three weeks. All were applying for permission to leave. Every day the KGB police, Russian secret police, were at the doors, calling out a list of men. They were taken to prison work camps in Siberia, and most were never seen again. One night the dreaded knock came to our door. They read every name in that room. Then came the surprise announcement, "You may leave!" Crying jubilation brought tears even to the hardened eyes of the police! 15,000 thousand refugees had applied for permission to leave. Our family of four were among approximately 5,000 allowed to go. Father's brother Johann lived in Ontario, Canada. We knew our destination.

Now here I was in Japan. Can you imagine our surprise when we read the announcement that Gorbachev, President of Russia, would be speaking at a Peace Forum in Fukuoka? Peter and I immediately bought tickets. We received ear phones with simultaneous translation. The hall was packed.

Peter and Gorbachev had one thing in common. Both were bald. People sometimes told Peter that he looked like Gorbachev. Years later when Peter had to have two biopsies on his forehead that left scars, he looked even more like Gorbachev whose trademark was a big scar on his forehead.

When we sat in our places in the rapidly filling hall, I felt as if I was sitting on pins and needles. We had fled Russia as refugees in 1929. Relatives and friends in Russia suffered terrible hardships. Two of my cousins spent years in prison for preaching the Gospel, one for ten years and one for six. In Beppu I had collected three hundred signatures on an Amnesty International program to release my younger cousin still suffering in a Russian prison.

Shortly after Gorbachev came to power, he introduced "*Perestroika,"* and most religious prisoners were released, including my cousin. In his talk, Gorbachev said, "The Communists made a big mistake in denying the importance of religion." He said, "Christianity is a trustworthy religion," and repeatedly emphasized the importance of spiritual things as the world faces the twenty-first century.

1995 HAPPENINGS

The church was excited when Satoru and Toshimi, a Christian who had moved to Fukuoka and came to our church, announced their engagement. Toshimi, a young Christian lady, had moved to Fukuoka recently and was attending our church. Our biggest problem was that we had no place for a wedding. The local Baptist church kindly loaned us their facilities. A ladies group from our church sang, and Peter married the happy couple. Both were very active in church. A year later their daughter Midori was born. Now we had the whole range of ages in our church: a baby, children, youth, parents and grandparents.

Koji Honda Sensei, 83, was called the Billy Graham of Japan. Honda Sensei had one big desire. He wanted to traverse Japan from one end to the other to share the love of God. We were happy to be included in the twenty-five Fukuoka churches, joining in praying for a year for this three-day crusade. Tomoko Koga, formerly from Oita, and I had the privilege of singing in the mass choir. Honda Sensei's messages drew a full house of eight hundred for the meetings. He preached in the power of the Spirit, and many people made decisions for Christ, including Anai San, our elderly business lady.

This year marked the fiftieth anniversary of the end of World War II. To reflect on the problems of war and peace, we initiated a Peace Sunday. During worship service, we read Koji Honda's confession fifty years after the war and joined in repentance and renewed dedication to be peacemakers in our world in Jesus' name. Peace begins as we first seek Christ's peace in each of our hearts.

Our daughter Rose, husband John, and Ben 13, Luke 10, and Tali 8, visited us in May and June. It was so special to have our kids and grandkids for three weeks. No one complained about our squished quarters. Ben enjoyed Japanese internet games, and every time Luke saw a plane coming, ran out to our sixth-floor entrance to watch the planes land at Fukuoka International Airport nearby.

Tali surprised us one day by bringing a computer print-out of her art. She had watched Opa (grandpa) carefully, and presto. We realized how far we lagged behind the new computer generation.

We were quite surprised when a strange lady, the second wife of a man who had passed away, came with a request. She asked for a Christian memorial service for the first wife of her deceased husband, who had been a sincere Christian. However, the husband had arranged for a Buddhist funeral. That was twenty-five years ago. The second wife, although not a Christian, felt bad that her husband had not honored the first wife's Christian faith. Perhaps this will lead to the second wife becoming a Christian one day.

MINI FURLOUGH

In the summer of 1996 we went on a two-month North American assignment for our mission board. Rick and Marilyn were also on a short furlough with their children. It's hard to describe the joy of grandkids dashing into your arms at the airport after a long absence! Our biggest encouragement was the love and support we received from children and grandchildren.

September was packed with travels and meetings in churches, nursing homes, private homes, and colleges. Meetings took us to BC, Saskatchewan, Manitoba, Ontario, Michigan and Kansas. Strong impressions carried us through our remaining years.

- Strong support for missions by elderly and contemporaries
- Meeting people who had been praying for us thirty years or more
- Finding kids excited about missions
- Young people's positive view of missionaries (different from a decade ago)
- Visits with former Japan COM coworkers
- Meeting with our many PARTNERS IN MISSION

The Japan Mennonite Conference called us to serve in Japan once more. You gave us thumbs up to return to Japan! What a privilege to be your missionaries.

The Hakata Mennonite Church had started a fund for a future building soon after we started meetings. The mission board, COM, suggested a few years ago that we retire. We didn't agree. How could we leave a new struggling church without a leader? Thus began our earnest prayer that God would provide a Japanese pastor.

Mayumi Sensei, pastor of the Fukuoka sister church, had recently married a pastor from another city, so that church was left without a pastor. No, I never aspired to preach, but of necessity, Peter and I took turns serving both churches on Sunday mornings.

After a strong typhoon, the upstairs patio of the Fukuoka church had crashed. Peter went to clean it up. He moved huge slabs of cement into a pile for easy pick-up by the garbage trucks. He came home with his face red from the exertion.

PETER IN THE HOSPITAL

Peter was having more angina pain and used nitro often. Dr. Orita, our Christian family doctor, said it was time for angioplasty, or ballooning, as it was called. He might be in the hospital for two weeks.

After another severe angina attack, Dr. Orita make an appointment for Peter to enter a hospital that specialized in heart problems in the neighboring city of Kurume, an hour south on the toll road, for August the 18, 1997. That was our wedding anniversary, so I packed a picnic lunch to enjoy at a park before going to the hospital. Had I known how serious Peter's condition was, I would have been driving.

We had just entered Kurume when the car began to shake. Oh no! A flat tire! Peter opened the trunk to get at the spare. I said, "Peter, you can't do this. We have to get help." He straightened, and we looked across the street. There in bold English letters we read: TIRE SHOP! I ran over, and two kind workers rushed to our aid. In fifteen minutes we were on our way again. What a miracle! We even had time for our mini picnic in the park.

Peter's appointment was with a top heart specialist in Japan. After the consultation, Peter was admitted for the angiogram. The results shocked us. "You have five blockages; two arteries are 50% blocked, one is 75% blocked, one is 90% blocked, and one is 99% blocked. No doctor would do angioplasty in your condition. You need open heart surgery. Your country (Canada) is much farther advanced in heart surgeries than Japan, so if you prefer to return, we will accept that," the doctor said.

We wanted to have the surgery in Japan. Recently our children had encouraged us to join Email, so we had subscribed. How very convenient. Now we had instant contact with each of our children. All agreed that Dad should have the operation in Japan if that was his preference. Some offered to come. We said, "No, Bill is here, and we have our church family. No one needs to come."

When we told the doctor that we wanted him to operate, he was pleased that we chose to trust him. "However," he said, "I have a full schedule until September 1."

Peter answered, "Fine. We'll just go home and come back."

"Oh, no, you won't!" the doctor said. "That would be very irresponsible of me. I am admitting you today." Thus Peter was hospitalized for the first time in his life! The doctor wouldn't even let him walk a block to the new hospital but sent him by ambulance.

With a monitor hanging around his neck, and a blue gown flapping around his legs, he walked the hospital hall, often with another patient beside him, questioning him. "Where do you live? What are you doing in Japan? Why are you here?" He soon had many friends, including his three roommates.

HEALTH INSURANCE

The next morning an office clerk came to us. "Do you have Japanese health insurance?" she asked. Foreigners were not allowed to get Japanese health insurance until a few years ago, when they finally passed a law giving foreigners the rights to their insurance. We declined; we had been quite healthy until recently, so decided to depend on COM.

However, in the consultation with the doctor, he also told us that the operation would be approximately $50,000 U.S. Shocking! Who would have the nerve to ask COM for such an enormous sum?

The office lady told us to return to Fukuoka immediately and ask for health insurance. "What?" I asked. "Are they going to give us insurance when they know the cost and risk?"

"Just go," she said.

It was 4 PM. All offices close at 5 PM. Bill and I rushed off on an express train, took a taxi, and arrived at the city office at 4:45 PM. At 5 PM I walked out with Japanese health insurance. The cost was reduced to $12,000. How could that be?

A few days later I went to the city office again to take care of minor business. An official called me aside and said, "Your husband will be 70 on his next birthday. We are giving him complete senior's benefits. You will need to pay three years of retroactive insurance fees." Total cost? $3,000. What kind of a miracle was God giving us? We will be forever indebted to the Japanese.

Our son Rick wrote from Congo, "I'm coming!" What an emotional reunion when Rick arrived on August 26. What a pillar of strength Rick was for us that month.

Congo was in the midst of turmoil. He had daily email contact with Marilyn and the kids. One day Marilyn wrote that a native pastor had been driving in the city when a fifteen-year-old stopped him and demanded his keys. The pastor refused, and the young soldier shot him. We were quite concerned, but Rick said, "Mom, when we are in God's hand, we are just as safe in Africa as anywhere else."

On operation day, Rick and Bill watched Dad and Mom say goodbye. The possibility that we might never see each other again on earth was real. A few church people came to sit with us. I would have preferred to be just us three, but later realized that God had sent them. Their quiet presence was our strength. Tomoko brought lunch for us all.

Seven long hours! We jumped up when the doctor came in. His face was serious. Yes, the operation was a success, but they would not know until the following day how he really was. There could be brain damage.

Rick, Bill and I were allowed to visit Peter. We wore long white gowns and white masks. It took a while to collect myself when I saw Peter lying there with tubes coming out of every opening. He opened his eyes. The nurse brought a writing tablet and pen so he could express himself. I leaned over him and said, "Hi, darling! Here are your three angels!"

He could barely hold the pen but scrawled something we could not read. Later he told us, "I didn't know if I was still on earth or had gone to heaven!"

The doctor asked one of us to stay for night, and Rick offered. Bill and I drove home, and spent the evening connecting with our other children and extended family. Ringgggggg! I jumped up when the phone rang at 7 AM next morning. It was Rick. The doctor had just told him, "Your Dad is fine. He's going to make it." Joyful news!

We took turns staying one night with Peter. Probably customs regarding visiting the sick are similar the world over. Flowers are always in style! But in Japan people also bring money gifts. We experienced an outpouring of generosity as friends came to visit. Yes, there were lovely flower bouquets, but people brought money, so much that the three-year monthly insurance payments were covered.

DAILY MERCIES

Our daily trips to the hospital and meals out were also covered. It was good to see our boys spending time together. How Rick enjoyed the abundance of Japanese food! We were indebted to all our Japanese friends, and to Japan for giving us health insurance.

Peter went through agonizing pain, but day by day he improved. One day the Hirakawas drove five hours from Nichinan, where we had spent our first three years of service, to visit Peter. We were surrounded by several visitors that day. Peter was walking with a walker, and when these friends left, we walked them to the elevator. Hirakawa was so excited to see Peter walking with a walker, that he suddenly raised his hand and gave Peter a resounding smack on his back. Ouch! But before anyone could stop him, he slapped once more. I thought Peter's heart would fly out of his body!

Before his release, Peter had to endure one more angiogram to make sure he was ready for life outside the hospital. After the angiogram, he was not to move for six hours.

What a nightmare! The three of us tried in vain to comfort him. Finally, he blurted out, "You are all a bunch of Job comforters!" Rick held Dad's hand throughout the six painful hours. The positive outcome? A pale Peter was released from the hospital on September 19, a month since entering. How we thanked God that Peter was home again. A few days later Peter, Bill and I were at the airport to see Rick fly back to Congo. We had experienced one miracle after another. What a journey for each of us.

Slowly Peter's strength returned. We took short walks every day. Exhausting work! Our schedule was gradually returning to normal, and he was eager to preach on Sundays.

Satoru had been taking Bible correspondence courses. One day he and Toshimi surprised us. "We feel God is calling us to pastor the Hakata church," they said. What an answer to prayer. Satoru was teaching English, and in summer he went to Tokyo for short seminary courses.

OITA'S THIRTIETH

The Oita church asked Peter to speak at their thirtieth anniversary celebrations in November 1997. Sasaki Sensei had been pastor in Oita for 15 years. Former members came from Tokyo, Hiroshima, Fukuoka and elsewhere. What a gathering! The church had purchased the land and building from the mission by faithful giving through the years and had made numerous renovations and additions. The sun shone brightly through the south windows adding to the festive spirit.

The church had grown from small gatherings in our home, to a congregation of 118, scattered throughout Japan. Many involved in churches in other cities returned for this event; others who had dropped out, joined the celebration. Hugs and tears mingled. We could feel with Jeremiah 30:19, *From them will come songs of thanksgiving and the sound of rejoicing…and their community will be established before me…their leader will be one of their own…*

Our son Bill was working in Minami, Oita in cooperation with the Oita church. He was amazed at how the church members took the initiative in preparing for this milestone event. In reporting the celebration, he wrote: "The commemorative booklet of letters, the huge meal of onigiri rice balls and home-cooked dishes, five panels of photographs depicting the life history of our church, the neatly weeded and trimmed yard, and of the course the morning worship service of praise and offerings each had the flavor of a people's church blessed by God."

He also wrote: "Dad's energetic and sincere preaching that morning is something I will never forget. I understood in a new way why the work of his hands, together with Mom, over the past thirty years in Oita has affected so many people."

Another highlight for Bill happened during self-introductions in the afternoon. All were seated around tables laden with food. A friend who attended his church and had been hospitalized for years, seldom had the opportunity to attend church. When the microphone was handed to him, he sang a Christmas carol, ***Joy to the World**, perhaps* with anticipation that someday life could be joyful. He was not much of a singer, but grinning at the applause, he continued with ***Jingle Bells**!*

Sasaki Sensei commented on the message according to I John 1:1-4, "We must believe Christ and share Christ, who never changes from generation to generation. Without turning to the left or to the right, we will continue to be a church that simply and purely believes in Christ and shares only Christ. This is the challenge I received."

Four young men, all pastors now who had met Christ in the Oita church, were present. "I am one of those," said Sasaki Sensei. "I was an atheist," he continued, "but I was led to faith in Christ. I went to Bible College and am now pastoring this church. Twenty years have passed since my confession of faith."

At the time of this writing, Sasaki Sensei has been pastoring the Oita church for 37 years. Soon after this celebration, a new building replaced the old. The Oita church invited Peter and me to attend their fortieth in 2007, long after we had retired. What a homecoming for all!

One thing Peter always emphasized in all his talks on furlough about missions was the need for each Christian to be a missionary wherever they are, at their job, at home, or abroad.

Peter also shared his feelings about the Japanese people thus: "Throughout our many years in Japan we learned and received so much. I shall always be deeply grateful to the people of Japan for all that they have taught me!"

HOPE

The Japanese often asked us a hard question, "Why is the Christian church so divided?" It was difficult enough to explain the difference between Catholic and Protestant, let alone the many denominations. What an experience to join 300 Christians from different denominations on a **MARCH FOR JESUS** in the city of Fukuoka. We walked the city streets singing and chanting, "*God loves you! God loves Fukuoka! God loves Japan*!" Is there hope for Japan?

Japan's national educational TV channel featured Bible studies for several months with a Japanese Bible scholar/pastor. One week when the lesson was on the Book of Acts, the pastor told the interviewer, "I will never forget my incredible joy on baptism day. The Holy Spirit's power is just something I cannot explain."

In a country where God's Word has been proclaimed for centuries; where Christianity was almost wiped out four hundred years ago when approximately one million Christians lost their lives for the sake of Christ; and where today less than 1% of the population is Christian, such a national broadcast gives new hope. We claim God's promise in Isaiah 55:11, *My Word.....will not return empty.*

The airport waiting room was filled with friends coming to say good-bye. Our hearts rejoiced with the many who had become Christians, but our hearts ached knowing we were saying good-bye, perhaps for the last time. We had experienced great joy but also great pain, both in the church and in the family. The physical pains had gradually melted away. We were torn at leaving our beloved Japan, our home for 45 years.

One of our favorite Bible verses was Isaiah 54:10, *Though the mountains be shaken and the hills be removed, yet my unfailing love for you will not be shaken, nor my covenant of peace be removed, says the Lord…* Our comfort? *God's unfailing love will be with you! And with us!*

Sayonara, our dear friends! Sayonara, our beloved Japan!

COM Japan missionaries, 1995

Excellent Parents

Reaching out - one by one

Peter leading English Bible study

Let me help you

Mary holding meeting for neighbour kids and moms - full house

Rick & Marilyn, our African family presents missions in Zaire

Peter leading outdoor worship

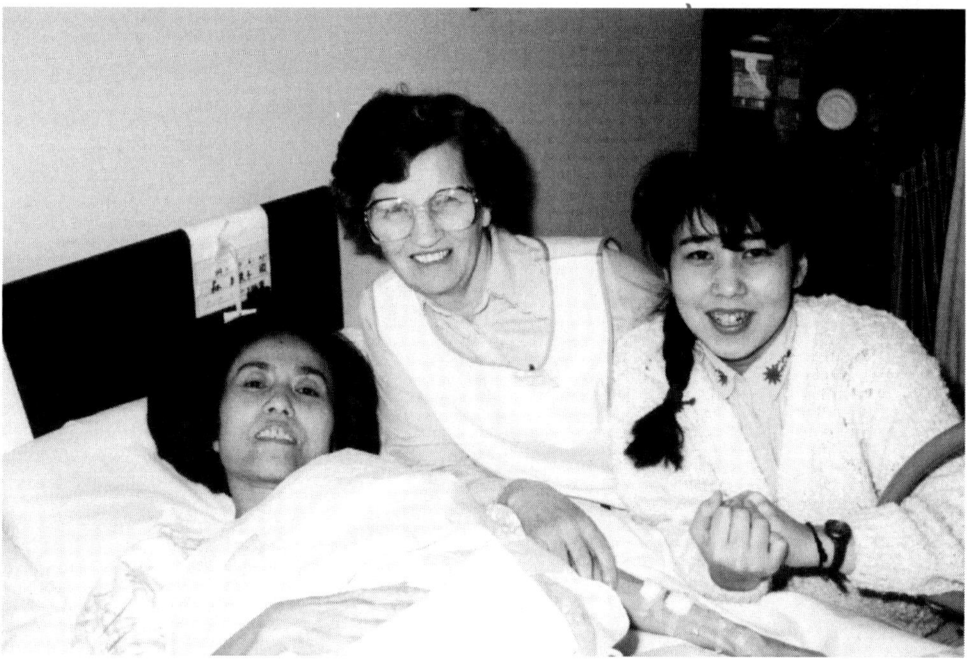

Mary volunteering at Eiko hospice

Greta & friend help prepare for Christmas Eve

Ladies' Christmas choir

Airport farewell

Peter and Mary with grandchildren, 1994
Micah, Jayden, Jeremiah, Ben, Erica, Luke,
Carissa, Tali, Tessia, Karina, Brina

Peter Derksen, 1928 — 2014

ACKNOWLEDGEMENTS

A big thank-you to my editor, Alvin Ens. You have patiently and kindly led me through the intricacies of writing a book, my first. Thank-you for not giving up on me.

A big thank-you to my publisher, Dave Loewen, for working on the layout, for making sure the pictures are all in place, and for the big job of publishing my book.

Thank you, Eden Mennonite Church and West Abbotsford Mennonite Church for commissioning us to mission work in Japan in 1954, and for supporting us with prayer and finances via our mission board COM, throughout our 45 years in Japan.

Wanda, thank you for the many pictures you scanned for me. I could not have done it without you. Thank you for patiently answering the many calls for help with computer technology, and walking me through the glitches.

Ernie, thank you for computer help, especially for storing my manuscripts in case I hit some wrong buttons!

Thank-you, my family, for your encouragement and care for me, so that I could finish this, which for me, was a big project.

Thank you, my friends who have encouraged me and prayed for me, waiting expectantly for the finished product.

Thank you to all my friends in Japan who have given permission to use your stories, excited about what you might find! Some whose stories I share have joined the throng in heaven, waiting for us to join them.

おかげさまでこの本を書くことはできて本当にありがとうございました。お祈りも感謝いたします。この本は神様に栄光を与えるように...

My dear Peter, who was my best writing critic, shared these 45 awesome years with me. Peter joined the heavenly hosts in 2014.

And THANK YOU, my LORD and SAVIOR, for calling us to serve you in the beautiful land of Japan that you created for your glory!

THANK YOU, GOD, for the beautiful Japanese people you created in your image, many now friends and coworkers!

Till we meet again!

Credits:

Cover photo: ad.wikimedia.org/wikipedia/commons/thumb/e/e4/
Numazu_and_Mount_Fuji.jpg

Map of Japan: Commission on Overseas Mission of the General Conference Mennonite Church

Photos: personal Derksen family collection